Appetite

Pleasers

FAVORITE RECIPES® of
PENNSYLVANIA 4-H FAMILIES

©Favorite Recipes Press, A Division of Great American Opportunities Inc. MCMLXXXIII
P. O. Box 77, Nashville, Tennessee 37202
Library of Congress Cataloging in Publication Data on page 136.

Cover recipe on page 42.
Page 1 recipes on pages 20 and 60.
Page 2 recipes on pages 27, 29 and 42.

4-H Club Pledge

I pledge

my head to clearer thinking,

my heart to greater loyalty,

my hands to larger service, and

my health to better living, for

my club,

my community,

my country, and

my world.

4-H Club Motto

"To make the best better"

To The Reader

4-H is the largest youth organization in the United States. In Pennsylvania, it reaches over 145,000 boys and girls, ages 8 to 19, from urban and rural areas. Supported by over 15,000 adult and teen volunteer leaders and the educational resources of Penn State and the U. S. Department of Agriculture, 4-H helps these boys and girls learn practical skills, achieve their goals, and understand the meaning of responsible citizenship.

Food and Nutrition projects have been part of the 4-H program almost since its beginnings in 1912. While 4-H has branched into many, many areas with 112 projects available, almost one-third of the membership in Pennsylvania is still enrolled in the nine basic food and nutrition projects. Members also have a chance to do independent study in this area if they have an interest in a particular subject area.

The following recipes represent favorite recipes of Pennsylvania 4-H members and leaders from across the Commonwealth. The diversity of these recipes represents the diversity of the 4-H program. Many more recipes were received than space allowed us to print. *Favorite Recipes Press* has edited the recipes and provided the pictures for this 4-H cookbook. The Cooperative Extension Service of The Pennsylvania State University is not recommending or endorsing these recipes nor were these recipes tested by the university faculty. The Pennsylvania State University also cannot be responsible for the nutritional analysis provided at the end of each recipe if ingredients are substituted.

Proceeds from the sale of this cookbook will be used to benefit the 4-H program in Pennsylvania. Your purchase of this cookbook will provide new opportunities and educational programs for many Pennsylvania 4-H'ers. Your support is very much appreciated.

Congratulations to those 4-H members and leaders whose names appear in this cookbook and we thank them and all those who contributed recipes for helping to "make the best better."

Sincerely,

Maurice S. Kramer

Maurice S. Kramer
State 4-H Program Director

VEGETABLES A LA ESPANA, recipe on page 76.

Contents

EDITOR'S NOTE

The editors and publishers have attempted to present these tried-and-true family recipes in a form that allows approximate nutritional values to be computed. Persons with dietary or health problems or whose diets require close monitoring should not rely on the nutritional information provided. They should consult their physicians or a registered dietitian.

ABBREVIATIONS FOR NUTRITIONAL ANALYSIS

Cal . . . . Calories	Sod . . . . , ...Sodium
Prot .Protein	Pot . . . . .Potassium
T Fat . . . . Total Fat	g . . . . .gram
Chl . . . . .Cholesterol	mg . . . . milligram
Car . . . . Carbohydrates	

PINEAPPLE GODDESS SALAD, recipe on page 54.

VIP Recipes

"PLAINS SPECIAL" CHEESE RING

1 lb. sharp cheese, grated
1 c. finely chopped nuts
1 c. mayonnaise
1 sm. onion, finely grated
Pepper to taste
Dash of cayenne pepper
Strawberry preserves (opt.)

Combine first 6 ingredients in bowl; mix well. Spoon into lightly greased 5 cup ring mold. Chill until firm. Unmold on serving plate. Fill center with preserves. Serve with crackers.

Mrs. Jimmy Carter

CHOCOLATE DELIGHT

1 1/2 c. flour
1 1/4 sticks butter, melted
1/2 c. chopped pecans
1   8-oz. package cream cheese, softened
1 c. confectioners' sugar
1 med. carton whipped topping
2 pkg. chocolate instant pudding mix
3 c. milk

Combine first 3 ingredients in bowl; mix well. Pat into 9 x 13-inch baking dish. Bake at 350 degrees for 20 to 25 minutes or until lightly browned; cool. Blend cream cheese and confectioners' sugar in bowl until smooth. Add 1 cup whipped topping; mix well. Spread over crust. Combine pudding mix with milk in bowl; mix well. Pour over cream cheese layer. Top with remaining whipped topping. Chill for 24 hours.

Howard H. Baker, Jr.
Senator from Tennessee

SPECIAL APPLE PIE

1/2 to 2/3 c. sugar
1/8 tsp. salt
1 to 1 1/2 tbsp. cornstarch
1/4 tsp. cinnamon
1/8 tsp. nutmeg
5 to 6 c. thinly sliced peeled apples
1 recipe 2-crust pie pastry
1 tbsp. lemon juice
1/2 tsp. grated lemon rind
1 tsp. vanilla extract
2 tbsp. cream (opt.)

Combine first 5 ingredients in small bowl; mix well. Sprinkle over apples; stir gently until apples are well coated. Spoon into 9-inch pie plate lined with half the pastry. Sprinkle with lemon juice, rind, vanilla and cream. Top with remaining pastry. Seal and flute edge; cut vents. Bake at 450 degrees for 10 minutes. Reduce temperature to 350 degrees. Bake for 35 to 50 minutes longer or until brown.

Variations:

Substitute sliced green tomatoes for half the apples. Substitute brown sugar for sugar. Substitute 1 teaspoon fennel or aniseed for cinnamon, nutmeg and vanilla if pie is to be served with cheese. Prepare pie without top crust, bake at 450 degrees for 20 minutes, sprinkle with 1 cup grated cheese and place under broiler until cheese melts. Brush top crust lightly with milk and sprinkle with sugar and cinnamon before baking.

David A. Stockman
Executive Office of the President
Office of Management and Budget

POTATO FRUITCAKE

1 c. shortening
2 c. sugar
4 eggs
1 c. hot mashed Irish potatoes
2 c. flour
3 tsp. baking powder
1/4 tsp. soda
1/2 tsp. salt
1 tsp. each nutmeg, cloves, cinnamon
1/4 c. cocoa
1/2 c. milk
8 oz. pitted dates, halved
1/2 c. cooked raisins, drained
8 oz. mixed candied fruits
8 oz. glazed cherries
8 oz. candied pineapple
4 oz. candied orange peel
2 c. coarsely chopped pecans
1 tsp. each butter, rum, brandy extract

Cream shortening and sugar in bowl. Add eggs 1 at a time, beating well after each addition. Stir in potatoes gradually. Mix dry ingredients together. Stir into batter. Add milk; mix well. Add remaining ingredients; mix well. Spoon into large tube pan lined with greased foil. Bake in preheated 275-degree oven for 2 hours until cake pulls away from pan and is firm to touch. Glaze cooled cake. Yields: 25-30 servings.

Dr. Bryce Jordan
President, Pennsylvania State University

HOT WEATHER CAKE

Whole graham crackers
Bananas, cut in half lengthwise
Chocolate frosting

Layer graham crackers and bananas in cake pan to within 1/2 inch of top, beginning and ending with graham crackers. Ice with chocolate frosting. Chill in refrigerator for 24 hours. Good at picnics and a favorite with children.

Dr. and Mrs. W. Wayne Hinish
Associate Dean, College of Agriculture and
Associate Director, Cooperative Extension Service

CORN BREAD DRESSING

1 pkg. stuffing mix
1 pkg. corn bread stuffing mix
2 bunches scallions, chopped
1 1/2 c. chopped celery
1 med. bunch parsley, chopped
3 eggs
Salt and pepper to taste
Crisp-cooked bacon, crumbled
Chopped turkey and giblets
Turkey broth

Combine first 5 ingredients in bowl; mix well. Add enough boiling water to moisten; mix well. Stir in eggs. Add remaining ingredients except broth to taste. Spoon into greased 5 x 9-inch baking dish and muffin cups. Add turkey broth. Bake at 350 degrees until brown and crusty. Add additional broth before reheating.

Mrs. Jonelle Jordan (Wife of Dr. Bryce Jordan)

CRAB IMPERIAL

1 lb. crab meat
4 tbsp. mayonnaise
1 tbsp. Worcestershire sauce
1 tsp. prepared mustard
1/2 tsp. Old Bay seasoning
Butter
Bread crumbs

Combine first 5 ingredients together with 3 teaspoons melted butter in bowl; mix lightly. Place in shallow dish or individual baking shells. Dot with butter; sprinkle with crumbs. Bake at 400 degrees for 10 to 15 minutes or until browned. Yields: 2-3 servings.

Dr. and Mrs. Samuel H. Smith
Dean, College of Agriculture and
Director, Cooperative Extension Service

CHICKEN-MACARONI CASSEROLE

2 c. chopped cooked chicken
1 7-oz. package elbow macaroni
1/2 lb. Cheddar cheese, shredded
2 cans cream of mushroom soup
2 c. milk
1/2 green pepper, chopped
1 2-oz. jar chopped pimento
4 hard-boiled eggs, chopped
1 tsp. salt
Dash of pepper
1 5-oz. can sliced water chestnuts, drained
1 sm. onion, minced

Combine all ingredients in large bowl; mix well. Chill overnight. Spoon into 8 x 13-inch baking dish. Bake at 350 degrees for 1 1/4 hours. May substitute tuna, shrimp or crab meat for chicken.

Dr. and Mrs. Maurice Kramer
State 4-H Program Director

CUCUMBER MOLD SALAD

1 3-oz. package lemon gelatin
1/4 tsp. salt
1 3-oz. package cream cheese, softened
1/4 c. white vinegar
Dash of Tabasco sauce
1/8 tsp. dried horseradish
1 med. cucumber, peeled, quartered

Dissolve gelatin and salt in 1 1/2 cups boiling water. Beat cream cheese in bowl. Add 6 tablespoons gelatin mixture 1 tablespoon at a time, mixing well after each addition. Stir in remaining gelatin and remaining ingredients except cucumber. Chill until partially set. Seed cucumber and slice

paper thin. Stir into gelatin mixture. Spoon into mold. Chill until firm. Unmold on serving plate. Serve with chicken.

Mr. and Mrs. Mark Branstetter
Pennsylvania Friends of 4-H Board Member

SUPER OATMEAL COOKIES

3/4 c. melted butter
1/2 c. packed brown sugar
1/2 c. confectioners' sugar
1/2 c. sugar
1 egg
1/4 c. milk
1 tsp. vanilla extract
3 c. oats
1 c. flour
1/2 tsp. baking powder
1 c. chocolate chips
36 wlanut halves

Beat butter, sugars, egg, milk and vanilla in bowl until creamy. Add remaining ingredients except walnuts; blend well. Shape into ping pong-sized balls on buttered cookie sheet. Press walnut half into each cookie. Bake at 350 degrees for 15 minutes. Let stand for 3 minutes before removing from cookie sheet; Yields: 36 servings.

Cas Welch
Pennsylvania Friends of 4-H Board Member

CHILI TEX

1 can chili and beans
1 c. grated Cheddar cheese
1 c. chopped onions
1 can hominy

Alternate layers of chili, cheese, onions and hominy in baking dish until all ingredients are used, ending with cheese. Bake at 350 degrees until onions are tender and cheese melted.

Dale Evans Rogers
4-H Alumni

SPINACH SOUFFLE

1 c. cooked spinach, drained
3 tbsp. butter
4 tbsp. flour
1 c. light cream
6 egg yolks
Pinch of nutmeg
1/8 tsp. pepper
7 egg whites
1/2 tsp. salt
1/8 tsp. cream of tartar

Process spinach in blender container until pureed. Melt butter in saucepan. Stir in flour and cream. Simmer until thickened, stirring constantly. Add a small amount of hot sauce to egg yolks; add egg yolks to hot sauce. Blend in spinach, nutmeg and pepper. Beat egg whites until soft peaks form. Add salt and cream of tartar; beat until stiff. Fold spinach mixture into egg whites. Spoon into greased and floured souffle dish with greased and floured foil collar attached. Cut 1-inch circle in center of souffle. Place in preheated 400-degree oven. Reduce temperature to 375 degrees. Bake for 25 to 35 minutes or until golden brown. Serve with Mornay Sauce. Yields: 6 servings.

Mornay Sauce

1 tbsp. butter
1 tbsp. flour
1 c. milk
1/2 tsp. mild prepared mustard, (Dijon type)
Salt and pepper to taste
1 tbsp. grated Parmesan cheese

Melt butter in saucepan. Stir in flour and milk. Simmer until thickened, stirring constantly. Add seasonings. Stir in cheese until melted. Serve over Spinach Souffle.

Florence Henderson
4-H Alumni

HOMERLINE'S PECAN PIE

2 tbsp. flour
1/2 c. sugar
3 eggs, beaten
1/4 c. butter, softened
1 c. pecan pieces
1 c. light corn syrup
Pinch of salt
1 unbaked pie shell

Combine flour and sugar. Add to eggs with next 4 ingredients; mix well. Pour into pie shell. Bake at 350 degrees for 50 minutes.

Jerry Clower

SISTER MABEL'S CARAMEL CORN

2 c. packed light brown sugar
1/2 c. light corn syrup
1/2 lb. margarine
1/4 tsp. cream of tartar
1 tsp. salt
1 tsp. baking soda
6 qt. popped Orville Redenbacher's
Gourmet Popping Corn

Combine first 5 ingredients in 2 1/2-quart saucepan. Cook over medium heat to hard ball-stage, 260 degrees on candy thermometer, stirring constantly. Remove from heat and stir in soda quickly. Pour over popped popcorn in large baking pan. Stir gently to coat kernels. Bake at 200 degrees for 1 hour, stirring 2 or 3 times. Spread on waxed paper to cool. Break apart and store in tightly covered container.

Orville Redenbacher

Appetizers, Soups

DANISH SALAD TRAY, recipe on page 16.

& Sandwiches

BACON QUICKIES

1 can mushroom soup
24 bread slices, trimmed
8 slices bacon, cut into thirds

Spread ..... soup on bread slices.
Cut .... each slice into thirds.
Roll .... as for jelly roll.
Wrap .... piece of bacon around bread roll, securing with toothpick.
Place .... on baking sheet.
Broil .... for several minutes or until bacon is brown, turning to brown evenly.
Yields ...... 8 servings.

Approx Per Serv: Cal 460, Prot 10.5 g, T Fat 25.3 g, Chl 25.4 mg, Car 46.4 g, Sod 920.1 mg, Pot 156.7 mg.

Betsy Will, Somerset

CHEESE PUFFS

1/2 c. butter
1 c. sifted flour
1/4 tsp. salt
4 eggs
1/2 c. Parmesan cheese

Melt .... butter in 1 cup boiling water in saucepan.
Add .... flour and salt, mixing well.
Cook .... over medium heat until mixture leaves side of pan, stirring constantly; remove from heat.
Let .... stand for 1 minute.
Add ...... eggs 1 at a time, beating well after each addition.
Stir .... in cheese, mixing well.
Drop .... by teaspoonfuls onto greased baking sheet.
Bake .... at 425 degrees for 18 to 20 minutes or until golden brown.
Yields ...... 48 servings.

Puffs may be stored in refrigerator for 1 to 3 days before baking.

Approx Per Serv: Cal 37.3, Prot 1.2 g, T Fat 2.7 g, Chl 28.2 mg, Car 1.9 g, Sod 48.7 mg, Pot 10.1 mg.

Jennifer Lathrop, Susquehanna

CHEEZ WHIZ APPETIZERS

20 slices bread, trimmed, halved
1 lg. jar Cheez Whiz
20 slices bacon, halved

Roll .... bread to flatten.
Spread ..... with Cheez Whiz.
Place .... bread cheese side up on top of bacon.
Roll .... as for jelly roll; secure with toothpick.
Place .... on rack in broiler pan.
Broil .... for 10 minutes or until bacon is crisp.
Yields ...... 40 servings.

Approx Per Serv: Cal 150, Prot 4.4 g, T Fat 11 g, Chl 16.5 mg, Car 8.1 g, Sod 330 mg, Pot 55.6 mg.

David Dickson, Bucks

CHICKEN DRUMMETTES

16 chicken drummettes
1 pkg. buttermilk dressing mix
1 pkg. corn bread stuffing mix
Pepper to taste

Coat .... chicken with buttermilk dressing mix.
Roll .... in stuffing mix.
Season ..... with pepper.
Place .... in 9 x 11-inch baking pan.
Bake .... at 350 degrees for 45 minutes.
Yields ...... 4 servings.

Kenneth Brush, Cambria

FANCY GRANOLA

6 c. oats
4 c. raw sunflower seed
2 c. wheat germ
1 c. bran
1 1/2 c. nonfat dry milk
2 tsp. salt
3 tbsp. cinnamon
3/4 c. molasses
1/2 c. honey
1 c. peanut oil
3 tbsp. vanilla extract
2 c. each coconut, raisins, chopped raw cashews

Combine .... first 7 ingredients in large bowl, mixing well.
Blend ...... molasses, honey, peanut oil and vanilla in bowl.
Add .... to oat mixture, mixing well.
Spread ..... on large baking pan.

Bake . . . . at 250 degrees until light brown, stirring occasionally.
Turn . . . . onto paper-covered surface.
Add . . . . remaining 3 ingredients, mixing well.
Store . . . . while warm in tightly sealed containers.
Yields . . . . . . 24 servings.

Approx Per Serv: Cal 677, Prot 10.8 g, T Fat 52.6 g, Chl 5.8 mg, Car 45.1 g, Sod 226.8 mg, Pot 580.6 mg.

Nutritional information does not include bran and cashews.

Sharon Custer, Montgomery

GOLDEN MICROWAVE GRANOLA

3 c. oats
1 c. coconut
1 c. coarsely chopped nuts
1/4 c. honey
1/4 c. butter, melted
1 1/2 tsp. cinnamon
1/2 tsp. salt
2/3 c. raisins

Combine . . . . all ingredients, except raisins, in 9 x 13-inch glass baking dish, mixing well.
Microwave . . on High for 8 to 10 minutes or until light golden brown, stirring several times.
Mix . . . . in raisins; cool.
Store . . . . tightly covered, in cool dry place.
Yields . . . . . . 6 cups.

Photograph for this recipe on page 104.

MICROWAVE NACHOS

16 lg. tortilla chips
4 slices crisp-cooked bacon, crumbled
4 oz. Cheddar cheese, shredded

Place . . . . tortilla chips on waxed paper-lined paper plate.
Top . . . . with bacon and cheese.
Microwave . . on Medium for 1 to 2 minutes or until cheese is melted.
Yields . . . . . . 16 servings.

Approx Per Serv: Cal 79.4, Prot 3.1 g, T Fat 6.2 g, Chl 12 mg, Car 3 g, Sod 125.8 mg, Pot 19 mg.

Cheryl Keifer, Northampton

PIZZA POPCORN

1/3 c. butter, melted
1/4 c. Parmesan cheese
1/2 tsp. each garlic salt, oregano, basil, salt
1/4 tsp. onion powder
10 c. freshly popped popcorn

Combine . . . . butter, Parmesan cheese and seasonings in bowl, mixing well.
Place . . . . popcorn in shallow baking pan.
Pour . . . . butter mixture over popcorn, stirring to mix.
Bake . . . . at 300 degrees for 15 minutes, stirring occasionally.
Yields . . . . . . 10 servings.

Approx Per Serv: Cal 107, Prot 2 g, T Fat 8.9 g, Chl 21.7 mg, Car 5.4 g, Sod 309.6 mg, Pot 6.2 mg.

Beth Hilterman, Butler

BETSY'S QUICHE LORRAINE APPETIZERS

1/2 lb. ground beef
1 1/3 c. coarsely shredded Swiss cheese
1/3 c. chopped onion
1 pkg. pie crust sticks
1 1/3 c. sour cream
1 tsp. salt
1 tsp. Worcestershire sauce
4 eggs, lightly beaten

Brown . . . . . . ground beef in skillet, stirring until crumbly.
Add . . . . cheese and onion, mixing well.
Prepare . . . . . pastry for 2-crust pie using package directions.
Cut . . . . into eighteen 4-inch circles.
Place . . . . in medium muffin cups.
Fill . . . . 1/2 full with ground beef mixture.
Blend . . . . . . sour cream, salt and Worcestershire sauce into eggs in bowl.
Spoon . . . . . . over ground beef mixture.
Bake . . . . at 375 degrees for 30 minutes or until lightly browned.
Cool . . . . for 5 minutes.
Yields . . . . . . 18 servings.

Approx Per Serv: Cal 220.8, Prot 7.8 g, T Fat 16.6 g, Chl 80.6 mg, Car 10.1 g, Sod 334 mg, Pot 100.7 mg.

Sonja Westover, Columbia

HOT SAUSAGE BALLS

2 c. biscuit mix
8 oz. sharp Cheddar cheese, shredded
1 lb. hot sausage

Combine .... all ingredients in bowl, mixing well.
Shape ...... into bite-sized balls.
Place .... on baking sheet.
Bake .... at 325 degrees for 20 to 25 minutes or until golden brown.
Yields ...... 48 servings.

Approx Per Serv: Cal 87.1, Prot 2.5 g, T Fat 7 g, Chl 10.5 mg, Car 3.5 g, Sod 168 mg, Pot 21.1 mg.

Eleanor Walker, Blair

SWEDISH MEATBALLS

2 lb. ground beef
2 eggs, beaten
1/4 c. bread crumbs
1 pkg. dry onion soup mix
1/2 bottle of hot catsup
1 10-oz. can pizza sauce
1 10-oz. jar apple jelly

Mix .... first 4 ingredients in bowl.
Shape ...... into small balls.
Brown ...... in skillet, stirring frequently.
Mix .... catsup, pizza sauce and apple jelly in saucepan.
Cook .... over low heat until jelly is melted, stirring constantly.
Pour .... over meatballs.
Simmer ..... for several minutes, stirring often.
Yields ...... 8 servings.

Approx Per Serv: Cal 498.6, Prot 23.4 g, T Fat 26.3 g, Chl 148.3 mg, Car 42.3 g, Sod 735.3 mg, Pot 501.6 mg.

Nutritional information does not include pizza sauce.

Michelle Witt, Somerset

SHRIMP TOAST APPETIZER

1 lb. cooked shrimp, mashed
1 tsp. ginger
4 tbsp. minced celery
3 tbsp. minced onion
1 tsp. salt
2 tsp. sesame oil
2 eggs, lightly beaten
2 tbsp. cornstarch

10 to 15 slices white bread, trimmed
1/4 c. sesame seed
Oil for frying

Combine .... first 8 ingredients in bowl, mixing well.
Roll .... out bread to flatten.
Spread ..... with shrimp mixture.
Sprinkle .... sesame seed over top.
Cut .... into triangles.
Place .... shrimp side down in 375-degree oil in electric skillet.
Cook .... until brown, turning once; drain.
Yields ...... 36 servings.

Approx Per Serv: Cal 55.4, Prot 4.5 g, T Fat 1.1 g, Chl 33.3 mg, Car 6.6 g, Sod 141.3 mg, Pot 35.6 mg.

Nutritional information does not include oil for frying.

Jennifer Mease, Bucks

DANISH SALAD TRAY

1/2 c. vinegar
1/2 tsp. sugar
1 lg. cucumber, peeled, thinly sliced
2 tsp. curry powder
1 tbsp. lemon juice
3/4 c. mayonnaise
1/2 c. whipping cream, whipped
1 lb. shrimp, cooked, shelled
1/2 c. sour cream
1/4 lb. Danish blue cheese, crumbled
1 10-oz. package frozen French-style green beans, cooked, drained
2 heads lettuce, cored, separated
2 6-oz. jars marinated artichoke hearts, drained
1 6-oz. can mushrooms, drained
Caraway cheese slices
Green pepper strips
Radish roses

Combine .... vinegar and sugar with 1/2 cup water in bowl, mixing well.
Add .... cucumber slices, mixing well.
Chill .... in refrigerator.
Stir .... curry powder into lemon juice in small bowl.
Blend ...... in mayonnaise.
Fold .... in whipped cream and shrimp.
Chill .... in refrigerator.
Combine .... sour cream and blue cheese in bowl, mixing well.
Add .... green beans, tossing to mix.

Chill . . . . in refrigerator.
Arrange . . . . . large lettuce leaves on serving tray; shred remaining lettuce.
Place . . . . shredded lettuce in lettuce leaves.
Fill . . . . each lettuce leaf with cucumber mixture, shrimp mixture, green bean mixture, artichokes or mushrooms.
Arrange . . . . . remaining 3 ingredients around cups.
Serve . . . . with Danish rye or pumpernickel.
Yields . . . . . . 6 servings.

Photograph for this recipe on page 13.

TUNA PATE'

2   7-oz. cans tuna
4 hard-boiled eggs
4 tbsp. margarine
13 sm. stuffed olives
3 tbsp. herb mix
1/4 tsp. dry mustard
6 drops of hot pepper sauce

Drain . . . . . . tuna, reserving liquid.
Place . . . . with remaining ingredients in blender container; process for several seconds, adding reserved liquid if necessary.
Shape . . . . . . into mound on serving platter.
Chill . . . . for 2 hours.
Garnish . . . . . with parsley.
Serve . . . . with crackers and fresh vegetable sticks.
Yields . . . . . . 10 servings.

Approx Per Serv: Cal 185.4, Prot 11.6 g, T Fat 15.1 g, Chl 121.4 mg, Car .3 g, Sod 496 mg, Pot 140.8 mg.

Nutritional information does not include herb mix.

Andrea Palguta, Somerset

HOT BEAN DIP

1   8-oz. package cream cheese, softened
1   10-oz. can bean dip
20 drops of Tabasco sauce
1/8 tsp. salt
1 c. sour cream
1/2 c. sliced green onion
1/2 pkg. taco seasoning mix
1/4 lb. each Cheddar cheese, Monterey Jack cheese, grated

Mix . . . . first 7 ingredients in glass serving dish.
Add . . . . cheeses, mixing well.
Microwave . . on High for 3 to 5 minutes, stirring frequently.
Yields . . . . . . 36 servings.

Approx Per Serv: Cal 62.7, Prot 2.3 g, T Fat 5.8 g, Chl 16 mg, Car .6 g, Sod 71.3 mg, Pot 22.2 mg.

Nutritional information does not include bean dip and taco seasoning mix.

Katie Rhoads, Dauphin

SAUSA CORN CHIP DIP

1   28-oz. can tomatoes
1 sm. can chopped green chiles
1/4 tsp. chopped onion
1/4 tsp. salt
Pinch each of chili powder, cayenne pepper

Combine . . . . all ingredients in bowl, mixing well.
Add . . . . more chili powder and cayenne pepper to taste.
Yields . . . . . . 12 servings.

Approx Per Serv: Cal 20.4, Prot .9 g, T Fat .2 g, Chl 0 mg, Car 4.3 g, Sod 132.7 mg, Pot 174.4 mg.

Heather Furman, Northumberland

ZIPPY VEGETABLE DIP

2 eggs
4 tbsp. vinegar
2 tbsp. sugar
1   8-oz. package cream cheese, softened
2 tbsp. each horseradish, chopped onion, chopped green pepper

Combine . . . . eggs, vinegar and sugar in saucepan, mixing well.
Cook . . . . until thick, stirring frequently.
Chill . . . . in refrigerator.
Whip . . . . cream cheese in bowl.
Combine . . . . with egg mixture and remaining 3 ingredients in serving bowl, mixing well.
Serve . . . . with assorted fresh vegetables.
Yields . . . . . . 8 servings.

Approx Per Serv: Cal 142, Prot 4 g, T Fat 12.1 g, Chl 94.7 mg, Car 4.8 g, Sod 90.4 mg, Pot 64.4 mg.

Carol Hall, Venango

HOLIDAY PARTY DIP

1 c. salad dressing
1 c. sour cream
1 8-oz. can water chestnuts, drained, chopped
2 tbsp. chopped pimento
1 tbsp. chopped green onion
2 tsp. beef instant bouillon
1/2 tsp. Worcestershire sauce
1/4 tsp. garlic powder

Combine .... all ingredients in bowl, mixing well.
Chill .... covered, until serving time.
Yields ...... 8 servings.

Approx Per Serv: Cal 194, Prot 1.4 g, T Fat 18.8 g, Chl 28 mg, Car 5.9 g, Sod 31.5 mg, Pot 56.8 mg.

Christine Rumbold, Monroe

SPINACH DIP

1 16-oz. carton sour cream
1 c. mayonnaise
1/2 c. chopped onion
1 10-oz. package frozen chopped spinach, thawed, drained
1 pkg. dry vegetable soup mix

Combine .... all ingredients in bowl, mixing well.
Chill .... for 3 hours or longer.
Serve .... with fresh vegetables.
Yields ...... 18 servings.

Approx Per Serv: Cal 163.3, Prot 1.9 g, T Fat 15.7 g, Chl 20 mg, Car 4.9 g, Sod 339.4 mg, Pot 111.1 mg.

Mary T. Hosterman, Centre

FRESH VEGETABLE DIP

1 16-oz. carton sour cream
1 1/2 c. shredded Cheddar cheese
1/4 c. each minced onion, sweet potato
1/2 tsp. hot sauce
1 tbsp. milk
1/4 tsp. salt (opt.)

Combine .... all ingredients in bowl, mixing well.
Serve .... with fresh vegetables.
Yields ...... 12 servings.

Approx Per Serv: Cal 140, Prot 4.9 g, T Fat 12.6 g, Chl 31 mg, Car 2.3 g, Sod 165.5 mg, Pot 74.2 mg.

Crossroads Community Center, Philadelphia

GOAT'S MILK CHEESE SPREAD

1/4 c. white vinegar
1 tsp. soda
1 gal. goat's milk, scalded
1/2 c. butter
1/2 tsp. each onion powder, garlic salt

Stir .... vinegar and soda into hot goat's milk.
Cool .... and strain, discarding whey.
Knead ...... butter into curds in bowl.
Add .... seasonings, mixing well.
Pack .... into small container.
Chill .... until serving time.
Yields ...... 50 servings.

Approx Per Serv: Cal 68.7, Prot 2.5 g, T Fat 5 g, Chl 16.6 mg, Car 3.7 g, Sod 86.7 mg, Pot 142.3 mg.

Tracy L. Bowen, Juniata

SHRIMP BALL

1 tbsp. lemon juice
1 8-oz. package cream cheese, softened
2 7-oz. cans shrimp, rinsed, drained, chopped
2 tsp. grated onion
1 tsp. horseradish
1/4 tsp. liquid smoke
1/4 tsp. salt
1/2 c. chopped pecans

Blend ...... lemon juice into cream cheese in bowl.
Add .... remaining ingredients except pecans, mixing well.
Chill .... until firm.
Shape ...... into 2 balls.
Roll .... in pecans.
Serve .... with crackers.
Yields ...... 36 servings.

Approx Per Serv: Cal 47.8, Prot 3.3 g, T Fat 3.7 g, Chl 23.5 mg, Car .5 g, Sod 46.1 mg, Pot 29.3 mg.

David Clyde, Lawrence

OLD-FASHIONED BEAN SOUP

1 lb. navy beans
1 ham bone with meat
1/2 c. chopped green pepper
1 c. chopped celery
2 c. diced potatoes
1 med. onion, diced

3 carrots, sliced
1 tbsp. salt
1/4 tsp. pepper
1 c. tomato juice

Simmer . . . . . beans and ham bone in 12 cups water in soup pot for 2 hours.
Remove . . . . ham from bone; place ham in soup pot.
Add . . . . remaining ingredients, mixing well.
Simmer . . . . . for 2 hours longer.
Yields . . . . . . 8 servings.

Approx Per Serv: Cal 248.4, Prot 14.5 g, T Fat 1.1 g, Chl 0 mg, Car 47.4 g, Sod 906 mg, Pot 1081.5 mg.

Nutritional information does not include ham bone.

Doris Beck, Forest

VIOLET'S CREAM OF BROCCOLI SOUP

1   10-oz. package frozen chopped broccoli
3/4 c. finely chopped onion
2 tsp. each salt, monosodium glutamate, white pepper
1 tsp. garlic powder
8 to 10 oz. American cheese, shredded
1 c. each milk, cream
1/4 c. butter
1/3 c. flour

Add . . . . broccoli and onion to 6 cups boiling water in 3-quart saucepan.
Cook . . . . for 10 to 12 minutes or until tender.
Add . . . . next 5 ingredients, mixing well.
Cook . . . . until cheese melts, stirring constantly.
Add . . . . milk, cream and butter, mixing well.
Blend . . . . . . 1/2 cup water into flour in bowl, stirring until smooth.
Add . . . . to soup, stirring rapidly.
Bring . . . . to a boil, stirring constantly.
Yields . . . . . . 16 servings.

Approx Per Serv: Cal 154.9, Prot 5.4 g, T Fat 12.4 g, Chl 40.3 mg, Car 6.1 g, Sod 601.2 mg, Pot 136.4 mg.

Violet Ray, Butler

FRENCH ONION SOUP

1 tsp. flour
2 tsp. margarine, melted

1 c. thinly sliced onion
1 1/2 c. beef bouillon
1/8 tsp. pepper
4 slices French bread, toasted
4 oz. Gruyere cheese, grated

Stir . . . . flour into margarine in double boiler over boiling water until smooth.
Add . . . . onion.
Cook . . . . for 15 minutes or until onion is tender, stirring occasionally.
Mix . . . . in bouillon and pepper.
Cook . . . . for 20 minutes longer.
Pour . . . . half the soup into 2 small casseroles.
Top . . . . with bread and cheese.
Pour . . . . remaining soup over top.
Place . . . . on baking sheet.
Bake . . . . at 400 degrees for 15 minutes or until cheese is melted.
Yields . . . . . . 2 servings.

Approx Per Serv: Cal 457, Prot 25.7 g, T Fat 21.6 g, Chl 76.4 mg, Car 39.9 g, Sod 1332.3 mg, Pot 351.4 mg.

Wilma Mohr, Lehigh

NEW ENGLAND CLAM CHOWDER

1/4 c. finely chopped salt pork
1/3 c. chopped onion
1/4 c. finely chopped celery
2 c. finely chopped potatoes
1 tsp. salt
1/8 tsp. white pepper
1 6 1/2-oz. can chopped clams
2 c. milk, scalded
1/4 c. butter

Cook . . . . salt pork in skillet.
Add . . . . onion.
Saute . . . . . . until lightly brown.
Add . . . . 1 cup boiling water and next 5 ingredients, mixing well.
Bring . . . . to a boil.
Add . . . . hot milk.
Pour . . . . into bowls.
Dot . . . . with butter and garnish with paprika.
Yields . . . . . . 6 servings.

Approx Per Serv: Cal 285, Prot 8.4 g, T Fat 22.1 g, Chl 56.1 mg, Car 13.7 g, Sod 647.2 mg, Pot 392.4 mg.

Gladys Leiby, Lehigh

FISH CHOWDER

6 strips bacon, chopped
2 lg. onions, chopped
6 lg. potatoes, cubed
2 pkg. frozen haddock, thawed, cut into
    pieces
1 c. light cream
4 c. milk
1 green pepper, chopped
3 or 4 carrots, chopped
3 stalks celery, chopped
1/4 c. minute rice
3 tbsp. butter
1/8 tsp. Tabasco sauce
1/8 tsp. each thyme, salt, pepper

Cook .... bacon in large skillet until crisp.
Add .... onions.
Cook .... for 5 minutes.
Stir .... in potatoes and 2 cups boiling water.
Cook .... for 5 minutes longer.
Add .... haddock.
Simmer ..... covered, for 10 minutes.
Combine .... with remaining ingredients in soup pot, mixing well.
Simmer ..... for 1 hour.
Yields ...... 6 servings.

Approx Per Serv: Cal 564, Prot 30.3 g, T Fat 24.8 g, Chl 99.1 mg, Car 56.2 g, Sod 778.1 mg, Pot 1568.1 mg.

Christine M. Dickson, Bucks

PARSLIED POTATO SOUP

2 1/2 c. diced potatoes
1 tbsp. salt
1/4 tsp. each pepper, celery salt,
    onion salt
4 c. milk
2 tbsp. butter
3/4 c. flour
1 tbsp. (or more) parsley flakes

Cook .... first 5 ingredients in 2 cups water in saucepan until potatoes are tender; drain, reserving liquid.
Combine .... reserved liquid, milk and 2 cups water in large saucepan.
Simmer ..... for several minutes.
Cut .... butter into flour in bowl until crumbly.
Brown ...... in skillet, stirring constantly.

Spoon ...... slowly into milk mixture, stirring constantly.
Cook .... for 5 minutes, stirring constantly.
Add .... parsley and potatoes.
Cook .... for 5 minutes longer.
Yields ...... 8 servings.

Approx Per Serv: Cal 183, Prot 6.5 g, T Fat 7.3 g, Chl 26 mg, Car 23 g, Sod 1030.7 mg, Pot 384.9 mg.

Karol and Amy Sherman, Adams

CREAMY POTATO SOUP

6 to 8 potatoes, sliced
1 med. onion, chopped
1 tbsp. parsley flakes
2 tbsp. butter
Milk
1 can evaporated milk
1/2 tsp. each salt, pepper

Cook .... potatoes with onion and parsley flakes in salted water to cover in saucepan until tender; drain, reserving 2 cups liquid.
Mash .... potatoes with butter and a small amount of milk in bowl.
Add .... evaporated milk, reserved potato liquid, salt and pepper to taste.
Bring .... to a boil over low heat, stirring frequently.
Add .... additional milk or water if necessary.
Yields ...... 8 servings.

Approx Per Serv: Cal 246.4, Prot 7.9 g, T Fat 7.3 g, Chl 8.9 mg, Car 38.6 g, Sod 237.9 mg, Pot 954.8 mg.

Michelle Underkoffler, Clinton

CLASSIC VICHYSSOISE

2 c. sliced leeks
2 tbsp. butter, melted
2 tbsp. flour
2 tsp. salt
1/4 tsp. pepper
2 1/2 c. diced peeled potatoes
2/3 c. whipping cream
2 tbsp. chopped chives

Cook .... leeks in butter in saucepan over medium heat for 5 minutes.
Add .... flour, mixing well.
Cook .... for 2 minutes, stirring constantly.

Stir . . . . in 4 cups water, seasonings and potatoes gradually.
Simmer . . . . . for 30 minutes.
Place . . . . in blender container when slightly cooled.
Process . . . . . until smooth.
Chill . . . . in refrigerator.
Stir . . . . in whipping cream and chives.
Yields . . . . . . 6 servings.

Photograph for this recipe on page 1.

CREAMED SPINACH SOUP

1/2 c. chopped onion
2 tbsp. margarine
1/3 c. flour
1/8 tsp. nutmeg
2 1/2 c. skim milk
3/4 c. cubed Velveeta cheese
1 10-oz. package frozen spinach, thawed

Saute . . . . . . onion in margarine in skillet until tender.
Stir . . . . in flour and nutmeg until well blended.
Add . . . . milk and 1 cup water gradually.
Simmer . . . . . until thickened, stirring constantly.
Add . . . . cheese and spinach.
Cook . . . . . . until cheese is melted, stirring frequently.
Yields . . . . . . 10 servings.

Approx Per Serv: Cal 74, Prot 4 g, T Fat 3 g, Chl 2.6 mg, Car 8.3 g, Sod 111.6 mg, Pot 212.4 mg.

Michael Watkins, Huntingdon

VEGETABLE RICE SOUP

2 tbsp. beef base
1/2 c. chopped onion
2 c. rice
4 cans mixed vegetables, drained
1 tsp. each salt, pepper

Combine . . . . 12 cups boiling water, beef base, onion and rice in stock pot.
Simmer . . . . . until rice is tender.
Add . . . . vegetables, salt and pepper.
Heat . . . . to serving temperature.
Yields . . . . . . 24 servings.

Approx Per Serv: Cal 96, Prot 3 g, T Fat .3 g, Chl 0 mg, Car 20.8 g, Sod 121.9 mg, Pot 135.8 mg.

Nutritional information does not include beef base.

Michele Kunes, Elk

SAN FRANCISCO STEW

3/4 lb. ground beef
1/2 green pepper, chopped
4 med. onions, chopped
1 clove of garlic, minced
2 15-oz. cans pork and beans
2 tbsp. brown sugar
2 15-oz. cans tomatoes
1/2 tsp. mustard
3 slices bacon, crisp-fried

Brown . . . . . . ground beef with green pepper, onions and garlic in skillet, stirring until crumbly.
Add . . . . remaining ingredients, mixing well.
Cook . . . . for several minutes.
Spoon . . . . . . into casserole.
Bake . . . . in moderate oven for 1 1/2 hours.
Yields . . . . . . 6 servings.

Approx Per Serv: Cal 465, Prot 24.4 g, T Fat 18.8 g, Chl 48.7 mg, Car 51.2 g, Sod 1073.4 mg, Pot 1021.8 mg.

Tammy Wert, Union

CHILI CON CARNE

1 lb. ground beef
1 lg. onion, chopped
2 1/2 c. kidney beans
1 1/3 c. tomato soup
1 can corn
1 tbsp. chili powder
1 tbsp. flour
1 tsp. salt
1 tbsp. Worcestershire sauce

Brown . . . . . . ground beef with onion in soup pot, stirring until crumbly.
Add . . . . next 3 ingredients, mixing well.
Cook . . . . for 10 minutes.
Mix . . . . 3 tablespoons water with chili powder, flour, salt and Worcestershire sauce in bowl until smooth.
Stir . . . . into ground beef mixture.
Simmer . . . . . for 45 minutes, stirring frequently.
Yields . . . . . . 5 servings.

Approx Per Serv: Cal 482, Prot 27.1 g, T Fat 21.7 g, Chl 61.7 mg, Car 47 g, Sod 1177.5 mg, Pot 866 mg.

Lila M. Newhard, Berks

SPECIAL BEEF SANDWICHES

2 onions, sliced
1 c. catsup
2 tbsp. each Worcestershire sauce, vinegar
1 tsp. each salt, paprika, chili powder
2 tsp. pepper
1/2 tsp. red pepper
1 tsp. garlic salt
1 3-lb. beef chuck roast

Combine .... onions, catsup and next 7 seasonings in roasting pan, mixing well.
Sprinkle .... garlic salt on roast.
Place .... in sauce in roasting pan.
Bake .... at 300 degrees for 4 to 5 hours or until very tender; remove from pan.
Shred ...... with fork when cool.
Return ..... to roasting pan, mixing well.
Cook .... until heated through.
Yields ...... 24 servings.

Approx Per Serv: Cal 143, Prot 11.4 g, T Fat 8.9 g, Chl 38.6 mg, Car 4 g, Sod 327.2 mg, Pot 240 mg.

Leslie, Mark and Matthew Kralevich, Mercer

BEEF BARBECUE

1 lb. ground beef
3 tbsp. Worcestershire sauce
1/2 c. chopped onion
1/2 tsp. salt
Pepper to taste
2 tbsp. vinegar
1 c. catsup
2 tbsp. sugar
8 round rolls

Mix .... first 8 ingredients in large saucepan.
Simmer ..... for 1 hour, stirring frequently.
Serve .... on rolls.
Yields ...... 8 servings.

Approx Per Serv: Cal 328, Prot 14.4 g, T Fat 14.4 g, Chl 41 mg, Car 35 g, Sod 783 mg, Pot 389.8 mg.

Teresa A. Murren, Adams

ZIPPY HOT DOG SAUCE

3 onions, chopped
1 (or more) cloves of garlic, minced
1/2 c. oil

3 lb. ground beef
1 sm. can tomato paste
1/2 sm. can paprika
1/2 sm. can chili powder
1/4 tsp. red pepper
3 tsp. salt
3 tsp. pepper

Cook .... onions with garlic and oil in 3 cups water in large saucepan until tender.
Stir .... in remaining ingredients.
Simmer ..... until ground beef is cooked through and mixture thickens, stirring frequently.
Yields ...... 36 servings.

Sauce may be frozen in ice cube trays, reheating 1 cube sauce per hot dog to serve.

Approx Per Serv: Cal 139, Prot 7.2 g, T Fat 11.1 g, Chl 25.7 mg, Car 2.5 g, Sod 213.3 mg, Pot 178.4 mg.

Myrtle Gozikowski, Wyoming

PEPPERONI BREAD

1 loaf frozen bread dough, thawed
4 tbsp. pizza sauce
1/2 lb. cheese, grated
1/2 lb. pepperoni, thinly sliced

Roll .... dough on floured surface to 1-inch thick rectangle.
Spread ..... pizza sauce over dough.
Top .... with cheese and pepperoni.
Roll .... as for jelly roll.
Cut .... 4 or 5 slits on top.
Place .... on baking pan.
Bake .... at 350 degrees for 20 to 25 minutes or until brown.
Yields ...... 10 servings.

Faye A. Blass, Columbia

JUDITH'S SLOPPY JOES

1 lb. ground beef
1 tbsp. vinegar
1 tbsp. dry mustard
3/4 c. catsup
1/2 tsp. Worcestershire sauce
2 tbsp. sugar
1/2 c. chopped onion
1 tsp. each salt, pepper

Combine .... all ingredients in skillet, mixing well.

Simmer . . . . . for 2 hours, stirring occasionally.
Serve . . . . on hamburger buns.
Yields . . . . . . 8 servings.

Approx Per Serv: Cal 195, Prot 10.8 g, T Fat 12.1 g, Chl 38.6 mg, Car 10.6 g, Sod 572.8 mg, Pot 276.5 mg.

Judith A. Rudy, Allegheny

BARBECUED HAM SANDWICHES

1/2 c. packed brown sugar
1/2 c. vinegar
1 bottle of chili sauce
1/2 tsp. dry mustard
1/2 c. chopped onion
1/2 c. finely chopped celery
1 1/2 lb. ham, chopped
6 buns

Combine . . . . first 6 ingredients in saucepan, mixing well.
Simmer . . . . . for 1 hour, stirring occasionally.
Stir . . . . in ham.
Serve . . . . on buns.
Yields . . . . . . 6 servings.

Approx Per Serv: Cal 589, Prot 28.5 g, T Fat 27.6 g, Chl 103.3 mg, Car 56.9 g, Sod 1695.3 mg, Pot 660.5 mg.

Katrina Harbach, Clinton

HOT CHIPPED HAM SANDWICHES

1/2 lb. chipped ham
1/2 c. grated American cheese
1/2 c. chili sauce
1/4 c. chopped onion
2 tbsp. mayonnaise
6 hamburger buns

Mix . . . . first 5 ingredients in bowl.
Spoon . . . . . . into buns.
Wrap . . . . in foil.
Bake . . . . at 350 degrees for 20 minutes.
Yields . . . . . . 6 servings.

Approx Per Serv: Cal 331, Prot 15 g, T Fat 18.5 g, Chl 51.8 mg.

Beverly Sekol, Pike

MORNING DELIGHT

1 tsp. butter
1 slice bread
1 tsp. sugar
1 c. sliced peaches

Spread . . . . . butter on bread.
Sprinkle . . . . sugar over top.
Cover . . . . . . with peaches.
Place . . . . on baking sheet.
Broil . . . . for 12 minutes.
Yields . . . . . . 1 serving.

Approx Per Serv: Cal 258, Prot 3.6 g, T Fat 12.6 g, Chl 36.4 mg, Car 34.8 g, Sod 285.6 mg, Pot 376.6 mg.

Althea Molyneux, Sullivan

JACK-O-LANTERN PIZZAS

1 tbsp. oil
4 English muffins, cut into halves
1 8-oz. can pizza sauce
8 slices mozzarella cheese

Brush . . . . . . a small amount of oil on each muffin half.
Place . . . . muffins cut side up, on broiler rack.
Broil . . . . 4 inches from heat source until lightly browned.
Spread . . . . . 1 tablespoon pizza sauce over muffins.
Trim . . . . cheese slices into a circle.
Cut . . . . jack-o-lantern face into each slice.
Place . . . . over pizza sauce.
Broil . . . . 4 inches from heat source for 3 to 5 minutes or until cheese is melted.
Yields . . . . . . 8 servings.

Hope Keister, Union

PIZZA MOUNTAIN PIE

2 slices bread
Spaghetti sauce
Mozzarella cheese
Muenster cheese
Pepperoni

Place . . . . bread on each side of greased pie iron.
Spread . . . . . spaghetti sauce on one slice of bread.
Top . . . . with cheeses and pepperoni.
Close . . . . iron.
Cook . . . . over open fire until toasted on both sides.
Yields . . . . . . 1 serving.

Marc States, Indiana

FRUITY PUNCH SLUSH

2 c. sugar
1 24-oz. can frozen orange juice
  concentrate
1 46-oz. can pineapple juice
4 or 5 bananas, mashed
8 c. ginger ale

Combine .... sugar with 6 cups water in large saucepan.
Simmer ..... for 1/2 hour or until thickened, stirring occasionally; cool.
Stir .... in next 3 ingredients.
Freeze ...... until firm.
Spoon ...... into glasses and fill with ginger ale.
Yields ...... 20 servings.

Approx Per Serv: Cal 240, Prot 1.6 g, T Fat .2 g, Chl 0 mg, Car 60.1 g, Sod 2 mg, Pot 495.7 mg.

Clay Snyder, Venango

GOOD LUCK PUNCH

4 c. grape juice
1 c. sugar
4 c. unsweetened pineapple juice
2 qt. ginger ale

Mix .... grape juice, sugar, pineapple juice and 8 cups cold water in 2-gallon container.
Add .... ginger ale at serving time.
Yields ...... 40 servings.

Approx Per Serv: Cal 52.5, Prot .1 g, T Fat 0 g, Chl 0 mg, Car 13.4 g, Sod .4 mg, Pot 44.7 mg.

Venus Seaman, Juniata

PEACHY KEEN NOG

1 1/2 c. vanilla or peach ice cream
2 fresh peaches, sliced
2 eggs

Combine .... all ingredients in blender container.
Process ..... on medium speed for 15 seconds or until smooth.
Serve .... immediately.
Yields ...... 2 servings.

Approx Per Serv: Cal 366, Prot 10 g, T Fat 23.7 g, Chl 316.1 mg, Car 30.1 g, Sod 98.8 mg, Pot 372.3 mg.

Debby Long, Union

STRAWBERRY MILK PUNCH

6 c. fresh strawberries, sliced
3 c. sugar
1 gal. cold milk
2 qt. strawberry ice cream, softened
2 qt. mint ice cream, softened

Place .... strawberries and sugar in mixer bowl.
Beat .... with electric mixer until well blended.
Combine .... with milk and ice cream in punch bowl.
Yields ...... 25 servings.

Approx Per Serv: Cal 417, Prot 8.2 g, T Fat 20.9 g, Chl 75.9 mg, Car 51.6 g, Sod 109.9 mg, Pot 374.2 mg.

Barbara Rader, Butler

HOT SPICED APPLE CIDER

2 tsp. whole cloves
1/2 tsp. allspice
2 sticks cinnamon
1 gal. apple cider
1 tsp. liquid artificial sweetener
2 oranges, sliced

Tie .... spices in cheesecloth.
Combine .... with next 2 ingredients in large saucepan.
Simmer ..... covered, for 20 minutes.
Add .... orange slices.
Yields ...... 16 servings.

Renee Mullowney, Bucks

SPICED TEA

1 c. instant tea
2 c. Tang
3 oz. Wyler's lemonade mix
1 1/4 c. sugar (opt.)
1 tsp. each cloves, allspice
1 1/2 tsp. cinnamon

Combine .... all ingredients in large bowl, mixing well.
Store .... in airtight container.
Mix .... 2 teaspoons or more with 1 cup hot or cold water.
Yields ...... 80 servings.

Lenora Aquilani, Montgomery

Main Dishes:

SAUERBRATEN SUPPER, recipe on page 26.

Meats

BROILED MARINATED FLANK STEAK

1/4 c. oil
2 tbsp. catsup
2 tbsp. soy sauce
1 sm. onion, finely chopped
1 clove of garlic, minced
1   1-lb. flank steak, scored

Mix . . . . first 5 ingredients and 2 table-spoons water in jar, shaking well.
Place . . . . flank steak in plastic bag.
Pour . . . . marinade over top; tie bag.
Marinate . . . . overnight or for several days in refrigerator, turning frequently.
Broil . . . . to desired degree of doneness.
Slice . . . . cross grain.
Yields . . . . . . 4 servings.

Approx Per Serv: Cal 307, Prot 25.5 g, T Fat 20.2 g, Chl 77.1 mg, Car 4.8 g, Sod 825.4 mg, Pot 189.4 mg.

Roberta C. Burdick, Allegheny

SAUERBRATEN SUPPER

1 c. dill pickle juice
1 c. sliced onion
1/2 tsp. ginger
1/8 tsp. pepper
1 bay leaf
1 beef bouillon cube
1   3 1/4 to 3 1/2-lb. beef brisket
7 med. carrots, cut into chunks
1 tbsp. sugar
1 sm. head cabbage, cut into wedges
1 1/2 c. sliced dill pickles
1 tbsp. flour

Combine . . . . first 6 ingredients and 2 cups water in stock pot.
Bring . . . . to a boil.
Add . . . . brisket.
Simmer . . . . . covered, for 2 1/2 to 3 hours or until brisket is tender.
Chill . . . . and skim.
Add . . . . carrots and sugar.
Bring . . . . to a boil.
Cook . . . . covered, over low heat for 10 minutes.
Add . . . . cabbage and pickles.
Cook . . . . for 15 to 20 minutes or until cabbage is tender-crisp.
Remove . . . . brisket, pickles and vegetables to warm serving platter.

Stir . . . . in flour mixed with 2 table-spoons water.
Cook . . . . until thick, stirring constantly.
Serve . . . . with brisket.
Yields . . . . . . 8 servings.

Photograph for this recipe on page 25.

DRIED BEEF CASSEROLE

1 can mushroom soup
2 c. milk
1 med. onion, minced
1 c. macaroni
1 c. chopped Velveeta cheese
2 hard-boiled eggs, chopped
1/4 lb. dried beef, cut up
1/2 c. bread crumbs
1 tbsp. butter, melted

Combine . . . . first 7 ingredients in baking dish, mixing well.
Chill . . . . for 4 hours or overnight.
Bake . . . . covered, at 350 degrees for 40 minutes.
Toss . . . . bread crumbs with butter in bowl.
Sprinkle . . . . over top.
Bake . . . . uncovered, for 20 minutes longer.
Yields . . . . . . 6 servings.

Approx Per Serv: Cal 329, Prot 18.4 g, T Fat 16.2 g, Chl 130 mg, Car 27.1 g, Sod 1615 mg, Pot 336.3 mg.

Judy A. Sterner, Adams

ROCK SPRING FARM BEEF BRISKET

1   2 to 3-lb. beef brisket
1/2 tsp. (or more) each onion salt,
*   seasoned salt*
Pepper to taste
1 env. dry onion soup mix
3 or 4 tbsp. chili sauce

Season . . . . . brisket with onion salt, seasoned salt and pepper.
Place . . . . in baking dish.
Chill . . . . covered, overnight.
Bake . . . . uncovered, at 400 degrees until browned, turning once.
Sprinkle . . . . with soup mix.
Bake . . . . covered, at 250 degrees for 1 hour.

Top . . . . with chili sauce.
Bake . . . . for 1 hour longer.
Yields . . . . . . 12 servings.

Approx Per Serv: Cal 361, Prot 20.3 g, T Fat 29.1 g, Chl 82.4 mg, Car 3.2 g, Sod 538 mg, Pot 353.7 mg.

Sue Blain, Schuylkill

TEXAS BARBECUE

1 2-lb. steak
1 c. catsup
1/4 c. vinegar
2 tbsp. brown sugar
2 tbsp. Worcestershire sauce
2 tbsp. chopped green pepper
1 med. onion, chopped
1/2 tsp. salt
1/2 tsp. pepper
1 tsp. prepared mustard

Pound . . . . . . steak with meat mallet to tenderize.
Place . . . . in baking dish.
Combine . . . . remaining ingredients in sauce-pan, mixing well.
Bring . . . . to a boil.
Pour . . . . over steak.
Bake . . . . at 325 degrees for 2 hours, turn-ing once.
Yields . . . . . . 8 servings.

Approx Per Serv: Cal 387, Prot 18.9 g, T Fat 28.3 g, Chl 71.7 mg, Car 13.9 g, Sod 525.6 mg, Pot 487.7 mg.

Danny Graybill, Juniata

FUND-RAISER HAMBURGER BARBECUE

10 lb. ground beef
5 lg. onions, chopped, cooked
2 bunches celery, chopped, cooked
2 lb. carrots, chopped, cooked
4 green peppers, chopped, cooked
4 bottles of catsup
2 bottles of chili sauce

Brown . . . . . . ground beef in soup pot, stirring until crumbly; drain.
Add . . . . vegetables, catsup and chili sauce.
Simmer . . . . . for 20 minutes.
Yields . . . . . . 150 servings.

Mary T. Hosterman, Centre

MEXICALI MEAT LOAVES

1 lb. ground beef
1/2 c. oats
1 egg
1 tsp. chili powder
1/2 tsp. salt
1 8-oz. can tomato sauce
1 4-oz. can chopped green chilies, drained
4 tsp. instant minced onion
1/8 tsp. garlic powder
1/2 c. shredded Cheddar cheese

Combine . . . . first 5 ingredients, 1/4 cup tomato sauce, 2 tablespoons green chilies and 3 teaspoons minced onion, mixing well.
Shape . . . . . . into 4 loaves and place in baking dish.
Microwave . . on High for 6 to 7 minutes, ro-tating every 2 minutes.
Mix . . . . garlic powder, remaining tomato sauce, green chilies and minced onion in glass bowl.
Microwave . . on High for 1 minute.
Spoon . . . . . . over meat loaves.
Top . . . . with cheese.
Yields . . . . . . 4 servings.

Photograph for this recipe on page 2.

SPICY MEAT LOAF

1 1/2 lb. ground beef
3 slices bread, torn into pieces
3/4 c. milk
1 egg, beaten
2 tsp. catsup
1 tbsp. horseradish
1 tbsp. Worcestershire sauce
1/4 c. minced onion
1/2 tsp. pepper
1/4 tsp. garlic salt

Combine . . . . all ingredients in bowl, mixing well.
Shape . . . . . . into loaf in baking pan.
Bake . . . . at 350 degrees for 1 hour.
Yields . . . . . . 8 servings.

Approx Per Serv: Cal 287, Prot 17.9 g, T Fat 19.9 g, Chl 93 mg, Car 7.8 g, Sod 226.6 mg, Pot 329.1 mg.

Edith A. Riker, Allegheny

SPICED MEATBALL CASSEROLE

1 lb. ground beef
2 tbsp. each minced onion, green pepper
1/2 c. cornmeal
1 1/2 tsp. dry mustard
1 tsp. each salt, chili powder
1/8 tsp. pepper
1/2 c. milk
1 egg
1/4 c. flour
1/4 c. shortening, melted
1/4 c. catsup
2 tbsp. Worcestershire sauce
4 carrots, cut in halves
4 potatoes, quartered
6 sm. onions

Combine . . . . first 10 ingredients in large bowl.
Shape . . . . . . into 12 balls.
Roll . . . . each in flour.
Brown . . . . . . in shortening in Dutch oven.
Mix . . . . remaining flour, 1 cup water, catsup and Worcestershire sauce in bowl.
Add . . . . to meatballs with carrots, potatoes and onions, mixing well.
Bake . . . . at 400 degrees for 35 to 45 minutes or until done.
Yields . . . . . . 6 servings.

Approx Per Serv: Cal 540, Prot 21.7 g, T Fat 27.6 g, Chl 96.4 mg, Car 51.9 g, Sod 631.5 mg, Pot 1177.8 mg.

Penny Ritenour, Somerset

TWIN MEAT LOAVES

2 lb. ground beef
1/4 c. chopped onion
2 tbsp. chopped celery
2 tsp. salt
1/4 tsp. each pepper, sage, dry mustard poultry seasoning
4 slices bread, cubed
1 c. warm milk
2 eggs, beaten
1 tbsp. Worcestershire sauce
1/2 c. dry bread crumbs
1/2 c. chili sauce

Combine . . . . first 8 ingredients in bowl, mixing well.
Soak . . . . cubed bread in warm milk in bowl.

Add . . . . eggs and Worcestershire sauce, beating well.
Mix . . . . into ground beef mixture.
Shape . . . . . . into 2 loaves.
Coat . . . . with bread crumbs.
Place . . . . in greased baking pan.
Spread . . . . . chili sauce over loaves.
Pour . . . . 1/2 cup boiling water around loaves.
Bake . . . . at 350 degrees for 1 hour, basting with pan juices every 15 minutes.
Yields . . . . . . 10 servings.

Approx Per Serv: Cal 343.1, Prot 20.4 g, T Fat 21.9 g, Chl 116.3 mg, Car 14.8 g, Sod 761 mg, Pot 400.6 mg.

Ann Powell, Lackawanna

MEATBALLS AND SAUCE

1/3 c. minced onion
1/2 c. butter
2 eggs
2 c. milk
1 c. fine bread crumbs
4 tsp. salt
1 tsp. pepper
3 lb. ground beef
1 lb. ground pork
3 tbsp. flour
4 beef bouillon cubes
1 1/2 tbsp. lemon juice
4 bay leaves

Saute . . . . . . onion in 1 tablespoon butter in skillet.
Combine . . . . with next 7 ingredients in bowl, mixing well.
Shape . . . . . . into 1-inch balls.
Brown . . . . . . in remaining butter in skillet.
Mix . . . . flour and 1/2 cup water in small bowl until smooth.
Dissolve . . . . bouillon cubes in 1 cup boiling water in large bowl.
Add . . . . lemon juice and 3 1/2 cups water, mixing well.
Stir . . . . in flour mixture.
Pour . . . . over meatballs.
Add . . . . bay leaves.
Simmer . . . . . for 1 hour.
Yields . . . . . . 100 servings.

Approx Per Serv: Cal 65, Prot 3.8 g, T Fat 4.9 g, Chl 19.7 mg, Car 1.2 g, Sod 153.2 mg, Pot 63.9 mg.

Tish Avery, Wayne

PIZZA MEATBALLS

1/2 lb. Monterey Jack cheese
1 lb. ground beef
1 c. soft bread crumbs
1/2 c. milk
1 egg
1 onion, chopped
1/2 tsp. pepper
2 tbsp. oil
1   15-oz. jar spaghetti sauce

Cut . . . . cheese into twenty 1/2-inch cubes; shred remaining cheese.
Combine . . . . shredded cheese with next 6 ingredients in bowl, mixing well.
Shape . . . . . . into 1 1/2-inch balls around cheese cubes.
Brown . . . . . . in oil in skillet; drain.
Pour . . . . spaghetti sauce over meatballs.
Simmer . . . . . covered, until cooked through.
Yields . . . . . . 20 servings.

Approx Per Serv: Cal 303, Prot 7.7 g, T Fat 29.4 g, Chl 40.1 mg, Car 2.7 g, Sod 110.4 mg, Pot 81.8 mg.

Nutritional information does not include spaghetti sauce.

Priscilla Bush, Susquehanna

WAIKIKI MEATBALLS

1 1/2 lb. ground beef
2/3 c. cracker crumbs
1/3 c. minced onion
1 egg
1 1/2 tsp. salt
1/4 tsp. ginger
1/4 c. milk
1 tbsp. shortening
1 can pineapple tidbits
2 tbsp. cornstarch
1/2 c. packed brown sugar
1/3 c. vinegar
1 tbsp. soy sauce
1/3 c. chopped green pepper
1 sm. can mushrooms, drained (opt.)

Combine . . . . first 7 ingredients in bowl, mixing well.
Shape . . . . . . into balls.
Brown . . . . . . in shortening in skillet; remove and keep warm.
Drain . . . . . . excess pan drippings from skillet.

Drain . . . . . . pineapple, reserving syrup.
Mix . . . . cornstarch, brown sugar, reserved syrup, vinegar and soy sauce in bowl until smooth.
Pour . . . . into skillet.
Cook . . . . over medium heat until thick and bubbly, stirring constantly.
Add . . . . meatballs, pineapple, green pepper and mushrooms.
Cook . . . . until heated through.
Serve . . . . . . over rice.
Yields . . . . . . 6 servings.

Approx Per Serv: Cal 456, Prot 22.4 g, T Fat 21.3 g, Chl 120.2 mg, Car 44.5 g, Sod 909.7 mg, Pot 439.4 mg.

Barbara Carpenter, Wyoming

ITALIAN MEAT PIE

1 lb. ground beef
2/3 c. oats
1/2 c. chopped onion
1 egg
3/4 tsp. salt
1/8 tsp. each pepper, garlic powder
1 c. catsup
2 med. zucchini, sliced 1/4 in. thick
1/2 c. sliced ripe olives
1/2 tsp. each oregano, basil
1 c. shredded mozzarella cheese
2 tbsp. Parmesan cheese (opt.)

Combine . . . . first 5 ingredients with pepper, garlic powder and 1/2 cup catsup in bowl, mixing well.
Press . . . . into 9-inch pie plate.
Microwave . . at High for 6 to 7 minutes, rotating once; drain.
Combine . . . . zucchini, olives, oregano, basil, 1/2 cup mozzarella cheese and remaining 1/2 cup catsup in bowl, mixing well.
Spoon . . . . . . into ground beef shell.
Top . . . . with remaining 1/2 cup mozzarella cheese and Parmesan cheese.
Microwave . . at High for 7 to 8 minutes, turning every 2 minutes.
Yields . . . . . . 4-6 servings.

Photograph for this recipe on page 2.

BURGER BUNDLES

1 lb. ground beef
1/3 c. evaporated milk
1 c. herb-seasoned stuffing mix
1 can mushroom soup
2 tsp. Worcestershire sauce
1 tbsp. catsup

Combine .... ground beef and evaporated milk in bowl, mixing well.
Shape ...... into 5 patties with well in center of each.
Prepare ..... stuffing mix using package directions.
Spoon ...... stuffing into wells, folding to enclose filling.
Place .... in baking dish.
Mix .... remaining 3 ingredients in bowl.
Pour .... over patties.
Bake .... at 350 degrees for 45 to 50 minutes or until cooked through.
Yields ...... 5 servings.

Approx Per Serv: Cal 332, Prot 19.9 g, T Fat 19.7 g, Chl 67 mg, Car 17.9 g, Sod 769.3 mg, Pot 333.7 mg.

Nutritional information does not include ingredients used in preparing stuffing mix.

Mary Foster, Susquehanna

FIESTA CASSEROLE

1 1/2 lb. hamburger
1/4 tsp. Tabasco sauce
Pepper to taste
1 med. onion, chopped
1/2 green pepper, chopped
1/4 tsp. garlic powder
1/2 tsp. chili powder
1/2 tsp. salt
1 1/2 c. macaroni, cooked
1/2 c. (about) Parmesan cheese
1 can tomato soup
1 soup can milk
1/2 c. bread crumbs

Brown ...... hamburger in skillet, stirring until crumbly.
Stir .... in next 7 ingredients.
Layer ...... macaroni, hamburger mixture and cheese alternately in greased 2-quart casserole until all ingredients are used.
Mix .... soup and milk in bowl.
Pour .... over casserole.

Sprinkle .... bread crumbs over top.
Bake .... at 350 degrees for 30 to 40 minutes or until heated through.
Yields ...... 8 servings.

Approx Per Serv: Cal 407, Prot 23.2 g, T Fat 22.6 g, Chl 70.7 mg, Car 26.5 g, Sod 586.3 mg, Pot 464 mg.

Heather Lyn Temple, Union

PIZZA CASSEROLE

1 lb. ground beef
1/4 c. chopped onion
1/4 c. chopped green pepper
1/2 tsp. salt
Pepper to taste
Garlic powder to taste
5 oz. curly noodles, cooked
1 can tomato soup
1/2 c. chopped mushrooms
1 tsp. oregano
6 oz. mozzarella cheese, shredded

Brown ...... ground beef with onion and green pepper in skillet, stirring until crumbly; drain.
Stir .... in salt, pepper and garlic powder to taste.
Combine .... with noodles in 2-quart casserole, mixing well.
Cook .... soup, mushrooms, oregano and half the cheese in saucepan until heated through, stirring frequently.
Pour .... over casserole.
Top .... with remaining cheese.
Bake .... covered, at 350 degrees for 45 minutes.
Bake .... uncovered, for 15 minutes longer.
Yields ...... 6 servings.

Approx Per Serv: Cal 398, Prot 23.4 g, T Fat 22.4 g, Chl 98 mg, Car 25.2 g, Sod 732.2 mg, Pot 344.3 mg.

Dolores Simasek, Delaware

THREE-CHEESE LASAGNA

1 lb. ground beef
1/2 c. chopped onion
1 15-oz. jar spaghetti sauce with mushrooms
1 tsp. each garlic salt, oregano
1/2 tsp. basil

8 oz. lasagna noodles, cooked, drained
1 1/2 c. cottage cheese
2 c. shredded mozzarella cheese
3/4 c. Parmesan cheese

Brown . . . . . . ground beef with onion in skillet, stirring until crumbly; drain.
Stir . . . . in spaghetti sauce, garlic salt,
oregano and basil.
Layer . . . . . . 1/3 of the noodles, sauce, cottage cheese, mozzarella cheese
and Parmesan cheese in buttered
2-quart baking dish.
Repeat . . . . . l a y e r s   w i t h   r e m a i n i n g
ingredients.
Bake . . . . at 350 degrees for 45 minutes.
Let . . . . stand for 10 minutes before
serving.
Yields . . . . . . 8 servings.

Approx Per Serv: Cal 345, Prot 25.4 g, T Fat 16.1 g,
Chl 90.5 mg, Car 23.2 g, Sod 508.9 mg, Pot 226.6 mg.

Nutritional information does not include spaghetti
sauce.

Danielle Yoder, Berks

HAMBURGER HEAVEN

1 lb. ground beef
1/2 lb. American cheese, sliced
1 c. chopped celery
1 sm. can sliced ripe olives
1 20-oz. can tomatoes
2 c. noodles
1/2 tsp. onion salt

Brown . . . . . . ground beef in skillet, stirring
until crumbly.
Layer . . . . . . next 5 ingredients over ground
beef in order given.
Dissolve . . . . onion salt in 1/4 cup water in
bowl.
Pour . . . . over noodles.
Simmer . . . . . covered, for 30 minutes.
Yields . . . . . . 8 servings.

Approx Per Serv: Cal 387, Prot 20.3 g, T Fat 22 g, Chl
85.6 mg, Car 26.3 g, Sod 796.9 mg, Pot 473.1 mg.

Doris S. Hollingshead, Franklin

WHIMPIES

1 lb. ground beef
1 onion, chopped
2 tbsp. mustard

1 tbsp. each Worcestershire sauce, vinegar
3 tbsp. sugar
3/4 c. catsup

Brown . . . . . . ground beef with onion in skil-
let, stirring until crumbly; drain.
Mix . . . . in remaining ingredients.
Simmer . . . . . for 1 1/2 hours.
Yields . . . . . . 8 servings.

Judy Muller, Wayne

SPAGHETTI-CABBAGE ROLL DINNER

12 med. cabbage leaves
1 lb. ground beef
1 sm. onion, chopped
1 clove of garlic, minced
1 tbsp. oil
1 egg, slightly beaten
1/4 tsp. pepper
4 tsp. salt
8 oz. spaghetti
Grated Parmesan cheese
1 15-oz. jar marinara or tomato sauce

Cook . . . . cabbage in 12 cups boiling water
in large saucepan for 5 minutes
or until tender; drain, reserving
liquid.
Brown . . . . . . ground beef with onion and garlic in oil in large skillet, stirring
until crumbly; remove.
Add . . . . egg, pepper and 1 teaspoon salt,
mixing well.
Place . . . . 2 tablespoons ground beef mixture in center of each cabbage
leaf.
Fold . . . . sides to center to enclose filling.
Roll . . . . as for jelly roll from narrow end.
Place . . . . seam side down in skillet.
Add . . . . 1 cup boiling water.
Simmer . . . . . covered, for 20 minutes or until
heated through.
Cook . . . . spaghetti in reserved liquid with
remaining 3 teaspoons salt until
tender; drain.
Place . . . . cabbage rolls on spaghetti in
serving dish.
Garnish . . . . . with Parmesan cheese.
Serve . . . . with marinara sauce.
Yields . . . . . . 4 servings.

Photograph for this recipe on page 69.

BASIC CASSEROLE

1 1/2 lb. ground beef
1 c. milk
4 c. chopped cooked potatoes
1 can each minestrone, cream of mushroom
   soup
1 onion, chopped (opt.)

Brown . . . . . . ground beef in skillet, stirring
                 until crumbly; drain.
Add . . . . remaining ingredients, mixing
                 well.
Spoon . . . . . . into greased casserole.
Bake . . . . at 350 degrees for 1/2 hour.
Yields . . . . . . 6 servings.

Approx Per Serv: Cal 290, Prot 13.5 g, T Fat 12.5 g,
Chl 44.4 mg, Car 31.6 g, Sod 850.4 mg, Pot 754 mg.

Margie Russell, Lancaster

SIX-LAYER CASSEROLE

2 c. sliced potatoes
2 c. chopped celery
2 c. sliced carrots
2 c. ground beef
1 c. sliced onions
2 c. canned tomatoes
2 tsp. salt
1/4 tsp. pepper

Layer . . . . . . first 6 ingredients in order given
                 in greased casserole, seasoning
                 each layer with salt and pepper.
Bake . . . . at 350 degrees for 2 hours.
Yields . . . . . . 6 servings.

Approx Per Serv: Cal 493, Prot 30.1 g, T Fat 32.4 g,
Chl 102.8 mg, Car 19.6 g, Sod 981.6 mg, Pot 1116.9
mg.

Janie Baer, Somerset

CROCK•POT HAMBURGER
VEGETABLE CASSEROLE

1 1/2 lb. ground beef
2 lg. potatoes, sliced
2 med. carrots, sliced
1 sm. can peas
3 med. onions, chopped
2 stalks celery, sliced
1/2 tsp. salt
Pepper to taste
1 can tomato soup

Brown . . . . . . ground beef in skillet, stirring
                 until crumbly.
Place . . . . vegetables in Crock•Pot in order
                 given, seasoning each layer with
                 salt and pepper.
Add . . . . ground beef.
Mix . . . . soup and 1 soup can water in
                 bowl.
Pour . . . . over ground beef.
Cook . . . . on Low for 6 to 8 hours.
Yields . . . . . . 6 servings.

Approx Per Serv: Cal 450, Prot 25.1 g, T Fat 25.4 g,
Chl 77.1 mg, Car 30.3 g, Sod 754.5 mg, Pot 929.4 mg.

Cheryl A. Wessner, Lehigh

DINNER-IN-A-DISH

1 lb. ground beef
1 onion, finely chopped
4 potatoes, sliced
1 can cream of chicken soup
1 soup can milk

Brown . . . . . . ground beef with onion in skil-
                 let, stirring until crumbly; drain.
Layer . . . . . . ground beef mixture and pota-
                 toes alternately in 2-quart casse-
                 role until all ingredients are
                 used.
Combine . . . . soup and milk in bowl, mixing
                 well.
Pour . . . . over top.
Bake . . . . at 400 degrees for 1 hour.
Yields . . . . . . 6 servings.

Approx Per Serv: Cal 397, Prot 22.3 g, T Fat 19.1 g,
Chl 76.8 mg, Car 34 g, Sod 523.4 mg, Pot 945.8 mg.

George Messinger, Fulton

BARLEY HOT DISH

1 1/2 lb. ground beef
1 c. chopped onion
1/2 c. chopped celery
4 c. tomato juice
3/4 c. barley
1 lb. peas
1 lb. carrots, chopped
1 can cream of mushroom soup
2 1/2 tsp. salt
1/4 tsp. pepper
1 bay leaf

Brown . . . . . . ground beef with onion and celery in skillet, stirring until crumbly.
Stir . . . . in remaining ingredients with 2 1/2 cups water.
Bring . . . . to a boil.
Place . . . . in large baking dish.
Bake . . . . covered, at 375 degrees for 1 1/4 hours.
Yields . . . . . . 20 servings.

Approx Per Serv: Cal 170, Prot 8.8 g, T Fat 8.7 g, Chl 24.3 mg, Car 14.6 g, Sod 519.5 mg, Pot 359.4 mg.

Beth Adele Reed, Lancaster

BEST-IN-THE-WEST BARBECUED BEAN BAKE

1 lb. lean ground chuck
1 lb. bacon, chopped
1 onion, chopped
1/2 c. catsup
1/2 c. barbecue sauce
1 tsp. salt
4 tbsp. mustard
4 tbsp. molasses
1 tsp. chili powder
3/4 tsp. pepper
2   16-oz. cans each kidney beans, pork and beans, butter beans

Brown . . . . . . ground chuck with bacon and onion in Dutch oven, stirring until crumbly; drain.
Add . . . . next 7 ingredients, mixing well.
Stir . . . . in beans.
Bake . . . . at 350 degrees for 1 hour.
Yields . . . . . . 20-24 servings.

Approx Per Serv: Cal 300, Prot 12.6 g, T Fat 16.6 g, Chl 28.2 mg, Car 25.5 g, Sod 650.8 mg, Pot 435 mg.

Audrey Ridinger, Adams

JONAH-IN-THE-WHALE

1 lg. Hubbard squash
2 lb. ground beef
1/2 c. each chopped onion, celery
1 clove of garlic, chopped
1/2 tsp. each marjoram, pepper
1 tsp. each parsley flakes, salt
1/4 tsp. paprika
1 tbsp. oil

Cut . . . . squash in half lengthwise, removing seeds.
Place . . . . halves together.
Bake . . . . in moderate oven in 1/2 inch water in baking pan until tender.
Brown . . . . . . ground beef in skillet, stirring until crumbly; remove ground beef.
Saute . . . . . . onion, celery and garlic in pan drippings.
Add . . . . ground beef and seasonings, mixing well.
Brush . . . . . . cut edges of squash with oil.
Spoon . . . . . . ground beef mixture into squash halves.
Place . . . . in baking dish.
Bake . . . . covered with foil, for 15 minutes longer.
Yields . . . . . . 8 servings.

Approx Per Serv: Cal 349, Prot 21.4 g, T Fat 25.8 g, Chl 77.1 mg, Car 7.4 g, Sod 348.6 mg, Pot 575.9 mg.

Deborah Brown, Allegheny

SHIPWRECK

2 onions, sliced
2 potatoes, sliced
1 lb. ground beef
1/2 c. rice
1 c. chopped celery
1 c. sliced carrots
1 tsp. salt
Pepper to taste
Paprika
1 can cream of mushroom soup
1/2 c. grated American cheese

Layer . . . . . . first 6 ingredients in order given in buttered 9 x 13-inch baking dish, sprinkling each layer with salt, pepper and paprika.
Mix . . . . soup and 1 cup boiling water in bowl.
Pour . . . . over layers.
Bake . . . . covered, at 275 degrees for 3 to 4 hours or until vegetables are tender.
Sprinkle . . . . cheese over top.
Bake . . . . uncovered, for 10 minutes.
Yields . . . . . . 6 servings.

Approx Per Serv: Cal 424, Prot 19.9 g, T Fat 22.5 g, Chl 62.2 mg, Car 35.4 g, Sod 990.4 mg, Pot 767.2 mg.

Kelvin Lehman, Franklin

BACON-TOMATO SKILLET DINNER

10 slices bacon, chopped
1 med. onion, chopped
2 cans stewed tomatoes
1 lb. macaroni, cooked, drained

Cook . . . . bacon with onion in skillet until crisp; drain.
Add . . . . tomatoes.
Simmer . . . . . for several minutes.
Combine . . . . with macaroni in large serving bowl, tossing to mix.
Yields . . . . . . 4 servings.

Approx Per Serv: Cal 590, Prot 29.9 g, T Fat 11.6 g, Chl 16.6 mg, Car 98.5 g, Sod 491.7 mg, Pot 810.1 mg.

Robert Middleton, Schuylkill

HAM BARBECUE

2 c. catsup
1/4 c. chili sauce
1/2 c. relish
3 lb. chipped ham

Mix . . . . catsup, chili sauce, relish and 3 cups water in saucepan.
Simmer . . . . . for 30 minutes.
Stir . . . . in ham.
Serve . . . . on hamburger buns.
Yields . . . . . . 24 servings.

Approx Per Serv: Cal 163, Prot 11.3 g, T Fat 9.8 g, Chl 50.5 mg, Car 7.4 g, Sod 969.7 mg, Pot 217.6 mg.

Hilda Hearn, Blair

CHEESY BROCCOLI-HAM STRATA

5 slices bread, cubed
1 c. cooked ham
1   10-oz. package frozen broccoli in cheese sauce, thawed
1/2 c. shredded Cheddar cheese
3 eggs, slightly beaten
1 3/4 c. milk
1/4 tsp. each salt, dry mustard

Place . . . . half the bread cubes in bottom of buttered 8 x 8-inch baking dish.
Layer . . . . . . ham, broccoli and cheese over bread.
Top . . . . with remaining bread cubes.

Mix . . . . eggs, milk, salt and dry mustard in bowl.
Pour . . . . over bread cubes.
Chill . . . . covered, for several hours.
Bake . . . . uncovered, at 350 degrees for 45 to 50 minutes or until knife inserted in center comes out clean.
Let . . . . stand for 10 minutes before cutting into squares.
Yields . . . . . . 4 servings.

Approx Per Serv: Cal 384, Prot 22.5 g, T Fat 21.5 g, Chl 250.7 mg, Car 23.8 g, Sod 772.9 mg, Pot 333 mg.

Nutritional information does not include broccoli in cheese sauce.

Katrina Harbach, Clinton

SCALLOPED POTATOES AND HAM SLICES

7 or 8 med. potatoes, thinly sliced
1 lg. onion, thinly sliced
5 tsp. salt
4 tbsp. margarine, melted
5 tsp. (heaping) flour
Paprika
2 1/4 c. milk
1/2 tsp. pepper
Ham slices
Chopped parsley

Cook . . . . potatoes and onion with 3 teaspoons salt in boiling water to cover in saucepan for 5 minutes; drain.
Blend . . . . . . margarine, flour and 1/4 teaspoon paprika in saucepan.
Add . . . . milk slowly, mixing well.
Sprinkle . . . . with 2 teaspoons salt and pepper.
Cook . . . . over low heat until thick, stirring constantly.
Layer . . . . . . 1/3 of the ham slices, potatoes and white sauce in greased casserole, sprinkling each layer with parsley and paprika.
Repeat . . . . . layers with remaining ingredients.
Bake . . . . at 400 degrees for 40 minutes.
Yields . . . . . . 8 servings.

Dorothy Staudenmeier, Luzerne

Recipe on page 38.

EASY HAM AND SCALLOPED POTATOES

5 c. thinly sliced potatoes
1 lb. chopped cooked ham
1/2 c. sliced onion
1/4 c. sliced green pepper
1 can cream of mushroom soup
1/4 c. milk
2 tbsp. margarine

Layer . . . . . . half the potatoes and all the ham in greased 2-quart casserole.
Top . . . . with remaining potatoes, onion and green pepper.
Mix . . . . soup and milk in bowl.
Pour . . . . over casserole.
Dot . . . . with margarine.
Bake . . . . covered, at 350 degrees for 1 hour.
Bake . . . . uncovered, for 45 minutes or until potatoes are tender.
Yields . . . . . . 4 servings.

Approx Per Serv: Cal 507, Prot 34.9 g, T Fat 22.5 g, Chl 107.8 mg, Car 41.2 g, Sod 1704.3 mg, Pot 1213.8 mg.

Fay Yoder, Berks

HAM-POTATO AND CHEESE CASSEROLE

1 med. onion, chopped
3 tbsp. chopped green pepper
4 tbsp. margarine
2 1/2 tbsp. flour
2 c. milk
3 c. chopped cooked ham
3 c. chopped cooked potatoes
1/2 tsp. (or more) salt
Pepper to taste
3/4 c. shredded cheese

Saute . . . . . . onion and green pepper in margarine in skillet for 5 minutes.
Stir . . . . in flour until well blended.
Add . . . . milk gradually, mixing well.
Cook . . . . until thick, stirring constantly.
Combine . . . . with ham, potatoes, salt and pepper in 2-quart casserole, mixing well.
Top . . . . with cheese.

Recipes on pages 75 and 76.

Bake . . . . at 350 degrees for 25 to 30 minutes or until heated through.
Yields . . . . . . 4 servings.

Approx Per Serv: Cal 725, Prot 36.1 g, T Fat 46 g, Chl 131.5 mg, Car 41.3 g, Sod 1439.9 mg, Pot 1194.8 mg.

Nancy Honeywell, Luzerne

PORK CHOPS AND RICE

2 tbsp. instant chicken bouillon
1 tbsp. instant minced onion
1 can each cream of chicken, cream of mushroom soup
1 c. long grain rice
4 1/2-in. thick pork chops, trimmed

Combine . . . . bouillon and onion with 2 cups boiling water in 9 x 9-inch baking pan, stirring until bouillon dissolves.
Stir . . . . in soups until smooth.
Mix . . . . in rice.
Arrange . . . . . pork chops over rice.
Bake . . . . tightly covered, at 350 degrees for 1 hour.
Yields . . . . . . 4 servings.

Approx Per Serv: Cal 622, Prot 26.3 g, T Fat 34.5 g, Chl 83.6 mg, Car 49.5 g, Sod 1965.5 mg, Pot 388.2 mg.

Denise Rupert, Mercer

SKILLET-BARBECUED PORK CHOPS

4 pork chops
1 tbsp. oil
1/3 c. chopped celery
2 tbsp. lemon juice
1/2 tsp. each salt, dry mustard
1/8 tsp. pepper
2 tsp. brown sugar
2 8-oz. cans tomato sauce

Brown . . . . . . pork chops in oil in skillet; drain.
Sprinkle . . . . next 6 ingredients over chops.
Pour . . . . tomato sauce over top.
Simmer . . . . . covered, for 1 hour or until chops are tender.
Yields . . . . . . 4 servings.

Approx Per Serv: Cal 368, Prot 20.3 g, T Fat 28.3 g, Chl 69.4 mg, Car 8 g, Sod 654.9 mg, Pot 499.3 mg.

Marjorie Hackenburg, Snyder

SCALLOPED POTATOES WITH PORK CHOPS

6   1/2-in. thick pork chops
1 tbsp. oil
1/2 c. chopped green onions
1 can cream of celery soup
1 1/4 c. milk
5 c. sliced potatoes
6 slices American cheese
1 tsp. salt
1/4 tsp. pepper

Brown . . . . . . pork chops on one side in oil in skillet; remove chops.
Saute . . . . . . onions in pan drippings until tender. Do not brown.
Add . . . . soup and milk, mixing well.
Cook . . . . until heated through.
Layer . . . . . . half the potatoes and all the cheese in greased 9 x 13-inch baking pan.
Top . . . . with remaining potatoes and pork chops, browned side down.
Sprinkle . . . . with salt and pepper.
Pour . . . . soup mixture over top.
Bake . . . . tightly covered, at 350 degrees for 1 hour.
Bake . . . . uncovered, for 30 minutes longer or until chops and vegetables are tender.
Yields . . . . . . 6 servings.

Approx Per Serv: Cal 641, Prot 32.3 g, T Fat 39.6 g, Chl 105 mg, Car 38.8 g, Sod 1150.9 mg, Pot 1120.6 mg.

Janice Beck, Forest

FLORIDA-BAKED PORK CHOP DINNER

6 pork chops, trimmed
1/2 c. orange juice
1/2 tsp. each salt, dry mustard
1/4 tsp. pepper
1/4 c. packed brown sugar
1   16-oz. can whole onions, drained
1   16-oz. can sliced carrots, drained
1 orange, thinly sliced

Place . . . . pork chops in large shallow baking dish.
Combine . . . . next 5 ingredients in bowl, mixing well.

Pour . . . . over chops.
Bake . . . . at 350 degrees for 45 minutes, basting occasionally.
Add . . . . onions, carrots and orange slices.
Bake . . . . for 5 minutes longer, basting once.
Yields . . . . . . 4 servings.

Approx Per Serv: Cal 593, Prot 31.6 g, T Fat 37.5 g, Chl 104.1 mg, Car 35 g, Sod 623.2 mg, Pot 798.6 mg.

Kathleen Lillicrapp, Delaware

SWEET AND SOUR PORK CHOPS

1/4 c. sugar
1/2 c. cider vinegar
1/4 c. packed brown sugar
2 tbsp. soy sauce
3/4 tsp. (or more) salt
1/4 c. chopped onion
1 green pepper, coarsely chopped
1/2 c. (or more) flour
1/4 tsp. (or more) pepper
6 to 8 pork chops

Mix . . . . first 4 ingredients with 1/4 teaspoon salt in saucepan.
Cook . . . . until thick.
Add . . . . onion and green pepper.
Combine . . . . flour with remaining salt and pepper to taste on plate.
Dredge . . . . . pork chops in seasoned flour.
Brown . . . . . . in skillet; drain.
Pour . . . . syrup over chops.
Simmer . . . . . covered, for 1 hour or until tender.
Yields . . . . . . 6 servings.

Approx Per Serv: Cal 421, Prot 20.9 g, T Fat 24.9 g, Chl 69.4 mg, Car 27.9 g, Sod 758.2 mg, Pot 328.7 mg.

Nutritional information includes 6 pork chops.

Dorothy Houtz, Centre

FRESH VEGETABLE SKILLET STEW

1 bunch broccoli
1 lb. lean pork, cut into 1/4-in. strips
1 clove of garlic, minced
2 tbsp. oil

1 med. onion, quartered, cut into
    1/4-in. strips
2 carrots, cut into 1/4-in. strips
1/4 c. soy sauce
1 tbsp. cornstarch
2 tsp. sugar
1/8 tsp. each salt, ginger

Slice . . . . broccoli stems into 1/8-inch slices and separate heads into flowerets.

Stir-fry . . . . . pork, broccoli stems and garlic in oil in skillet over high heat for 5 minutes or until pork is brown.

Add . . . . broccoli flowerets, onion and carrots.

Cook . . . . covered, over medium heat for 5 minutes or until vegetables are tender-crisp, stirring occasionally.

Blend . . . . . . remaining 5 ingredients with 3/4 cup water in bowl.

Stir . . . . into skillet.

Simmer . . . . . for 2 minutes or until thick, stirring frequently.

Yields . . . . . . 4 servings.

Photograph for this recipe on page 35.

EASY PORK CASSEROLE

4 c. chopped cooked pork
2 med. onions, chopped
2 stalks celery, chopped
4 c. wide noodles, cooked, drained
1 can each cream of mushroom, cream
    of celery soup
2 c. pork broth

Saute . . . . . . pork, onions and celery in a small amount of oil in Dutch oven.

Add . . . . remaining ingredients, mixing well.

Bake . . . . at 350 degrees for 1 1/2 to 2 hours or until pork and vegetables are tender.

Yields . . . . . . 6 servings.

Approx Per Serv: Cal 642, Prot 31.7 g, T Fat 35 g, Chl 137.3 mg, Car 48.3 g, Sod 869.8 mg, Pot 522.2 mg.

Nutritional information does not include pork broth.

Barbara Wessner, Lehigh

SAUERKRAUT AND SAUSAGE BAKE

1 1/2 lb. pork sausage
1 28-oz. can sauerkraut, drained
1 tbsp. chopped onion
4 servings instant mashed potatoes
4 tbsp. grated sharp cheese

Brown . . . . . . sausage in skillet, stirring until crumbly; drain.

Mix . . . . sauerkraut and onion in 1 1/2-quart casserole.

Cover . . . . . . with sausage.

Prepare . . . . . potatoes using package directions.

Stir . . . . cheese into hot potatoes.

Spread . . . . . over sausage.

Bake . . . . at 400 degrees for 35 to 40 minutes.

Yields . . . . . . 4 servings.

Approx Per Serv: Cal 547, Prot 20.4 g, T Fat 41.8 g, Chl 126.1 mg, Car 23.7 g, Sod 2619.7 mg, Pot 817.1 mg.

Nancy A. Hottle, Bucks

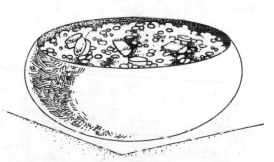

FRANKFURTER-BEAN CASSEROLE

1 16-oz. can pork and beans
1 16-oz. can kidney beans
2 tsp. prepared mustard
1/4 c. catsup
4 frankfurters, cut into chunks
1/4 c. packed brown sugar

Mix . . . . first 5 ingredients in bowl.

Place . . . . in shallow baking dish.

Add . . . . 1/2 cup water if necessary.

Sprinkle . . . . brown sugar over top.

Bake . . . . at 350 degrees for 30 minutes or until heated through.

Yields . . . . . . 4 servings.

Approx Per Serv: Cal 382, Prot 17.2 g, T Fat 7.8 g, Chl 13.8 mg, Car 62.6 g, Sod 939.9 mg, Pot 740.1 mg.

Sandy Yemm, Schuylkill

BREAKFAST PIZZA

1 pkg. refrigerator crescent rolls
1 lb. sausage
1 c. frozen hashed brown potatoes, thawed
1 c. grated Cheddar cheese
5 eggs
1/4 c. milk
1/4 tsp. salt
1/8 tsp. pepper
2 tbsp. Parmesan cheese

Press . . . . rolls over bottom and side of 12-inch pizza pan.
Brown . . . . . . sausage in skillet, stirring until crumbly; drain.
Layer . . . . . . sausage, potatoes and Cheddar cheese over dough.
Mix . . . . eggs, milk, salt and pepper in bowl.
Pour . . . . over Cheddar cheese.
Top . . . . with Parmesan cheese.
Bake . . . . at 375 degrees for 25 to 30 minutes or until crust is golden brown.
Yields . . . . . . 4 servings.

Approx Per Serv: Cal 692, Prot 31.7 g, T Fat 47.1 g, Chl 423.3 mg, Car 33.1 g, Sod 1256.7 mg, Pot 402.3 mg.

Wendy Leiby, Schuylkill

RABBIT CACCIATORE

2   4 1/2 to 6-lb. rabbits, cut up
3 or 4 cloves of garlic, crushed
3 sprigs of rosemary
1 tsp. salt
1/2 tsp. pepper
4 tbsp. oil
Flour

Place . . . . rabbit in roasting pan.
Rub . . . . with 3 cloves of garlic.
Add . . . . rosemary and 1 cup water.
Season . . . . . with salt and pepper.
Bake . . . . covered, at 350 degrees for 45 minutes or until tender; reserve pan drippings.
Brown . . . . . . rabbit with remaining clove of garlic in oil in large skillet; remove rabbit to serving platter.
Stir . . . . in enough flour to make smooth paste.

Mix . . . . in reserved pan drippings.
Cook . . . . until thick, stirring constantly.
Serve . . . . with rabbit.
Yields . . . . . . 4 servings.

Approx Per Serv: Cal 1711, Prot 215.5 g, T Fat 87.8 g, Chl 668.8 mg, Car .7 g, Sod 834.7 mg, Pot 2716.8 mg.

Karen Rosati, Lackawanna

BARBECUED RABBIT

3 tbsp. butter, melted
1/2 c. vinegar
1/2 tsp. garlic salt
Dash of pepper
2 rabbits, cut up

Mix . . . . first 4 ingredients in bowl.
Grill . . . . rabbits over hot coals for 1 hour or until tender, basting frequently with seasoned vinegar.
Yields . . . . . . 8 servings.

Approx Per Serv: Cal 702, Prot 89.8 g, T Fat 35.2 g, Chl 292 mg, Car .9 g, Sod 311.5 mg, Pot 1143.2 mg.

Carolyn B. Welty, Franklin

OVEN-BARBECUED RABBIT

1 rabbit, cut up
1 sm. onion, chopped
1/4 c. chili sauce
2 tbsp. each lemon juice, Worcestershire sauce
1/2 c. each catsup, vinegar
1 tbsp. brown sugar

Place . . . . rabbit in baking dish.
Bake . . . . at 325 degrees for 30 minutes.
Combine . . . . remaining ingredients in saucepan.
Cook . . . . until sugar is dissolved.
Pour . . . . over rabbit.
Bake . . . . for 35 minutes longer or until tender, basting every 15 minutes.
Yields . . . . . . 4 servings.

Approx Per Serv: Cal 742, Prot 91.2 g, T Fat 31.2 g, Chl 278.7 mg, Car 20.2 g, Sod 671.5 mg, Pot 1435.8 mg.

Happy Hoppers, Butler

Main Dishes:

MIXED FRESH VEGETABLES IN CHEESE SAUCE, recipe on page 50.

Seafood, Poultry, Vegetarian

ADD-A-CRUNCH BAKED CHICKEN

1 egg
1/3 c. milk
2 c. oats
1/2 c. melted butter
1/3 c. Parmesan cheese
1/3 c. chopped nuts
1/4 tsp. garlic salt
1   2 1/2 to 3-lb. chicken, cut up

Mix . . . . egg and milk in bowl.
Combine . . . . oats, butter, cheese, nuts and garlic salt in bowl, mixing well.
Dip . . . . chicken in milk mixture.
Roll . . . . in oat mixture.
Place . . . . in foil-lined baking dish.
Bake . . . . at 375 degrees for 45 to 55 minutes or until tender.
Yields . . . . . . 4 servings.

Photograph for this recipe on page 2.

CHICKEN BARBECUE

1 tsp. salt
1/2 tsp. pepper
1 tbsp. sugar
1 med. onion, chopped
1 c. catsup
1 tbsp. Worcestershire sauce
1 tbsp. margarine
1 chicken, cut up

Combine . . . . first 6 ingredients with 1/2 cup hot water in saucepan.
Bring . . . . to a boil.
Stir . . . . in margarine.
Pour . . . . over chicken in baking pan.
Bake . . . . covered, at 325 degrees for 1/2 hour.
Bake . . . . uncovered, for 1 to 2 hours or until tender.
Yields . . . . . . 4 servings.

Approx Per Serv: Cal 236, Prot 22.8 g, T Fat 6.5 g, Chl 0 mg, Car 21.7 g, Sod 934.1 mg, Pot 540.3 mg.

Jessica Barron, Schuylkill

CHICKEN AND BISCUITS CASSEROLE

Salt and pepper
1   3 1/2-lb. chicken, cut up
3 c. chicken broth
1 1/2 c. chopped celery
1 c. chopped onion
1 c. sliced carrots
Butter
1 1/2 c. flour
1/2 tsp. poultry seasoning
2 c. milk
1/2 c. shredded Cheddar cheese
1 1/2 tsp. baking powder

Sprinkle . . . . salt and pepper over chicken.
Place . . . . with next 4 ingredients in 4-quart saucepan.
Simmer . . . . . covered, for 45 minutes or until chicken is tender; drain, reserving broth.
Cut . . . . chicken into bite-sized pieces; set aside.
Combine . . . . 1/3 cup melted butter, 1/2 cup flour and poultry seasoning in large saucepan, stirring until smooth.
Cook . . . . until heated through, stirring constantly; remove from heat.
Stir . . . . in 1 1/2 cups each milk and broth gradually.
Bring . . . . to a boil, stirring constantly.
Cook . . . . for 1 minute, stirring constantly.
Stir . . . . in vegetables and chicken.
Spoon . . . . . . into 2-quart casserole.
Combine . . . . 1 cup flour, cheese, baking powder and 1/4 teaspoon salt in bowl, mixing well.
Cut . . . . in 3 tablespoons softened butter until crumbly.
Stir . . . . in 1/2 cup milk until mixture is moistened.
Drop . . . . by rounded tablespoonfuls onto chicken mixture.
Bake . . . . at 425 degrees for 20 to 25 minutes or until biscuits are golden.

Photograph for this recipe on cover.

CHICKEN DIVAN

1   10-oz. package frozen broccoli spears, cooked, drained
4 chicken breasts, cooked, boned
1 can cream of chicken soup
1/2 c. mayonnaise
1/2 tsp. curry powder
1/2 tsp. lemon juice

1/4 c. soft bread crumbs
2 tbsp. melted butter
1/2 c. shredded Cheddar cheese

Layer . . . . . . broccoli and chicken in shallow 1 1/2-quart baking dish.
Mix . . . . next 4 ingredients in bowl.
Pour . . . . over chicken.
Toss . . . . bread crumbs and butter in bowl.
Sprinkle . . . . cheese and buttered bread crumbs over casserole.
Bake . . . . at 350 degrees for 25 minutes.
Yields . . . . . . 4 servings.

Approx Per Serv: Cal 586, Prot 42.1 g, T Fat 41.5 g, Chl 140.3 mg, Car 11.5 g, Sod 1019.3 mg, Pot 568.9 mg.

Connie Lawrence, Wyoming

JUICY CHICKEN

3 c. finely crushed Cherrios
1 tsp. salt
1/8 tsp. each sage, garlic powder
1/2 tsp. each pepper, onion powder
1/2 tsp. each oregano, parsley flakes
1   2 1/2 to 3-lb. chicken, cut up
1/2 c. milk
2 tbsp. melted butter

Combine . . . . Cheerios with seasonings in bowl, mixing well.
Dip . . . . chicken in milk and coat with Cheerios mixture.
Place . . . . skin side up in foil-lined baking pan.
Drizzle . . . . . butter over chicken.
Bake . . . . at 350 degrees for 1 hour or until tender. Do not turn.
Yields . . . . . . 6 servings.

Approx Per Serv: Cal 177, Prot 16.2 g, T Fat 7.5 g, Chl 65.8 mg, Car 10.4 g, Sod 609.3 mg, Pot 191.5 mg.

Karan Heffelfinger, Carbon

QUICK CHICKEN PAPRIKA

1   2 1/2 to 3-lb. chicken, cut up
1 1/4 tsp. salt
Paprika
1 med. onion, chopped

1/4 c. butter, melted
1/2 c. sour cream

Sprinkle . . . . chicken with 1 teaspoon salt and paprika to taste.
Brown . . . . . . chicken with onion in butter in large skillet.
Add . . . . 1/2 cup water.
Simmer . . . . . covered, for 30 minutes or until chicken is tender; remove to heated platter.
Stir . . . . sour cream, remaining salt and 1 teaspoon paprika into pan drippings.
Heat . . . . to serving temperature, stirring
Pour . . . . over chicken.
Sprinkle . . . . with parsley.
Yields . . . . . . 4 servings.

Approx Per Serv: Cal 295, Prot 22.5 g, T Fat 20.9 g, Chl 124.9 mg, Car 4.1 g, Sod 882.9 mg, Pot 336.4 mg.

Shirley A. Wisser, Lehigh

FRIED CHICKEN

1 egg, beaten
1/2 c. milk
1 c. flour
1/4 c. cornmeal
1/2 tsp. baking powder
1/4 tsp. each garlic powder, paprika, basil
Pepper to taste
1/2 tsp. (or more) salt
1 chicken, cut up
Oil for deep frying

Mix . . . . egg and milk in bowl.
Combine . . . . remaining ingredients except chicken and oil in shallow bowl.
Dip . . . . chicken in egg mixture and coat with flour mixture.
Deep-fry . . . . for 20 to 30 minutes or until brown.
Arrange . . . . . on rack in roasting pan filled with boiling water.
Steam . . . . . . at 225 degrees for 10 to 15 minutes.
Yields . . . . . . 4 servings.

Approx Per Serv: Cal 306, Prot 27.6 g, T Fat 6.3 g, Chl 144.2 mg, Car 32.3 g, Sod 397 mg, Pot 342.4 mg.

Nutritional information does not include oil for deep frying.

Sharon Custer, Montgomery

CHICKEN WITH DUMPLINGS

1 5-lb. chicken, cut up
1 bunch celery
2 carrots, peeled, sliced
1 onion, sliced
3 tsp. salt
2 c. milk
2 1/3 c. flour
3 tsp. baking powder
1/4 c. minced parsley
1/4 c. shortening

Place . . . . first 4 ingredients and 2 teaspoons salt in 4 cups water in stock pot.
Simmer . . . . . covered, for 1 hour or until chicken is tender.
Cool . . . . chicken, bone and chop coarsely.
Strain . . . . . . broth, adding enough water to make 3 cups; return to stock pot.
Mix . . . . 1 cup milk and 1/3 cup flour in bowl until smooth.
Stir . . . . into hot broth gradually.
Cook . . . . for 5 minutes, stirring constantly.
Add . . . . chicken.
Sift . . . . 2 cups flour, baking powder and 1 teaspoon salt together in bowl.
Add . . . . parsley and cut in shortening until crumbly.
Stir . . . . in remaining 1 cup milk to make soft dough.
Drop . . . . by spoonfuls into bubbling chicken broth.
Simmer . . . . . for 10 minutes.
Simmer . . . . . covered, for 10 minutes longer.
Yields . . . . . . 8 servings.

Approx Per Serv: Cal 440, Prot 33.4 g, T Fat 17.4 g, Chl 84.7 mg, Car 36.4 g, Sod 1139.9 mg, Pot 803.1 mg.

Janice Beck, Forest

CHICKEN PATTIES

1 chicken, cooked
1/2 lb. fresh pork
1 onion, chopped
1/2 c. chopped celery
6 eggs
1 tsp. each oregano, garlic salt

Pepper to taste
1/2 tsp. (or more) salt

Put . . . . chicken, pork, onion and celery through food grinder.
Combine . . . . with remaining ingredients in bowl, mixing well.
Shape . . . . . . into patties.
Place . . . . in baking pan.
Bake . . . . at 350 degrees to desired degree of doneness.
Yields . . . . . . 6 servings.

Approx Per Serv: Cal 350, Prot 31.1 g, T Fat 22.9 g, Chl 341 mg, Car 2.7 g, Sod 683.4 mg, Pot 456.7 mg.

Judy Cain, Clinton

PEPSI CHICKEN

1 chicken, cut up
1 stick margarine, melted
1 12-oz. can Pepsi Cola
1 20-oz. bottle of catsup

Place . . . . chicken in margarine in electric skillet.
Pour . . . . Pepsi and catsup over top.
Cook . . . . at 250 degrees for 2 hours or until brown and tender.
Yields . . . . . . 4 servings.

Approx Per Serv: Cal 519, Prot 24.2 g, T Fat 27 g, Chl 76.7 mg, Car 47.4 g, Sod 1901.5 mg, Pot 792.7 mg.

Dawn Haney, Monroe

CHICKEN WAIKIKI BEACH

2 whole chicken legs
2 whole chicken breasts
1/2 c. flour
1/3 c. oil
1 tsp. salt
1/4 tsp. pepper
1 20-oz. can sliced pineapple
1 c. sugar
3/4 c. cider vinegar
1 tbsp. ginger
1 chicken bouillon cube
2 tbsp. cornstarch
1 lg. green pepper, sliced into 1/4-in. rings

Coat . . . . chicken with flour.
Brown . . . . . . in oil in skillet.
Place . . . . skin side up in baking dish.
Season . . . . . with salt and pepper.

Drain ...... pineapple, reserving syrup.
Add .... enough water to syrup to measure 1 1/4 cups.
Combine .... with next 5 ingredients in saucepan.
Boil .... for 2 minutes, stirring constantly.
Pour .... over chicken.
Bake .... at 350 degrees for 30 minutes.
Top .... with pineapple and green pepper.
Bake .... for 30 minutes longer or until tender.
Serve .... with rice.
Yields ...... 4 servings.

Approx Per Serv: Cal 1215, Prot 41.8 g, T Fat 28.4 g, Chl 87.3 mg, Car 268.7 g, Sod 882.8 mg, Pot 3517.1 mg.

Catherine Sterling, Carbon

CHICKEN ELEGANT

3 lg. chicken breasts, cooked, coarsely
chopped
1 pt. sour cream
1 can mushroom soup
1 c. mushrooms
2 sticks butter
1 c. chicken broth
1 pkg. herb-seasoned stuffing mix

Combine .... first 4 ingredients in bowl, mixing well.
Spoon ...... into 9 x 13-inch baking dish.
Melt .... butter in chicken broth in saucepan.
Stir .... in stuffing mix.
Spoon ...... over casserole.
Bake .... at 350 degrees for 45 minutes.
Yields ...... 8 servings.

Approx Per Serv: Cal 556, Prot 20.9 g, T Fat 41 g, Chl 138.6 mg, Car 27.5 g, Sod 1247.7 mg, Pot 365.6 mg.

Virginia Haist, Bucks

CHICKEN CASSEROLE

1 6-oz. box long grain and wild rice mix
1 can each cream of mushroom soup, cream
of celery soup
1 tbsp. chopped parsley
1/2 tsp. salt
1/4 tsp. pepper

Pinch of curry
10 pieces of chicken
3/4 pkg. dry onion soup mix
1/2 c. (or more) slivered almonds

Mix .... first 7 ingredients and 1 soup can water in buttered 9 x 13-inch baking dish.
Arrange ..... chicken, skin side up, in baking dish.
Top .... with soup mix and almonds.
Bake .... covered, at 350 degrees for 1 1/4 to 1 1/2 hours or to desired degree of doneness.
Yields ...... 10 servings.

Approx Per Serv: Cal 148, Prot 10.9 g, T Fat 8.4 g, Chl 39.6 mg, Car 7.6 g, Sod 819.7 mg, Pot 212.8 mg.

Nutritional information does not include rice.

Nina Lonchar, Allegheny

STUFFED CHICKEN DELIGHT

1/2 c. chopped onion
1/2 c. butter
2 c. bread cubes
1 tsp. each oregano, dry mustard
2 tsp. parsley flakes
4 chicken breasts, boned
1 tsp. seasoned salt
4 slices Monterey Jack cheese
1 can mushroom soup
Paprika

Brown ...... onion in butter in skillet.
Mix .... in next 4 ingredients.
Sprinkle .... inside of breasts with seasoned salt.
Top .... with cheese and spoonful of bread mixture.
Fold .... breasts to enclose filling, securing with toothpick.
Arrange ..... in baking dish.
Spoon ...... remaining bread mixture around edge.
Mix .... soup and 1 soup can water in bowl.
Pour .... over chicken.
Sprinkle .... with paprika.
Bake .... at 350 degrees for 1 hour.
Yields ...... 4 servings.

Approx Per Serv: Cal 672, Prot 45.3 g, T Fat 44 g, Chl 188.8 mg, Car 23.2 g, Sod 1800.5 mg, Pot 479.6 mg.

Aggie Arnold-Norman, Tioga

CHICKEN ON SUNDAY

1 c. rice
1 frying chicken, cut up
1/2 env. dry onion soup mix
1 can cream of chicken soup
1 can each cream of celery, cream of
    mushroom soup
2 c. milk

Layer ...... first 4 ingredients in greased casserole.
Combine .... cream of celery and cream of mushroom soup with milk in saucepan.
Cook .... until heated through.
Pour .... over top.
Bake .... at 350 degrees for 2 1/2 hours.
Yields ...... 12 servings.

Approx Per Serv: Cal 194, Prot 11.1 g, T Fat 7 g, Chl 39.4 mg, Car 20.9 g, Sod 756.1 mg, Pot 222.3 mg.

Audrey Ridinger, Adams

CHICKEN WITH RICE

1 stick margarine, melted
1 pkg. long grain and wild rice mix
1 pkg. dry onion soup mix
4 lg. chicken breasts

Layer ...... margarine, rice, rice seasonings and half the soup mix in 9 x 13-inch casserole.
Pour .... 2 cups hot water over all.
Arrange ..... chicken breasts over rice.
Sprinkle .... remaining soup mix on top.
Bake .... covered, at 325 degrees for 1 1/4 hours.
Bake .... uncovered, for 15 minutes longer.
Yields ...... 4 servings.

Approx Per Serv: Cal 431, Prot 35.5 g, T Fat 29.1 g, Chl 98.9 mg, Car 5.9 g, Sod 1048.4 mg, Pot 387.3 mg.

Nutritional information does not include rice.

Tracy Leigh Levan, Columbia

CORNISH HENS WITH RICE

1 6-oz. package long grain and wild
    rice mix
Lemon juice
Salt and pepper to taste

3 1 1/2-lb. Cornish game hens, halved
1/3 c. butter

Cook .... rice mix for 15 minutes using package directions.
Sprinkle .... lemon juice, salt and pepper over hens.
Place .... breast side up, in buttered shallow baking dish.
Bake .... at 450 degrees for 15 minutes; turn.
Fill .... cavities with rice.
Top .... with butter.
Bake .... at 350 degrees for 30 to 40 minutes or until cooked through.
Yields ...... 6 servings.

Nina Lochar, Allegheny

TURKEY-CHEESE CASSEROLE

1/2 c. chopped onion
1/4 c. butter
1/4 c. flour
1 tbsp. instant chicken bouillon
2 1/2 c. milk
13 slices American cheese
3 c. cubed cooked turkey
2 c. cooked elbow macaroni
2 tbsp. chopped pimento
1 c. soft buttered bread crumbs

Saute ...... onion in butter in medium saucepan until tender.
Stir .... in flour and bouillon.
Add .... milk and 10 slices cheese broken into pieces, mixing well.
Cook .... until cheese is melted and sauce thickens, stirring constantly; remove from heat.
Combine .... turkey, macaroni, pimento and cheese sauce in lightly greased 2-quart baking dish.
Sprinkle .... bread crumbs over top.
Bake .... at 350 degrees for 25 minutes or until bubbly.
Arrange ..... remaining 3 cheese slices, cut in half diagonally, over top.
Bake .... for 5 minutes longer or until cheese is melted.
Yields ...... 8 servings.

Approx Per Serv: Cal 450, Prot 33.2 g, T Fat 25.7 g, Chl 114.1 mg, Car 20.4 g, Sod 904.6 mg, Pot 422.3 mg.

Lucille A. Dashem, Centre

POOR MAN'S LOBSTER

1 tbsp. vinegar
1 tsp. seafood seasoning
1/2 tsp. salt
1 pkg. flounder

Combine . . . . vinegar, seafood seasoning and salt with 2 cups water in saucepan.
Bring . . . . to a boil.
Add . . . . flounder.
Simmer . . . . . for 15 to 20 minutes or until tender.
Place . . . . on rack in broiling pan.
Broil . . . . until browned.
Serve . . . . with drawn butter.
Yields . . . . . . 4 servings.

Approx Per Serv: Cal 140, Prot 27.3 g, T Fat 2.5 g, Chl 64.3 mg, Car .4 g, Sod 333.4 mg, Pot 266.4 mg.

Nutritional information does not include flounder.

Carolyn B. Welty, Franklin

MOCK LOBSTER

1 tbsp. vinegar
1/2 tsp. salt
1/8 tsp. sugar
1 1/2 tbsp. seafood seasoning
1 lb. frozen haddock

Mix . . . . first 4 ingredients and 2 cups water in large saucepan.
Bring . . . . to a boil.
Add . . . . haddock.
Simmer . . . . . for 30 minutes.
Serve . . . . with melted butter.
Yields . . . . . . 4 servings.

Approx Per Serv: Cal 117.7, Prot 25.8 g, T Fat .7 g, Chl 58.1 mg, Car .2 g, Sod 304.3 mg, Pot 261.2 mg.

Dave Spence, Adams

SLADE'S STUFFED BROOK TROUT

1 sm. onion, chopped
Butter
2 c. canned crab meat
1/2 tsp. salt
Freshly ground pepper

8 trout, rinsed, dried
Chopped parsley
1 tsp. lemon juice

Saute . . . . . . onion in 2 tablespoons butter in skillet until tender.
Stir . . . . in crab meat; remove from heat.
Add . . . . salt, pepper and enough water to moisten.
Spoon . . . . . . into trout.
Place . . . . in well-buttered baking dish.
Top . . . . with 1 stick melted butter, parsley and lemon juice.
Bake . . . . at 450 degrees for 20 minutes.
Yields . . . . . . 8 servings.

Approx Per Serv: Cal 471, Prot 72 g, T Fat 17.8 g, Chl 193.6 mg, Car 1.4 g, Sod 752.2 mg, Pot 713.1 mg.

Slade A. Davis, Pike

FISH CAKES

5 tbsp. flour
1/2 tsp. salt
7 tbsp. butter, melted
1 1/2 c. milk
1 1/2 tbsp. minced onion
1 1/2 tbsp. minced parsley
1 tsp. lemon juice
3 c. flaked cooked fish
1 egg, beaten
1 c. (or more) fine dry bread crumbs

Combine . . . . flour and salt with 5 tablespoons butter in saucepan, mixing well.
Add . . . . milk gradually, stirring constantly.
Cook . . . . until thick, stirring constantly.
Stir . . . . in onion, parsley, lemon juice and fish.
Chill . . . . in refrigerator.
Shape . . . . . . fish mixture into 12 cakes.
Mix . . . . egg with 2 tablespoons water in bowl.
Roll . . . . fish cakes in bread crumbs.
Dip . . . . in egg mixture then into bread crumbs.
Chill . . . . for 1 hour.
Cook . . . . in remaining 2 tablespoons butter in skillet until golden brown.
Yields . . . . . . 6 servings.

Approx Per Serv: Cal 301, Prot 24.9 g, T Fat 17.2 g, Chl 92.2 mg, Car 10.8 g, Sod 406.6 mg, Pot 125.1 mg.

Eileen Graham, Adams

FISH FILLETS

Flour
Flavored bread crumbs
Paprika to taste
Haddock, cut into serving-sized pieces
Lemon-pepper marinade to taste

Mix . . . . flour, bread crumbs and paprika in shallow bowl.
Dredge . . . . . haddock in seasoned flour.
Brown . . . . . . on both sides in a small amount of margarine in skillet.
Sprinkle . . . . with lemon-pepper marinade.

Karol and Amy Sherman, Adams

CRAB IMPERIAL

3 tbsp. margarine
1 tbsp. flour
1/2 c. milk
1 tsp. minced onion
1 1/2 tsp. Worcestershire sauce
2 slices bread, cubed
1/2 c. mayonnaise
1 tbsp. lemon juice
1/2 tsp. salt
Dash of pepper
1 lb. crab meat
Paprika

Mix . . . . 1 tablespoon margarine and flour in medium saucepan.
Stir . . . . in milk gradually.
Cook . . . . over medium heat until thick, stirring constantly.
Add . . . . next 3 ingredients, mixing well; cool.
Blend . . . . . . in mayonnaise, lemon juice, salt and pepper.
Brown . . . . . . remaining 2 tablespoons margarine in saucepan.
Add . . . . crab meat, tossing lightly.
Stir . . . . into sauce.
Spoon . . . . . . into greased 1-quart casserole.
Sprinkle . . . . paprika over top.
Bake . . . . at 350 degrees for 10 to 15 minutes or until lightly browned.
Yields . . . . . . 4 servings.

Approx Per Serv: Cal 451, Prot 22.6 g, T Fat 34.7 g, Chl 137.7 mg, Car 12 g, Sod 882.5 mg, Pot 298.4 mg.

Elisa D. Gagliardi, Philadelphia

TUNA IMPERIAL

2 7 1/2-oz. cans oil-pack chunky tuna
1/4 c. each chopped green onion, celery
2/3 c. flour
1/4 tsp. grated lemon rind
2 c. light cream
1 4-oz. can sliced mushrooms
1 5-oz. can sliced water chestnuts
1/4 tsp. salt
2 tbsp. parsley

Drain . . . . . . tuna, reserving oil.
Saute . . . . . . green onion and celery in reserved oil in saucepan.
Stir . . . . in flour and lemon rind.
Add . . . . cream slowly, stirring until well blended.
Cook . . . . over low heat until thick, stirring constantly.
Drain . . . . . . mushrooms, reserving liquid.
Add . . . . enough water to reserved liquid to measure 1 1/4 cups.
Stir . . . . into cream sauce.
Add . . . . water chestnuts, mushrooms, tuna and salt, mixing well.
Simmer . . . . . until bubbly.
Sprinkle . . . . with parsley.
Serve . . . . with rice.
Yields . . . . . . 6 servings.

Approx Per Serv: Cal 341, Prot 19.3 g, T Fat 22.1 g, Chl 68.1 mg, Car 15.4 g, Sod 625.4 mg, Pot 384.9 mg.

Annette Wright, Philadelphia

NOODLES AND TUNA FLAKES

3 pkg. Oodles of Noodles
1/2 c. each chopped celery, chopped onion
2 tbsp. butter
1 lg. can tuna

Prepare . . . . . Oodles of Noodles using package directions; drain.
Saute . . . . . . celery and onion in butter in skillet.
Combine . . . . tuna, noodles and vegetables in bowl, mixing well.
Chill . . . . for several hours.
Yields . . . . . . 6 servings.

Approx Per Serv: Cal 218, Prot 15.2 g, T Fat 16.4 g, Chl 45.6 mg, Car 1.6 g, Sod 551.4 mg, Pot 242. mg.

Nutritional information does not include Oodles of Noodles.

Millcreek Community Center, Philadelphia

TUNA LOAF

1 9-oz. can tuna
1 c. chopped celery
1 1/2 tbsp. chopped green pepper
2 tbsp. pickle relish
4 hard-boiled eggs, chopped
1/2 tsp. salt
1 tbsp. vinegar
2 c. mayonnaise
2 env. unflavored gelatin

Combine .... first 8 ingredients in bowl, mixing well.
Soften ...... gelatin in 3/4 cup water in double boiler.
Heat .... over boiling water until gelatin dissolves.
Stir .... into tuna mixture.
Spoon ...... into 1 1/2-quart mold.
Chill .... until firm.
Unmold .... onto serving dish.
Yields ...... 8 servings.

Approx Per Serv: Cal 557, Prot 13.9 g, T Fat 54.7 g, Chl 184.6 mg, Car 3.5 g, Sod 821.6 mg, Pot 219.8 mg.

Ruth Clapper, Wyoming

SCALLOPED EGGPLANT

1 lg. eggplant, peeled, cubed
1 can cream of mushroom soup
1/3 c. milk
1 egg, beaten
1 c. chopped onion
1 can sliced mushrooms
1 1/4 c. herb-seasoned stuffing mix
1 c. grated sharp cheese
2 tbsp. melted butter

Cook .... eggplant in salted water in saucepan for 7 minutes; drain.
Combine .... with next 5 ingredients and 3/4 cup stuffing mix, mixing well.
Spoon ...... into casserole.
Top .... with cheese.
Toss .... remaining 1/2 cup stuffing mix with butter.
Sprinkle .... over top.
Bake .... at 350 degrees for 20 minutes.
Yields ...... 6 servings.

Approx Per Serv: Cal 241, Prot 9.6 g, T Fat 15.8 g, Chl 78.8 mg, Car 16.5 g, Sod 852.7 mg, Pot 293.1 mg.

Ann Powell, Lackawanna

PEAS AND TOMATOES IN CASSEROLE

1 med. onion, chopped
1/4 c. finely chopped green pepper
2 tbsp. butter
1 16-oz. can tomatoes
1 17-oz. can peas, drained
2 c. cooked rice
1 1/4 tsp. salt
1/8 tsp. pepper
3/4 c. grated sharp cheese
1/3 c. pea liquid
Bread crumbs (opt.)

Saute ...... onion and green pepper in butter in skillet until tender.
Combine .... with next 7 ingredients in 1 1/2-quart casserole, mixing well.
Top .... with bread crumbs and additional cheese.
Bake .... at 375 degrees for 30 minutes.
Yields ...... 4 servings.

Approx Per Serv: Cal 359, Prot 13.1 g, T Fat 13.3 g, Chl 38.7 mg, Car 47.5 g, Sod 1619.9 mg, Pot 438.8 mg.

Ann Northup, Lackawanna

SPINACH PIE

1 10-oz. package frozen chopped spinach, cooked, drained
1 c. cottage cheese
2 eggs, beaten
1/2 tsp. salt
Pepper to taste
3 tbsp. Parmesan cheese
2 tbsp. butter

Combine .... first 5 ingredients in bowl, mixing well.
Spoon ...... into 8-inch pie plate.
Top .... with cheese.
Dot .... with butter.
Bake .... at 350 degrees for 30 minutes.
Yields ...... 4 servings.

Approx Per Serv: Cal 195, Prot 15.7 g, T Fat 12.8 g, Chl 160.9 mg, Car 4.9 g, Sod 587 mg, Pot 345.4 mg.

Sandra Ogden, Tioga

SPINACH CASSEROLE

1/2 c. chopped celery
1/4 stick butter, melted
1/2 c. milk
2 pkg. frozen spinach, thawed
1/4 c. grated cheese
3 hard-boiled eggs, sliced

Combine .... first 4 ingredients in casserole, mixing well.
Sprinkle .... with cheese.
Bake .... in moderate oven for 30 minutes or until set.
Top .... with egg slices; serve immediately.
Yields ...... 6 servings.

Approx Per Serv: Cal 120, Prot 6.7 g, T Fat 9.1 g, Chl 145.7 mg, Car 3.5 g, Sod 160 mg, Pot 268.2 mg.

Millcreek Community Center, Philadelphia

QUICK MACARONI AND CHEESE

2 c. macaroni
3 tbsp. melted margarine
1 1/2 tsp. salt
1/8 tsp. pepper
2 c. shredded cheese
4 c. milk

Toss .... macaroni with margarine in bowl until coated.
Stir .... in remaining ingredients.
Spoon ...... into casserole.
Bake .... at 350 degrees for 45 minutes.
Yields ...... 4 servings.

Approx Per Serv: Cal 670, Prot 29.8 g, T Fat 36 g, Chl 90.1 mg, Car 55.9 g, Sod 1423.1 mg, Pot 512 mg.

Christine Freidhoff, Cambria

JOE'S MACARONI AND CHEESE

2 tbsp. flour
1 tsp. each salt, dry mustard
2 tbsp. butter, melted
1 c. milk, heated
1 1/2 c. shredded sharp cheese
2 c. macaroni, cooked
1/4 c. buttered bread crumbs
1/4 tsp. paprika

Combine .... flour, salt and dry mustard with butter in saucepan, mixing well.
Stir .... in milk.

Simmer ..... for 1 minute, stirring constantly.
Stir .... in 1 cup cheese.
Cook .... until cheese is melted, stirring constantly.
Combine .... with macaroni in 2-quart casserole, mixing well.
Top .... with remaining 1/2 cup cheese, bread crumbs and paprika.
Bake .... at 375 degrees for 25 minutes.
Yields ...... 6 servings.

Approx Per Serv: Cal 334, Prot 13.7 g, T Fat 15.5 g, Chl 47.5 mg, Car 34.2 g, Sod 640.6 mg, Pot 162.5 mg.

Joe Zug, Forest

MIXED FRESH VEGETABLES IN CHEESE SAUCE

1/2 lb. fresh green beans, cut in half
1/2 lb. small onions
1 med. head cauliflower, separated into flowerets
1 c. julienned carrot
1/4 lb. mushrooms, sliced
5 tbsp. butter, melted
3 tbsp. flour
1 tsp. salt
1/4 tsp. dry mustard
Dash of pepper
2 c. milk
1 c. shredded sharp Cheddar cheese

Cook .... green beans and onions in a small amount of boiling water in covered saucepan for 5 minutes.
Add .... cauliflower and carrot.
Cook .... covered, just until vegetables are tender; drain.
Saute ...... mushrooms in 2 tablespoons butter in skillet for 5 minutes.
Add .... to cooked vegetables.
Mix .... flour, salt, dry mustard and pepper with remaining 3 tablespoons butter in saucepan.
Stir .... in milk gradually.
Cook .... over medium heat until thick, stirring constantly.
Add .... cheese.
Cook .... until cheese is melted, stirring constantly.
Combine .... with vegetable mixture in serving dish, mixing well.
Yields ...... 8 servings.

Photograph for this recipe on page 41.

Salads

SUMMER SALAD BOWL DELUXE, recipe on page 62.

ANGEL SALAD

1 c. chopped apples
2 tbsp. lemon juice
1 1/2 tsp. sugar
1 c. thinly sliced celery
1 tsp. salt
1/2 c. salad dressing
1 c. coarsely chopped walnuts
1 c. coconut
1 c. miniature marshmallows
1/2 c. raisins

Combine .... first 6 ingredients in bowl, tossing to mix.
Add .... walnuts, coconut, marshmallows and raisins, mixing well.
Serve .... on lettuce.
Yields ...... 8 servings.

Approx Per Serv: Cal 266, Prot 3.2 g, T Fat 19.2 g, Chl 7.6 mg, Car 23.4 g, Sod 400.5 mg, Pot 243.6 mg.

Jamie Chase, Sullivan

APPLE SALAD

1 6-oz. package strawberry gelatin
1 pkg. whipped topping mix, prepared
2 or 3 apples, chopped
2 c. crushed pineapple, drained
1 sm. jar maraschino cherries, quartered
4 tbsp. sugar

Prepare ..... gelatin using package directions.
Chill .... until partially set.
Fold .... in remaining ingredients.
Spoon ...... into mold.
Chill .... until set.
Unmold .... on serving plate.
Yields ...... 8 servings.

Approx Per Serv: Cal 201, Prot 1.9 g, T Fat 2.5 g, Chl 1.6 mg, Car 45.8 g, Sod 45.8 mg, Pot 195.1 mg.

Shelly Burkholder, Franklin

APRICOT GELATIN DELIGHT

2 pkg. apricot gelatin
1 20-oz. can crushed pineapple, drained
1 c. miniature marshmallows
2 bananas, sliced
1 egg, beaten
2 tsp. butter
1/2 c. pineapple juice
1/2 c. sugar

2 tsp. flour
1 sm. package cream cheese, softened
1 sm. container whipped topping

Prepare ..... gelatin using package directions.
Chill .... until partially congealed.
Fold .... pineapple, marshmallows and bananas into gelatin.
Chill .... until set.
Combine .... next 6 ingredients in saucepan, blending well.
Cook .... over low heat until thick, stirring constantly; cool.
Stir .... in whipped topping.
Spread ..... over gelatin mixture.
Chill .... for several hours.
Yields ...... 8 servings.

Approx Per Serv: Cal 374, Prot 4.7 g, T Fat 12.9 g, Chl 46.4 mg, Car 63.7 g, Sod 124 mg, Pot 231.8 mg.

Nancy Alexander, Tioga

APRICOT-PINEAPPLE SALAD

1 20-oz. can crushed pineapple
1 6-oz. package apricot gelatin
1 8-oz. package cream cheese, softened
1 sm. container whipped topping

Drain ...... pineapple, reserving juice.
Dissolve .... gelatin in 2 cups boiling water in serving bowl.
Add .... pineapple, mixing well.
Chill .... until partially congealed.
Beat .... reserved pineapple juice gradually into cream cheese in bowl until smooth.
Combine .... with gelatin mixture, mixing well.
Fold .... in whipped topping.
Chill .... until firm.
Yields ...... 8 servings.

Approx Per Serv: 333, Prot 4.9 g, T Fat 17.9 g, Chl 31.5 mg, Car 41.2 g, Sod 146.2 mg, Pot 147.1 mg.

Christine Freidhoff, Cambria

CRANBERRY SALAD

1 6-oz. package orange gelatin
1 1/2 c. sugar
1 env. unflavored gelatin
1 lb. cranberries
4 apples, cored
Rind of 1/4 orange

2 oranges, sectioned, chopped
1 18 1/4-oz. can crushed pineapple, drained

Dissolve .... orange gelatin and sugar in 1 1/2 cups boiling water in serving bowl.

Soften ...... unflavored gelatin in 1/2 cup cold water.

Add .... to orange gelatin mixture, mixing until dissolved; cool.

Put .... cranberries, apples and orange rind through food grinder.

Add .... all fruit to gelatin mixture, mixing well.

Chill .... until set.

Yields ...... 8 servings.

Approx Per Serv: Cal 381, Prot 3.8 g, T Fat 1.1 g, Chl 0 mg, Car 94.8 g, Sod 71.9 mg, Pot 339.9 mg.

Ann Harbach, Clinton

LIME PARTY SALAD

16 marshmallows
1 c. milk
1 3-oz. package lime gelatin
2 3-oz. packages cream cheese, softened
1 20-oz. can crushed pineapple
1 c. whipped topping
2/3 c. mayonnaise

Combine .... marshmallows and milk in top of double boiler over boiling water.

Cook .... until marshmallows are melted, stirring frequently.

Stir .... in gelatin until dissolved.

Add .... cream cheese, blending well; remove from heat.

Fold .... in pineapple; cool.

Stir .... in whipped topping and mayonnaise.

Spoon ...... into mold.

Chill .... until firm.

Unmold .... on serving plate.

Yields ...... 12 servings.

Approx Per Serv: Cal 269, Prot 3.1 g, T Fat 17.4 g, Chl 27.4 mg, Car 27.1 g, Sod 148.1 mg, Pot 111.4 mg.

Kerry Freese, Lancaster

ORANGE SALAD DELUXE

2 pkg. orange gelatin
1 20-oz. can crushed pineapple

4 oranges, sectioned, cut into pieces
1 c. grapes
1 c. pecans
1 tbsp. butter
1/2 tsp. salt
1/2 c. chopped dates
8 marshmallows
1 egg, beaten
1 c. whipped cream

Prepare ..... gelatin according to package directions using 4 cups water.

Chill .... until partially set.

Drain ...... pineapple, reserving juice.

Fold .... pineapple, oranges, grapes and pecans into gelatin.

Chill .... until firm.

Combine .... reserved pineapple juice with butter and next 3 ingredients in saucepan.

Cook .... until dates are soft, stirring frequently.

Cool .... for several minutes.

Stir .... in egg; cool to room temperature.

Fold .... in whipped cream.

Top .... gelatin with date mixture.

Yields ...... 10 servings.

Approx Per Serv: Cal 296, Prot 5.1 g, T Fat 10.5 g, Chl 28.9 mg, Car 54.4 g, Sod 205.9 mg, Pot 435.2 mg.

Shellie Reichart, Forest

ORANGE SHERBET MOLD

1 3-oz. package orange gelatin
1 pt. orange sherbet
1 11-oz. can mandarin oranges, drained
1 c. miniature marshmallows
1 8 1/2-oz. can crushed pineapple
1/2 c. chopped pecans
10 maraschino cherries, cut up

Dissolve .... gelatin in 1 cup boiling water in bowl.

Stir .... in sherbet.

Chill .... until partially set.

Fold .... in remaining ingredients.

Pour .... into 5-cup mold.

Chill .... until set.

Unmold .... onto serving dish.

Yields ...... 6 servings.

Approx Per Serv: Cal 295, Prot 3.4 g, T Fat 7.9 g, Chl .1 mg, Car 56.4 g, Sod 55.6 mg, Pot 189.5 mg.

Doris Beck, Forest

ORANGE SALAD MOLD

2 3-oz. packages orange gelatin
1 pt. orange sherbet
1 20-oz. can pineapple tidbits, drained
1 11-oz. can mandarin oranges, drained

Dissolve .... gelatin in 2 cups hot water in bowl.
Add .... sherbet, stirring until melted.
Chill .... for 30 to 45 minutes, or until partially set.
Fold .... in remaining ingredients.
Pour .... into 6-cup mold.
Chill .... until set.
Unmold .... onto serving dish.
Yields ...... 10 servings.

Approx Per Serv: Cal 153, Prot 2.2 g, T Fat .5 g, Chl 0 mg, Car 36.8 g, Sod 58.7 mg, Pot 108 mg.

Susan Woodhead, Sullivan

SUNSET SALAD

1 3-oz. package orange gelatin
1/2 tsp. salt
1 8-oz. can crushed pineapple
1 tbsp. lemon juice
1 c. ground carrots

Dissolve .... gelatin and salt in 1 cup boiling water in serving bowl.
Add .... pineapple, lemon juice and carrots, mixing well.
Chill .... until set.
Yields ...... 6 servings.

Approx Per Serv: Cal 92.3, Prot 1.7 g, T Fat .1 g, Chl 0 mg, Car 22.7 g, Sod 231.8 mg, Pot 136.7 mg.

Diane Reppy, Schuylkill

WALNUT PEACHERINO SALAD

1 6-oz. package lemon gelatin
2 tsp. lemon juice
3/4 c. peach syrup
1/3 c. sliced walnuts
16 canned peach slices
4 maraschino cherries, halved
1 c. sour cream

Dissolve .... gelatin in 1 3/4 cups boiling water in bowl.
Stir .... in lemon juice and peach syrup.
Chill .... until partially set.
Add .... walnuts, mixing well.

Arrange ..... peach slices and cherry halves in 5 x 9-inch loaf pan.
Spoon ...... 1 cup gelatin mixture carefully over fruit.
Chill .... until firm.
Stir .... sour cream into remaining gelatin mixture.
Pour .... over congealed gelatin layer.
Chill .... until set.
Unmold .... onto serving plate.
Garnish ..... with mayonnaise and walnut halves.
Yields ...... 8 servings.

Approx Per Serv: Cal 226, Prot 3.9 g, T Fat 9.3 g, Chl 12.6 mg, Car 34.5 g, Sod 84.2 mg, Pot 190.7 mg.

Deane B. Macgill, Sullivan

MELON BOAT

1 cantaloupe, cut in half
Blueberries
Watermelon balls
Grapes
Peaches, cut into wedges
Honeydew balls
Cherries

Cut .... half the cantaloupe into balls with melon ball cutter.
Place .... remaining half on bed of lettuce on serving plate.
Mix .... cantaloupe balls with remaining ingredients except cherries in bowl.
Spoon ...... into cantaloupe on plate.
Arrange ..... cherries around cantaloupe.

Tammi Millen, Indiana

PINEAPPLE GODDESS SALAD

2 tbsp. pineapple juice
2 tbsp. tarragon wine vinegar
1 tsp. dry mustard
1/2 tsp. salt
1/4 tsp. pepper
6 canned anchovies, mashed
2 tbsp. each finely chopped chives, parsley
1 c. sour cream
1/2 c. mayonnaise
1 20 1/2-oz. can pineapple chunks, drained
8 c. coarsely chopped romaine lettuce

Mix . . . . first 8 ingredients in bowl.
Add . . . . sour cream and mayonnaise, mixing well.
Chill . . . . covered, until serving time.
Toss . . . . pineapple and romaine together in salad bowl.
Add . . . . chilled dressing, tossing lightly to mix.
Yields . . . . . . 6-8 servings.

Photograph for this recipe on page 8.

PINEAPPLE AND COTTAGE CHEESE SALAD

1 sm. package each lime, lemon gelatin
1 can crushed pineapple
1 c. mayonnaise
1 can sweetened condensed milk
1 c. chopped pecans
3 tsp. horseradish
1 pt. small curd cottage cheese

Dissolve . . . . gelatins in 1 cup boiling water in bowl.
Add . . . . remaining ingredients in order given, mixing well after each addition.
Spoon . . . . . . into 9 x 13-inch dish.
Chill . . . . until set.
Yields . . . . . . 16 servings.

Approx Per Serv: Cal 362, Prot 9 g, T Fat 20.9 g, Chl 27.8 mg, Car 37.3 g, Sod 228.8 mg, Pot 243.3 mg.

Lucille A. Dashem, Centre

PINK SALAD

1 lg. carton whipped topping
1 16-oz. carton cottage cheese
1 18 1/4-oz. can crushed pineapple, drained
1 sm. box wild strawberry gelatin

Let . . . . ingredients come to room temperature.
Combine . . . . whipped topping and cottage cheese in bowl, mixing well.
Stir . . . . in pineapple.
Add . . . . dry gelatin, mixing well.
Chill . . . . overnight.
Yields . . . . . . 6 servings.

Approx Per Serv: Cal 231, Prot 12.8 g, T Fat 5.5 g, Chl 15.5 mg, Car 34.2 g, Sod 235 mg, Pot 187.3 mg.

Dolly Spaar, Lehigh

SAWDUST SALAD

1 sm. package cherry gelatin
1 c. sugar
1/4 c. lemon juice
1 sm. can evaporated milk, chilled, whipped
1 sm. can crushed pineapple, drained
1/2 c. pecans
28 graham crackers, crushed
1/4 c. melted butter
1/4 tsp. salt

Combine . . . . first 3 ingredients with 1 cup boiling water in bowl, stirring until dissolved.
Chill . . . . until partially set.
Add . . . . whipped evaporated milk, pineapple and pecans, mixing well.
Mix . . . . crushed crackers with butter and salt in medium bowl.
Press . . . . into bottom of 9 x 13-inch dish, reserving a small amount for topping.
Spread . . . . . gelatin mixture over crumbs.
Top . . . . with reserved crumbs.
Chill . . . . for 24 hours.
Yields . . . . . . 6 servings.

Approx Per Serv: Cal 516, Prot 7.1 g, T Fat 20.1 g, Chl 32.4 mg, Car 83.2 g, Sod 483.4 mg, Pot 359.8 mg.

Tammy Shick, Elk

PINEAPPLE-CREAM CHEESE SALAD

1 env. unflavored gelatin
1 3-oz. package cream cheese, softened
1 can crushed pineapple, drained
1/2 c. salad dressing
1/2 lb. miniature marshmallows
1 1/2 c. white grapes
1/2 c. chopped pecans
1/2 pt. whipping cream, whipped

Combine . . . . gelatin with cream cheese in bowl.
Add . . . . next 5 ingredients, mixing well.
Fold . . . . in whipped cream.
Chill . . . . until serving time.
Yields . . . . . . 8 servings.

Approx Per Serv: Cal 324, Prot 3.9 g, T Fat 15.9 g, Chl 19.6 mg, Car 44.9 g, Sod 153.6 mg, Pot 241.4 mg.

Lisa Gregus, Schuylkill

RHUBARB SALAD

3 c. chopped rhubarb
3/4 c. sugar
1/4 tsp. salt
2 3-oz. packages strawberry gelatin
1/4 c. lemon juice

Combine . . . . first 3 ingredients in saucepan.
Simmer . . . . . until rhubarb is soft, stirring frequently.
Mix . . . . in gelatin.
Add . . . . lemon juice and 2 cups water, mixing well.
Pour . . . . into mold.
Chill . . . . until set.
Yields . . . . . . 6 servings.

Approx Per Serv: Cal 213.7, Prot 3.1 g, T Fat .1 g, Chl 0 mg, Car 52.9 g, Sod 180.5 mg, Pot 227.7 mg.

Teresa Murren, Adams

LAYERED STRAWBERRY SALAD

1 lg. package strawberry gelatin
1 c. pineapple juice
1 16-oz. package frozen sliced strawberries
1 20-oz. can crushed pineapple, drained
1/2 c. chopped walnuts
1 pt. sour cream

Dissolve . . . . gelatin in boiling juice.
Stir . . . . in strawberries, pineapple and walnuts.
Pour . . . . half the mixture into glass bowl.
Chill . . . . until set.
Spread . . . . . sour cream over top.
Spoon . . . . . . remaining gelatin mixture carefully over sour cream.
Chill . . . . until firm.
Yields . . . . . . 8 servings.

Approx Per Serv: Cal 372, Prot 5.5 g, T Fat 17.1 g, Chl 25.3 mg, Car 53.6 g, Sod 99.6 mg, Pot 301.3 mg.

Suzie Moyer, Lehigh

STRAWBERRY-BANANA SALAD

1 3-oz. package strawberry gelatin
1 8-oz. can crushed pineapple
1 10-oz. package frozen strawberries
1 ripe banana, mashed
1 8-oz. carton sour cream

Dissolve . . . . gelatin in 1/2 cup boiling water in bowl.
Add . . . . pineapple, strawberries and banana, mixing well.
Pour . . . . 1/2 of the mixture into mold.
Chill . . . . until set.
Spread . . . . . sour cream over top, reserving 2 tablespoons for garnish.
Spoon . . . . . . remaining gelatin mixture carefully over sour cream.
Chill . . . . covered, until set.
Unmold . . . . onto serving plate.
Top . . . . with reserved sour cream.
Yields . . . . . . 8 servings.

Approx Per Serv: Cal 173, Prot 2.3 g, T Fat 6.2 g, Chl 12.6 mg, Car 29.3 g, Sod 49.8 mg, Pot 178.1 mg.

Myra Woroniak, Lehigh

STRAWBERRY SALAD MOLD

2 3-oz. packages strawberry gelatin
1 10-oz. package frozen strawberries, thawed
1 20-oz. can crushed pineapple, drained
3 ripe bananas, mashed

Dissolve . . . . gelatin in 1 1/4 cups hot water.
Chill . . . . until partially set.
Stir . . . . in remaining ingredients.
Pour . . . . into mold.
Chill . . . . until firm.
Unmold . . . . onto serving dish.
Yields . . . . . . 10 servings.

Approx Per Serv: Cal 167, Prot 2.3 g, T Fat .2 g, Chl 0 mg, Car 42.1 g, Sod 55.3 mg, Pot 236.8 mg.

Penny Woodhead, Sullivan

PRETZEL CRUST SALAD

2 c. crushed unsalted pretzels
3 tsp. sugar
3/4 c. melted margarine
1 8-oz. package cream cheese, softened
1 c. sugar
1 sm. carton whipped topping
1 6-oz. package strawberry gelatin
1 20-oz. package frozen strawberries
1 16-oz. can crushed pineapple

Combine . . . . first 3 ingredients in bowl, mixing well.
Press . . . . into 9 x 13-inch baking pan.

Bake . . . . at 350 degrees for 10 minutes; cool.

Blend . . . . . . cream cheese and sugar in medium bowl.

Fold . . . . in whipped topping.

Spread . . . . . over crust.

Dissolve . . . . gelatin in 2 cups hot water in bowl.

Stir . . . . in strawberries and pineapple.

Chill . . . . until partially set.

Spread . . . . . over cream cheese.

Chill . . . . until firm.

Yields . . . . . . 24 servings.

Approx Per Serv: Cal 255, Prot 2.7 g, T Fat 12.2 g, Chl 10.5 mg, Car 35.3 g, Sod 278 mg, Pot 84.6 mg.

Judy Muller, Wayne

EMILY'S FRUIT SALAD

1 sm. package vanilla instant pudding mix
2 c. cold milk
1 c. chilled pineapple juice
4 c. cantaloupe balls
4 c. watermelon chunks
4 c. blueberries
1 20-oz. can pineapple chunks, drained

Combine . . . . pudding mix and milk in mixer bowl.

Beat . . . . at low speed for 2 minutes or until blended.

Stir . . . . in pineapple juice.

Chill . . . . in refrigerator.

Combine . . . . with cantaloupe, watermelon, blueberries and pineapple in serving dish, mixing well.

Chill . . . . until serving time.

Yields . . . . . . 24 servings.

Approx Per Serv: Cal 81.8, Prot 1.4 g, T Fat 1 g, Chl 2.8 mg, Car 18.4 g, Sod 35.7 mg, Pot 172.5 mg.

Emily Ross, Indiana

FROZEN FRUIT SALAD

1 21-oz. can cherry pie filling
1 can sweetened condensed milk
1 sm. container whipped topping
1 16-oz. can crushed pineapple, drained
1 c. chopped pecans
1 c. miniature marshmallows
1 c. coconut

Combine . . . . all ingredients in bowl, mixing well.

Spoon . . . . . . into mold.

Freeze . . . . . . until firm.

Yields . . . . . . 8 servings.

Approx Per Serv: Cal 614, Prot 8.2 g, T Fat 27.1 g, Chl 24.4 mg, Car 88.8 g, Sod 112.1 mg, Pot 414 mg.

Reajean Hummel, Union

MIXED FRUIT SALAD

1 20-oz. can pineapple
1 lg. can fruit cocktail
1 8-oz. can mandarin oranges, drained
1 tbsp. lemon juice
1 3-oz. package lemon instant pudding mix
3 bananas, sliced

Drain . . . . . . pineapple, reserving half the juice.

Combine . . . . pineapple and reserved juice with next 4 ingredients in serving dish, mixing well.

Chill . . . . until partially set.

Add . . . . bananas, mixing well.

Chill . . . . for several hours.

Yields . . . . . . 8 servings.

Approx Per Serv: Cal 230, Prot 1.7 g, T Fat .5 g, Chl 0 mg, Car 59.7 g, Sod 71.9 mg, Pot 454.6 mg.

Maxine Frantz, Elk

SPEEDY SALAD

1 lg. package vanilla instant pudding mix
1 c. cream, whipped
1 16-oz. can fruit cocktail, drained
1 11-oz. can mandarin oranges, drained
1 4-oz. jar maraschino cherries, drained
1 c. miniature marshmallows

Prepare . . . . . pudding mix using package directions.

Fold . . . . in whipped cream.

Add . . . . remaining ingredients, mixing well.

Chill . . . . until set.

Yields . . . . . . 10 servings.

Approx Per Serv: Cal 202, Prot 4 g, T Fat 3 g, Chl 10.3 mg, Car 42.8 g, Sod 139.4 mg, Pot 306.8 mg.

Karen Sattazahn, Berks

STAINED GLASS SALAD

1 3-oz. package each lime, orange, raspberry gelatin
1 3-oz. package lemon gelatin
1 c. pineapple juice
1 sm. container whipped topping

Prepare . . . . . lime, orange and raspberry gelatins according to package directions, using 1/4 cup less cold water.
Pour . . . . each flavor gelatin into individual loaf pan.
Chill . . . . until firm.
Prepare . . . . . lemon gelatin according to package directions, using pineapple juice for cold water, in glass bowl.
Chill . . . . until partially set.
Fold . . . . in whipped topping.
Cut . . . . first 3 gelatins into cubes.
Fold . . . . into lemon gelatin mixture.
Chill . . . . until set.
Yields . . . . . . 18 servings.

Approx Per Serv: Cal 117, Prot 2 g, T Fat 3 g, Chl 0 mg, Car 21.4 g, Sod 63.3 mg, Pot 62.6 mg.

Ruth Clapper, Wyoming

HOT DIGGITYDOG SALAD

2 c. macaroni, cooked
1/2 c. Italian dressing
1 c. chopped celery
1/2 c. sweet pickle relish
5 hot dogs, cooked, thinly sliced
1/2 c. sour cream

Combine . . . . macaroni and dressing in bowl, mixing well.
Chill . . . . in refrigerator.
Add . . . . remaining ingredients, mixing well.
Chill . . . . until serving time.
Yields . . . . . . 6 servings.

Approx Per Serv: Cal 464, Prot 11.4 g, T Fat 29.3 g, Chl 37.4 mg, Car 39 g, Sod 1110.2 mg, Pot 316 mg.

Mary Stanislawczyk, Cambria

DIFFERENT TACO SALAD

1 lb. ground beef
1 pkg. dry taco seasoning mix

1 head lettuce, chopped
4 tomatoes, chopped
1 onion, chopped
8 oz. Cheddar cheese, shredded
1 15-oz. can chick peas, drained
1 pkg. nacho cheese chips, crumbled
1 8-oz. bottle of Thousand Island dressing
1 tbsp. mild taco sauce
1/4 c. sugar

Brown . . . . . . ground beef in skillet, stirring until crumbly.
Stir . . . . in seasoning mix, reserving 1 tablespoon.
Layer . . . . . . next 5 ingredients in salad bowl.
Add . . . . ground beef.
Chill . . . . in refrigerator.
Add . . . . chips, tossing to mix.
Mix . . . . reserved seasoning mix, dressing, taco sauce and sugar in bowl.
Pour . . . . dressing over all.
Yields . . . . . . 10 servings.

Approx Per Serv: Cal 443, Prot 16.7 g, T Fat 31.8 g, Chl 66.9 mg, Car 24.4 g, Sod 446.4 mg, Pot 422.4 mg.

Nutritional information does not include chick peas or taco seasoning mix.

Betty J. Geer, Elk

TASTY PORK TACO SALAD

1 lb. ground pork
1 pkg. dry taco seasoning mix
1/8 tsp. salt
Pepper
1 head lettuce, torn into bite-sized pieces
1/2 bag corn chips, coarsely crushed
2 tomatoes, cut into wedges
1/4 to 1/2 c. shredded Cheddar cheese

Brown . . . . . . ground pork in skillet, stirring until crumbly; drain.
Add . . . . taco seasoning mix and 3/4 cup water, mixing well.
Simmer . . . . . for 15 minutes or until liquid is very thick.
Season . . . . . with salt and pepper to taste.
Layer . . . . . . lettuce, ground pork mixture, corn chips, tomatoes and cheese on serving platter.
Yields . . . . . . 4 servings.

Approx Per Serv: Cal 579, Prot 26.7 g, T Fat 43.4 g, Chl 93.3 mg, Car 21.7 g, Sod 382.6 mg, Pot 730.4 mg.

Cheryl Keifer, Northampton

EASY TACO SALAD

1 lb. ground beef
1 pkg. dry taco seasoning mix
1 c. tomato juice
1 head lettuce, coarsely chopped
1 sm. package corn chips
1 c. shredded Colby cheese

Brown . . . . . . ground beef in skillet, stirring until crumbly; drain.
Stir . . . . in the seasoning mix and tomato juice.
Simmer . . . . . for 10 to 15 minutes or until flavors are blended; cool.
Combine . . . . with lettuce and corn chips in salad bowl, tossing lightly.
Top . . . . with cheese.
Yields . . . . . . 6 servings.

Approx Per Serv: Cal 455, Prot 21.6 g, T Fat 31.1 g, Chl 81.7 mg, Car 24.2 g, Sod 522.5 mg, Pot 442.4 mg.

Nutritional information does not include taco seasoning mix.

Jill Prichard, Erie

THE BEST MACARONI SALAD

1 lb. macaroni, cooked
12 hard-boiled eggs, chopped
3 tomatoes, cut into wedges
1 green pepper, chopped
1 onion, finely chopped
1 med. cucumber, chopped
1 c. mayonnaise
1 tsp. each celery salt, paprika

Place . . . . first 6 ingredients lightly in 3-quart bowl.
Mix . . . . mayonnaise, celery salt and paprika in small bowl.
Add . . . . to macaroni mixture, mixing well and adding additional 1/2 cup mayonnaise if necessary.
Yields . . . . . . 12 servings.

Approx Per Serv: Cal 370, Prot 12.1 g, T Fat 21.2 g, Chl 265.9 mg, Car 32.6 g, Sod 354.6 mg, Pot 271.2 mg.

Marjorie Eakin, Lawrence

SPAGHETTI SALAD

1 1-lb. box thin spaghetti, broken, cooked, drained
3 stalks celery, chopped

1 med. green pepper, chopped
1 sm. onion, chopped
1/2 jar McCormick Salad Supreme
1 pkg. dry Italian salad dressing mix, prepared

Combine . . . . all ingredients in large bowl, mixing well.
Chill . . . . for several hours.
Yields . . . . . . 10 servings.

Approx Per Serv: Cal 179, Prot 6.1 g, T Fat .6 g, Chl 0 mg, Car 36.6 g, Sod 219.4 mg, Pot 165 mg.

Kristin Corboy, Allegheny

BEAN SALAD

1 20-oz. can kidney beans, drained
1/4 c. chopped celery
3 pickles, chopped
1 sm. onion, minced
2 hard-boiled eggs, sliced
1/2 tsp. salt
1/8 tsp. pepper
1/4 c. mayonnaise

Combine . . . . all ingredients in bowl, mixing well.
Chill . . . . in refrigerator.
Place . . . . on lettuce-lined serving plate.
Garnish . . . . . with grated cheese.
Yields . . . . . . 6 servings.

Approx Per Serv: Cal 181, Prot 7.6 g, T Fat 9.8 g, Chl 90.8 mg, Car 16.4 g, Sod 728.1 mg, Pot 353.5 mg.

Julia A. Sproat, Westmoreland

BROCCOLI SALAD

4 c. broccoli flowerets
1/2 c. raisins
1 sm. onion, chopped
8 slices crisp-cooked bacon, crumbled
1 c. salad dressing
1/4 c. sugar
3 tbsp. vinegar

Combine . . . . first 4 ingredients in bowl, tossing to mix.
Mix . . . . salad dressing, sugar and vinegar in small bowl.
Pour . . . . over broccoli mixture.
Yields . . . . . . 6 servings.

Approx Per Serv: Cal 334, Prot 6.7 g, T Fat 22.5 g, Chl 28.9 mg, Car 30 g, Sod 351.7 mg, Pot 425.3 mg.

Eleanor Walker, Blair

STUFFED CUCUMBER RINGS

2 cucumbers, cut in half crosswise, seeded
2 tsp. chopped walnuts
1 sm. onion, chopped
1 sm. green pepper, chopped
1   3-oz. package cream cheese, softened

Chill . . . . cucumbers for several hours or until firm.
Combine . . . . next 4 ingredients in bowl, mixing well.
Stuff . . . . into cucumbers.
Chill . . . . wrapped in plastic wrap, in refrigerator.
Cut . . . . into 1/4-inch slices.
Yields . . . . . . 6 servings.

Approx Per Serv: Cal 73.1, Prot 1.9 g, T Fat 5.9 g, Chl 15.7 mg, Car 3.8 g, Sod 41.4 mg, Pot 139.9 mg.

Eleanor Walker, Blair

GREEN PEA-TUNA SALAD

1 can green peas, drained
1 lg. can tuna, drained
1 sm. sweet onion, chopped
2 hard-boiled eggs, chopped
1 tbsp. wine vinegar
2 tbsp. sugar
1/2 to 3/4 c. mayonnaise

Combine . . . . all ingredients in bowl, mixing well.
Chill . . . . in refrigerator.
Yields . . . . . . 6 servings.

Approx Per Serv: Cal 477, Prot 20.2 g, T Fat 37.1 g, Chl 137.6 mg, Car 15.8 g, Sod 813.4 mg, Pot 295 mg.

Roma Perrine, Fayette

HOT POTATO SALAD

1/2 lb. bacon
3/4 c. chopped onion
1/3 c. chopped green pepper
6 c. cubed cooked potatoes
3/4 c. mayonnaise
1/3 c. chopped pimentos
1/4 c. mustard
1/4 c. sugar
1 tsp. salt
1/8 tsp. pepper

Cook . . . . bacon with onion and green pepper in skillet until crisp; drain.

Combine . . . . with remaining ingredients in casserole, tossing lightly.
Bake . . . . in moderate oven until heated through.
Yields . . . . . . 6 servings.

Approx Per Serv: Cal 573, Prot 12.6 g, T Fat 36.1 g, Chl 41.8 mg, Car 51.7 g, Sod 915.8 mg, Pot 1069 mg.

Violet Ray, Butler

POTATO SALAD NICOISE

1/2 c. oil
1/4 c. white wine vinegar
2 tbsp. chopped parsley
1 tbsp. chopped capers
1 tsp. dry mustard
1/4 tsp. basil
1 clove of garlic, crushed
6 med. potatoes, cooked, peeled, sliced
1/2 lb. green beans, cooked, drained
1   1-pt. carton cherry tomatoes
2   7-oz. cans water-pack tuna, drained
4 hard-boiled eggs, sliced
Lettuce
6 anchovy fillets
6 ripe olives

Combine . . . . first 7 ingredients in bowl, mixing well.
Toss . . . . half the dressing with hot potatoes in bowl.
Stir . . . . remaining dressing into each of the next 4 ingredients in small bowls.
Chill . . . . until serving time.
Mound . . . . . tuna in center of lettuce-lined bowl.
Arrange . . . . . marinated vegetables and eggs around tuna.
Garnish . . . . . with anchovies, olives and chopped parsley.
Yields . . . . . . 6 servings.

Photograph for this recipe on page 1.

SAUERKRAUT RELISH

2 c. sugar
1 c. vinegar
1   27-oz. can sauerkraut, drained
2 c. finely chopped celery
1 c. finely chopped green pepper

1   16-oz. can chick peas, drained
1/2 c. finely chopped onion

Mix . . . . sugar and vinegar in saucepan.
Bring . . . . to a boil; cool.
Combine . . . . with remaining ingredients in salad bowl, mixing well.
Chill . . . . overnight.
Yields . . . . . . 10 servings.

Can be stored in refrigerator for 4 weeks.

Approx Per Serv: Cal 175, Prot .8 g, T Fat .1 g, Chl 0 mg, Car 45.2 g, Sod 383.3 mg, Pot 207.5 mg.

Nutritional information does not include chick peas.

Myrtle Gozikowski, Wyoming

FAVORITE SAUERKRAUT SALAD

4 c. sauerkraut, rinsed, drained
1 c. chopped celery
1/2 c. chopped onion
1 green pepper, chopped
1 sm. can pimentos, drained, chopped
1 1/2 c. sugar
1/4 c. vinegar
1/4 c. oil

Combine . . . . first 5 ingredients in bowl.
Mix . . . . sugar, vinegar and oil in small bowl.
Pour . . . . over sauerkraut mixture.
Toss . . . . until well mixed.
Chill . . . . covered, overnight.
Yields . . . . . . 10 servings

May store in refrigerator for 3 weeks.

Approx Per Serv: Cal 191, Prot 1.3 g, T Fat 5.7 g, Chl 0 mg, Car 36.2 g, Sod 719.5 mg, Pot 208.5 mg.

Cheryl Keifer, Northampton

SPINACH SALAD

1 lb. fresh spinach
1/4 lb. bacon, crisp-cooked, crumbled
1 hard-boiled egg, chopped
1 sm. red Italian onion, sliced into rings
1/2 c. oil
1/4 c. red wine vinegar
1 tbsp. lemon juice
1/8 tsp. oregano
1 tsp. salt
1 tsp. sugar
1/8 tsp. pepper

Combine . . . . spinach, bacon, egg and onion in bowl, tossing to mix.
Combine . . . . oil, vinegar, lemon juice and remaining ingredients in tightly covered jar.
Shake . . . . . . until well blended.
Pour . . . . over spinach mixture.
Toss . . . . lightly to coat.
Yields . . . . . . 4 servings.

Approx Per Serv: Cal 360, Prot 7.9 g, T Fat 33.9 g, Chl 71.5 mg, Car 9.2 g, Sod 724.4 mg, Pot 609.1 mg.

Pam Powers, Westmoreland

LAYERED SALAD WITH CHEESE

1 head lettuce, shredded
1 lg. green pepper, chopped
1 or 2 stalks celery, chopped
1 lg. red onion, sliced
1 10-oz. package frozen peas, thawed
1 c. mayonnaise
4 slices Swiss cheese
1/4 c. (or more) Parmesan cheese

Layer . . . . . . all ingredients in order given in 8-inch square glass dish.
Chill . . . . tightly covered, for 24 hours.
May . . . . store in refrigerator, tightly covered, for 5 days.
Yields . . . . . . 6 servings.

Approx Per Serv: Cal 542, Prot 26.1 g, T Fat 43.4 g, Chl 100.1 mg, Car 12.8 g, Sod 477 mg, Pot 517.8 mg.

Jennifer Seebold, Union

SUMMER SALAD WITH BACON

1 head cauliflower, cut into flowerets
1 bunch broccoli, cut into flowerets
1 lb. bacon, crisp-cooked, crumbled
1 bottle of Green Goddess creamy dressing

Combine . . . . all ingredients in large bowl, tossing to coat.
Chill . . . . for several hours.
Yields . . . . . . 12 servings.

Approx Per Serv: Cal 106, Prot 6.6 g, T Fat 6.8 g, Chl 11.1 mg, Car 6.4 g, Sod 142.6 mg, Pot 385.3 mg.

Nutritional information does not include Green Goddess creamy dressing.

Michael John Levan, Columbia

CRUNCHY SALAD

1 c. mayonnaise
1/2 tsp. sugar
1/2 c. Parmesan cheese
3 hard-boiled eggs, chopped
2 tbsp. (or more) bacon bits
1/2 c. sliced radishes
1/2 c. each chopped celery, green pepper,
   onion
1 8-oz. can water chestnuts,
   drained, sliced
1 10-oz. package frozen green peas,
   thawed

Combine . . . . mayonnaise, sugar, cheese, eggs
and bacon bits in bowl, mixing
well.
Pour . . . . over remaining ingredients in
salad bowl, tossing to mix.
Chill . . . . . . for 24 hours before serving.
Yields . . . . . . 8 servings.

Approx Per Serv: Cal 311, Prot 8.7 g, T Fat 28 g, Chl
125.4 mg, Car 7.4 g, Sod 327 mg, Pot 181.6 mg.

Nutritional information does not include water
chestnuts.

Julie H. Hughes, York

LAYERED LETTUCE SALAD

1 c. frozen peas
1 head lettuce, coarsely chopped
1 c. chopped celery
4 hard-boiled eggs, sliced
1/2 c. chopped green pepper
1 sweet onion, cut in rings
8 slices crisp-cooked bacon, crumbled
2 c. mayonnaise
2 tbsp. sugar
4 oz. cheese, grated

Cook . . . . peas, using package directions,
for 1 minute; drain.
Layer . . . . . . lettuce, celery, eggs, peas, green
pepper, onion and bacon in
order given in 9 x 13-inch glass
dish.
Mix . . . . mayonnaise and sugar in bowl.
Spread . . . . . over bacon, covering completely.
Sprinkle . . . . cheese over top.

Chill . . . . . . for 8 hours.
Yields . . . . . . 12 servings.

Approx Per Serv: Cal 464, Prot 15.7 g, T Fat 40.9 g,
Chl 149.4 mg, Car 9.3 g, Sod 406.8 mg, Pot 308.9 mg.

Heidi L. Orr, York

TWENTY-FOUR HOUR LETTUCE SALAD

1 head lettuce, torn
1 c. sliced celery
1 10-oz. package frozen peas, partially
   thawed
1/2 c. each chopped green pepper, onion
1/4 c. bacon bits
4 hard-boiled eggs, sliced
2 c. mayonnaise
2 tbsp. sugar
2 tsp. dry Italian salad dressing mix
1 c. grated Cheddar cheese

Layer . . . . . . lettuce, celery, peas, green
pepper, onion, bacon bits and
eggs in 9 x 13-inch baking dish.
Mix . . . . mayonnaise, sugar and dressing
mix in bowl.
Spread . . . . . over salad.
Sprinkle . . . . with cheese.
Chill . . . . for 24 hours.
Yields . . . . . . 12 servings.

Approx Per Serv: Cal 447, Prot 14.9 g, T Fat 39.7 g,
Chl 62.9 mg, Car 8.7 g, Sod 463.7 mg, Pot 285. 4 mg.

Tammie Lyn Boyer, Northumberland

SUMMER SALAD BOWL DELUXE

1/2 med. head Boston lettuce
1/2 med. head romaine lettuce
1/2 med. head endive
1 sm. bunch watercress
1 c. onion rings
1 c. diagonally sliced celery
2 tomatoes, quartered
1 tsp. each salt, dry mustard
1/2 tsp. pepper
3/4 tsp. tarragon
2 tsp. each lemon juice, cider vinegar
1/3 c. oil
1 sm. clove of garlic, crushed

Tear . . . . salad greens into bite-sized
pieces.

Combine . . . . greens with remaining vegetables in salad bowl, tossing to mix.
Combine . . . . seasonings, lemon juice, vinegar, oil and garlic in bowl, mixing well.
Pour . . . . over salad, tossing to coat.
Yields . . . . . . 6-8 servings.

Photograph for this recipe on page 51.

CONFETTI VEGETABLE SALAD

2 10-oz. packages frozen mixed vegetables, cooked, drained
3 hard-boiled eggs, finely chopped
1 1/2 c. finely chopped apples
1 tbsp. finely chopped onion
1 1/2 tsp. salt
1/8 tsp. pepper
3/4 c. salad dressing

Combine . . . . cooled mixed vegetables, eggs, apples, onion, salt and pepper in large bowl, tossing lightly.
Add . . . . salad dressing, mixing well.
Spoon . . . . . . into serving bowl.
Chill . . . . for 1 hour.
Garnish . . . . . with parsley and tomato wedges.
Yields . . . . . . 15 servings.

Approx Per Serv: Cal 50, Prot 2.6 g, T Fat 1.6 g, Chl 50.9 mg, Car 7 g, Sod 252.3 mg, Pot 105 mg.

Laura James, Mercer

COMPANY VEGETABLE SALAD

3/4 c. sugar
1/2 c. vinegar
1 1/2 tbsp. flour
1 tbsp. prepared mustard
2 pkg. frozen mixed vegetables, cooked, drained
1 onion, minced
4 stalks celery, minced
1/2 green pepper, chopped
1 can kidney beans, drained

Mix . . . . sugar, vinegar and flour in saucepan.
Cook . . . . until clear, stirring constantly.
Stir . . . . in mustard; cool.
Combine . . . . remaining 5 ingredients in bowl.
Add . . . . vinegar mixture, mixing well.

Chill . . . . covered, in refrigerator.
Yields . . . . . . 10 servings.

Approx Per Serv: Cal 179, Prot 6.1 g, T Fat .9 g, Chl 0 mg, Car 46 g, Sod 98.4 mg, Pot 548.1 mg.

Judy Muller, Wayne

DRESSING FOR TOSSED SALAD

2 c. sugar
3/4 c. cider vinegar
1 med. onion
1 c. oil
3 tsp. paprika
1/4 tsp. pepper
6 tbsp. catsup
1/2 tsp. each salt, garlic powder

Heat . . . . sugar and vinegar in saucepan until warm.
Place . . . . onion and oil in blender container.
Process . . . . . until onion is finely chopped.
Add . . . . remaining 5 ingredients.
Process . . . . . to blend, gradually adding sugar mixture; cool.
Store . . . . in refrigerator.
Yields . . . . . . 20 servings.

Approx Per Serv: Cal 182, Prot .2 g, T Fat 10.9 g, Chl 0 mg, Car 22.1 g, Sod 101.1 mg, Pot 35.9 mg.

Janet Norman, Tioga

HOMEMADE FRENCH DRESSING

1 can tomato soup
1 sm. onion, chopped
1 clove of garlic, crushed
1 tsp. salt
1 tsp. (scant) pepper
3/4 c. vinegar
1/2 tsp. paprika
1 1/2 c. oil
1/2 c. sugar
Dash of red pepper

Combine . . . . soup, onion and garlic in blender container.
Process . . . . . until smooth.
Add . . . . remaining ingredients.
Process . . . . . until well blended.
Yields . . . . . . 36 servings.

Approx Per Serv: Cal 98, Prot .2 g, T Fat 9.2 g, Chl 0 mg, Car 4.1 g, Sod 126.6 mg, Pot 20.5 mg.

Brian Spence, Adams

EASY FRENCH DRESSING

1 can tomato soup
1 c. oil
1/2 c. vinegar
3/4 c. sugar
1 tbsp. each salt, paprika
1 tbsp. each mustard, Worcestershire sauce
3 cloves of garlic, finely chopped

Place . . . . all ingredients in jar; cover.
Shake . . . . . . until well blended.
Yields . . . . . . 24 servings.

Approx Per Serv: Cal 116, Prot .3 g, T Fat 9.4 g, Chl 0 mg, Car 8.4 g, Sod 381.2 mg, Pot 36.9 mg.

Lucille Miller, Bucks

JAN'S FRENCH DRESSING

1/2 c. sugar
2/3 c. oil
1/3 c. vinegar
1 tsp. each celery seed, dry mustard
1 sm. onion, grated

Place . . . . all ingredients in blender container.
Process . . . . . until well blended.
Yields . . . . . . 12 servings.

Approx Per Serv: Cal 143, Prot .1 g, T Fat 12.1 g, Chl 0 mg, Car 9.3 g, Sod .9 mg, Pot 18 mg.

Jan Coutts, Pike

BACON DRESSING

8 strips bacon, cut into 1/2-in. pieces
2 eggs, beaten
1/2 c. sugar
1/2 c. vinegar
1/2 tsp. salt
Pepper to taste

Cook . . . . bacon in skillet until crisp.
Mix . . . . remaining ingredients in bowl.
Add . . . . to bacon and pan drippings in skillet.
Bring . . . . to a boil.
Cook . . . . until thick, stirring constantly.
Serve . . . . over lettuce or spinach.
Yields . . . . . . 12 servings.

Approx Per Serv: Cal 77, Prot 2.4 g, T Fat 3.6 g, Chl 46.6 mg, Car 9.1 g, Sod 150.3 mg, Pot 32.8 mg.

Nancy Myers, Columbia

DIET CREAMY SALAD DRESSING

8 pkg. artificial sweetener
1/2 c. diet mayonnaise
1/4 c. white vinegar
1/2 c. catsup
1 tbsp. mustard

Place . . . . all ingredients in blender container.
Process . . . . . until well blended.
Store . . . . in refrigerator.
Yields . . . . . . 10 servings.

Approx Per Serv: Cal 66, Prot .4 g, T Fat 5.1 g, Chl 6 mg, Car 5.1 g, Sod 197.5 mg, Pot 50.9 mg.

Nutritional information does not include artificial sweetener.

Julie A. Hughes, York

THOUSAND ISLAND DRESSING

1 c. mayonnaise
1/2 c. catsup
2 tbsp. pickle relish
1 tbsp. milk

Combine . . . . all ingredients, mixing well.
Add . . . . additional milk if necessary.
Yields . . . . . . 10 servings.

Approx Per Serv: Cal 177, Prot .6 g, T Fat 18 g, Chl 15.9 mg, Car 4.6 g, Sod 280.9 mg, Pot 59.3 mg.

Angie Finafrock, Adams

TOMATO SOUP SALAD DRESSING

1 med. onion, grated
1/2 c. vinegar
1 c. oil
1 1/2 c. sugar
1 1/2 tsp. Worcestershire sauce
1 1/2 tbsp. prepared mustard
1 tsp. each salt, paprika
1 c. tomato soup

Combine . . . . all ingredients in blender container.
Process . . . . . until well blended.
Yields . . . . . . 36 servings.

Approx Per Serv: Cal 94, Prot .2 g, T Fat 6.3 g, Chl 0 mg, Car 10 g, Sod 137.5 mg, Pot 27.6 mg.

Carol Nunn, Union

Vegetables &

SCANDINAVIAN-DILLED CARROTS, recipe on page 71.

Side Dishes

ASPARAGUS AND CORN CASSEROLE

2 tbsp. flour
5 tbsp. margarine
1 1/4 c. evaporated milk
1 tsp. salt
1/2 tsp. pepper
1 8-oz. can cream-style corn
2 hard-boiled eggs, chopped
1 10 1/2-oz. can cut asparagus
1/2 c. (about) bread crumbs
1/2 c. (about) grated cheese

Blend ......flour with 4 tablespoons melted margarine in saucepan.
Cook ....for 1 minute.
Add ......evaporated milk, mixing well.
Cook......until thickened, stirring constantly.
Season .....with salt and pepper.
Stir ....in corn, eggs and asparagus.
Spoon ......into 1 1/2-quart casserole.
Combine ....bread crumbs and cheese in bowl, mixing well.
Sprinkle ....over top of casserole.
Dot ....with remaining 1 tablespoon margarine.
Bake ....at 350 degrees for 1/2 hour or until golden brown.
Yields ......6 servings.

Approx Per Serv: Cal 288, Prot 10.8 g, T Fat 19.3 g, Chl 115.9 mg, Car 19.8 g, Sod 862.3 mg, Pot 322.4 mg.

Linda Messier, Centre

BAKED MARROWFAT BEANS

1 lb. dried marrowfat beans
1 tsp. salt
1 c. packed brown sugar
3/4 c. molasses
1/4 c. catsup
1 tsp. chopped onion (opt.)
1 tsp. prepared mustard
1/2 lb. sliced bacon, crisp-cooked, crumbled

Soak ....beans in water to cover in Dutch oven overnight; drain.
Add ....enough water to cover.
Cook ....until tender.
Add ....remaining ingredients, mixing well.

Bake ....at 350 degrees for several hours or until dark brown, adding water if necessary.
Yields ......8 servings.

Approx Per Serv: Cal 471, Prot 17.8 g, T Fat 8.6 g, Chl 13.3 mg, Car 83.1 g, Sod 538.3 mg, Pot 1010.5 mg.

Naomi Lauchnor, Lehigh

MRS. HOLLINGSHEAD'S BAKED BEANS

5 cans Great Northern beans
2 c. packed light brown sugar
1 c. molasses
1 med. onion, chopped
1/2 lb. bacon, chopped
1/2 c. (or more) catsup
2 tsp. salt
1 tbsp. mustard

Combine ....all ingredients in large baking dish, mixing well.
Bake ....at 375 degrees for 1 1/2 hours, stirring occasionally.
Yields ......16 servings.

Approx Per Serv: Cal 354, Prot 10.3 g, T Fat 10.6 g, Chl 9.9 mg, Car 56.5 g, Sod 470.4 mg, Pot 669 mg.

Doris Hollingshead, Franklin

BAKED LIMA BEANS

1 lb. dried baby lima beans
2 tsp. salt
1 14-oz. bottle of catsup
1 c. packed brown sugar
1 tbsp. vinegar
2 onions, chopped
4 strips bacon, chopped

Soak ....beans in salted water in Dutch oven overnight; drain.
Add ....enough cold water to cover.
Simmer .....for 1 hour.
Add ....remaining ingredients, mixing well.
Bake ....covered, at 325 degrees for 2 hours.
Yields ......8 servings.

Approx Per Serv: Cal 461, Prot 14.3 g, T Fat 11.1 g, Chl 9.9 mg, Car 79.5 g, Sod 1199.3 mg, Pot 1224.8 mg.

Beverly Sekol, Pike

PINTO BEANS

1 lb. bacon
2 lb. dried pinto beans, rinsed
1 med. onion, chopped
1 tbsp. chopped jalapeno pepper
2 tbsp. vinegar
1/4 tsp. garlic salt
1 tsp. (about) salt
Pepper to taste

Cook . . . . bacon in large skillet until crisp; drain and crumble, reserving pan drippings.
Place . . . . beans with water to cover in large saucepan.
Bring . . . . to a boil.
Add . . . . bacon, reserved pan drippings and remaining ingredients, mixing well.
Simmer . . . . . for 2 hours or until beans are tender, adding water if necessary to cover beans.
Yields . . . . . . 16 servings.

Approx Per Serv: Cal 275, Prot 7.9 g, T Fat 19.9 g, Chl 19.8 mg, Car 16.3 g, Sod 362.7 mg, Pot 290.1 mg.

Nancy Myers, Columbia

PATIO BAKED BEANS

1 c. packed brown sugar
1 tsp. instant coffee
1 tbsp. vinegar
1 tsp. each dry mustard, salt
2 1-lb. cans baked beans
1 onion, thinly sliced
4 slices bacon

Combine . . . . first 5 ingredients with 1/2 cup water in saucepan, mixing well.
Simmer . . . . . for 5 minutes.
Layer . . . . . . baked beans and onion alternately in 2-quart casserole.
Pour . . . . hot brown sugar mixture over all.
Bake . . . . covered, at 350 degrees for 45 minutes.
Top . . . . with bacon.
Bake . . . . . . uncovered, for 30 minutes longer.
Yields . . . . . . 6 servings.

Approx Per Serv: Cal 478, Prot 12.7 g, T Fat 14 g, Chl 13.2 mg, Car 77.3 g, Sod 1072.4 mg, Pot 658.2 mg.

Janet Reinninger, Union

BAKED GREEN BEANS AND MUSHROOMS

1 1/4 c. bread cubes
1/4 c. melted butter
2 3-oz. cans sliced mushrooms, drained
4 c. cut green beans
1/8 tsp. salt
Dash of pepper
1 tsp. chopped onion
1 can cream of mushroom soup
1/2 c. milk
1/4 c. toasted sliced almonds

Toss . . . . bread cubes with butter in bowl.
Layer . . . . . . half the bread cubes, all the mushrooms, green beans, salt, pepper and onion in greased 9 x 13-inch casserole.
Mix . . . . soup and milk in bowl.
Pour . . . . over layers.
Top . . . . with remaining bread cubes and almonds.
Bake . . . . at 400 degrees for 30 minutes.
Yields . . . . . . 8 servings.

Approx Per Serv: Cal 159, Prot 3.8 g, T Fat 11.6 g, Chl 23 mg, Car 11.6 g, Sod 594.9 mg, Pot 224.7 mg.

Nadine Long, Cambria

FAVORITE GREEN BEAN CASSEROLE

2 tbsp. butter, melted
2 tbsp. flour
1 tsp. each salt, sugar
1/4 tsp. pepper
1 sm. onion, grated
1 c. sour cream
2 pkg. frozen French-style green beans, cooked, drained
1/2 lb. Swiss cheese, shredded
1 c. corn flakes, crushed

Mix . . . . first 7 ingredients in bowl.
Layer . . . . . . half the beans, sour cream mixture and cheese in 3-quart casserole.
Repeat . . . . . layers.
Top . . . . with corn flake crumbs.
Bake . . . . at 400 degrees for 20 minutes.
Yields . . . . . . 6 servings.

Approx Per Serv: Cal 325, Prot 13.1 g, T Fat 24.2 g, Chl 66.1 mg, Car 15.6 g, Sod 732.2 mg, Pot 261.8 mg.

Tish Avery, Wayne

QUICK GREEN BEAN BAKE

4 c. canned green beans
1 can cream of mushroom soup
1 4-oz. can mushrooms, drained
1 c. bread crumbs

Cook . . . . green beans in saucepan until heated through; drain.
Add . . . . soup and mushrooms, mixing well.
Spoon . . . . . . into 1 1/2-quart baking dish.
Top . . . . with bread crumbs.
Bake . . . . at 350 degrees for 15 minutes or until golden brown.
Yields . . . . . . 6 servings.

Approx Per Serv: Cal 106, Prot 3.3 g, T Fat 4 5 g, Chl 4.3 mg, Car 14.1 g, Sod 656.9 mg, Pot 184.4 mg.

Teresa Grove, Westmoreland

VENUS' STRING BEANS

4 c. canned green beans
2 c. tomato juice
2 tbsp. sugar
1 tbsp. dry onion soup mix
3 slices bacon, finely chopped

Combine . . . . all ingredients in saucepan, mixing well.
Simmer . . . . . for 20 to 30 minutes.
Yields . . . . . . 6 servings.

Approx Per Serv: Cal 159, Prot 3.5 g, T Fat 10.9 g, Chl 13.2 mg, Car 13.3 g, Sod 596.9 mg, Pot 299.1 mg.

Venus Seaman, Juniata

CRUMB-TOPPED BROCCOLI CASSEROLE

1 egg, beaten
1/2 c. salad dressing
1 tbsp. grated onion
1/2 can mushroom soup
1 lg. bag frozen chopped broccoli, cooked, drained
Pepper to taste
1/2 tsp. (or more) salt
1/2 c. grated sharp cheese
1/4 c. bread crumbs

Combine . . . . first 4 ingredients in large bowl, mixing well.
Stir . . . . in broccoli and seasonings.
Spoon . . . . . . into 1-quart casserole.

Top . . . . with cheese and bread crumbs.
Bake . . . . at 400 degrees for 20 minutes.
Yields . . . . . . 8 servings.

Approx Per Serv: Cal 150, Prot 5.5 g, T Fat 11.1 g, Chl 47.6 mg, Car 8.6 g, Sod 447.5 mg, Pot 205.5 mg.

Janet M. Rudy, Allegheny

CHEESY BROCCOLI CASSEROLE

2 boxes frozen chopped broccoli, cooked, drained
1/4 lb. Velveeta cheese, cut into chunks
1 stick butter, melted
1 stack Ritz crackers, crushed

Place . . . . broccoli in 8-inch square baking pan.
Cook . . . . cheese and half the butter in saucepan until cheese melts, stirring constantly.
Pour . . . . over broccoli.
Toss . . . . crackers with remaining butter in bowl.
Sprinkle . . . . over cheese.
Bake . . . . at 350 degrees for 30 minutes.
Yields . . . . . . 4 servings.

Approx Per Serv: Cal 444, Prot 11.1 g, T Fat 34.1 g, Chl 89.1 mg, Car 27.1 g, Sod 1046.2 mg, Pot 445.9 mg.

Susan J. Athey, Snyder

MISSOURI BROCCOLI CASSEROLE

1 pkg. frozen chopped broccoli
1/4 c. butter, melted
3 tsp. chopped onion
1 c. cooked rice
1 sm. jar Cheez Whiz
1 can cream of celery soup

Cook . . . . broccoli in butter in skillet until thawed.
Stir . . . . in remaining ingredients.
Spoon . . . . . . into 2-quart casserole.
Bake . . . . at 350 degrees for 30 minutes.
Yields . . . . . . 4 servings.

Approx Per Serv: Cal 370, Prot 12.9 g, T Fat 25.1 g, Chl 70.6 mg, Car 24.9 g, Sod 1615.9 mg, Pot 357.2 mg.

Amy McNeal, Indiana

Recipe on page 31.

MOCK CABBAGE ROLL CASSEROLE

1 med. onion, chopped
3 tbsp. butter, melted
1/2 lb. ground beef
3/4 tsp. salt
1/8 tsp. pepper
6 c. coarsely shredded cabbage
1 can tomato soup

Saute ...... onion in butter in skillet.
Add .... ground beef and seasonings.
Cook .... until ground beef is heated through, stirring frequently. Do not brown.
Layer ...... half the cabbage and all the ground beef mixture in 2-quart baking dish.
Top .... with remaining cabbage and soup.
Bake .... covered, at 350 degrees for 1 hour.
Yields ...... 6 servings.

Approx Per Serv: Cal 214, Prot 8.9 g, T Fat 15 g, Chl 43.5 mg, Car 12.1 g, Sod 778.9 mg, Pot 401.9 mg.

Margaret Hutchko, Allegheny

SCANDINAVIAN-DILLED CARROTS

4 med. carrots, sliced
1 chicken bouillon cube
2 tbsp. butter, melted
1 tbsp. flour
1/4 c. milk
2 egg yolks, beaten
1 tbsp. lemon juice
1 tbsp. freshly chopped dillweed
1/4 tsp. salt
Dash of pepper

Cook .... carrots in 1 1/2 cups boiling water with bouillon cube in covered saucepan for 15 minutes or until tender-crisp; drain, reserving 1/4 cup liquid.
Blend ...... butter and flour in saucepan.
Stir .... in milk and reserved carrot liquid.
Cook .... over low heat until thick.
Combine .... egg yolks with lemon juice in small bowl.

Recipe on page 85.

Stir .... a small amount of hot mixture into egg yolks; stir egg yolks into hot mixture with dillweed, salt and pepper.
Cook .... for 1 minute longer, stirring constantly.
Pour .... over hot carrots in serving dish.
Yields ...... 4 servings.

Photograph for this recipe on page 65.

CAULIFLOWER SUPREME

1 lg. head cauliflower
1 box stuffing mix

Cook .... cauliflower in a small amount of boiling salted water in saucepan for 15 to 20 minutes; drain.
Prepare ..... stuffing mix using package directions.
Place .... cauliflower in baking dish.
Spread ..... stuffing over cauliflower to cover.
Bake .... at 350 degrees for 30 minutes.
Garnish ..... with pimento.
Yields ...... 8 servings.

Approx Per Serv: Cal 134, Prot 6.6 g, T Fat 1.3 g, Chl 1.1 mg, Car 26.1 g, Sod 391.6 mg, Pot 365.9 mg.

Nutritional information does not include ingredients used in preparing stuffing mix.

Pam Powers, Westmoreland

SUSAN'S BAKED CORN

2 tbsp. flour
1/2 tsp. salt
1/4 c. sugar
1/4 tsp. pepper
1 egg, beaten
1/4 c. milk
1 tbsp. butter, melted
2 c. corn

Combine .... all ingredients except corn in bowl, beating well.
Stir .... in corn.
Spoon ...... into casserole.
Bake .... at 400 degrees for 30 to 45 minutes or until bubbly.
Yields ...... 4 servings.

Approx Per Serv: Cal 202, Prot 5 g, T Fat 5.7 g, Chl 74.2 mg, Car 36.3 g, Sod 626.7 mg, Pot 167.1 mg.

Sonja Westover, Columbia

FAVORITE CORN PUDDING

3 eggs
1 1/4 c. sugar
1 tbsp. flour
3/4 can evaporated milk
1 lg. can cream-style corn
1 can Shoe Peg corn, drained
1/8 tsp. (or more) salt
1/2 stick butter

Beat . . . . eggs and sugar together in casserole.
Add . . . . flour, mixing well.
Stir . . . . in next 4 ingredients.
Place . . . . butter in center of corn mixture.
Bake . . . . at 350 degrees for 30 minutes; stir.
Bake . . . . for 30 minutes longer.
Yields . . . . . . 8 servings.

Approx Per Serv: Cal 338, Prot 7.2 g, T Fat 11.1 g, Chl 122.3 mg, Car 56.6 g, Sod 446.9 mg, Pot 240.1 mg.

Ann-Marie Dickson, Bucks

EASY CORN PUDDING

3 eggs, beaten
1 c. milk
4 tbsp. flour
1 tbsp. sugar
1/2 tsp. salt
Pepper to taste
1/4 c. melted butter
2 c. cream-style corn

Beat . . . . eggs and milk together in bowl.
Add . . . . remaining ingredients, mixing well.
Pour . . . . into 2-quart casserole.
Bake . . . . at 350 degrees for 1 hour.
Yields . . . . . . 6 servings.

Approx Per Serv: Cal 232, Prot 7.1 g, T Fat 12.5 g, Chl 155.8 mg, Car 25.3 g, Sod 523.5 mg, Pot 180.9 mg.

Margaret Weisenfluh, Elk

SCALLOPED ONIONS

8 med. onions, sliced
1 tsp. salt
1 c. cracker crumbs
1/4 c. butter

1 egg, beaten
1 3/4 c. milk
Pepper to taste

Cook . . . . onions in water with salt in saucepan for 1 hour; drain.
Arrange . . . . . in 2-quart casserole.
Mix . . . . cracker crumbs, butter, egg and milk in bowl.
Pour . . . . over onions.
Sprinkle . . . . with pepper.
Dot . . . . with additional butter.
Bake . . . . at 350 degrees for 25 minutes or until brown.
Yields . . . . . . 5 servings.

Approx Per Serv: Cal 291, Prot 8.7 g, T Fat 15.2 g, Chl 90.9 mg, Car 32.1 g, Sod 767.8 mg, Pot 475.7 mg.

Dorothy Houtz, Centre

CHEESE HASHED BROWN POTATOES

2 lb. frozen hashed brown potatoes, thawed
1/2 c. butter, melted
1 pt. sour cream
1/2 c. chopped onion
2 c. shredded Cheddar cheese
1 can cream of chicken soup
1 tsp. each salt, pepper

Combine . . . . potatoes and butter in bowl, mixing well.
Stir . . . . in remaining ingredients.
Spoon . . . . . . into greased 9 x 13-inch baking pan.
Bake . . . . covered, at 350 degrees for 30 minutes.
Bake . . . . uncovered, for 20 minutes longer or until browned.
Yields . . . . . . 8 servings.

Approx Per Serv: Cal 453, Prot 11.4 g, T Fat 34.5 g, Chl 91.7 mg, Car 26.3 g, Sod 946.3 mg, Pot 343.3 mg.

Julie A. Hughes, York

GOURMET POTATOES

2 c. shredded Cheddar cheese
6 tbsp. butter
6 med. potatoes, cooked, peeled, shredded
1 1/2 c. sour cream
1/3 c. finely chopped green onions

1 tsp. salt
1/4 tsp. pepper
Paprika

Combine . . . . cheese and 4 tablespoons butter in large saucepan.

Cook . . . . over low heat until cheese melts, stirring until smooth.

Stir . . . . in potatoes, sour cream, green onions, salt and pepper.

Place . . . . in greased 2-quart casserole.

Top . . . . with remaining 2 tablespoons butter and paprika.

Bake . . . . at 350 degrees for 30 minutes or until heated through.

Yields . . . . . . 8 servings.

Approx Per Serv: Cal 411, Prot 12.1 g, T Fat 27 g, Chl 73.6 mg, Car 31.7 g, Sod 597.4 mg, Pot 783.7 mg.

Sharon McCahren, Juniata

SCALLOPED POTATOES IN CHEESE SAUCE

3 tbsp. butter, melted
2 tbsp. flour
1 tsp. salt
Dash of pepper
2 c. hot milk
1 c. grated white American cheese
6 potatoes, sliced
1 onion, chopped
Parsley flakes

Blend . . . . . . butter, flour, salt and pepper in top of double boiler.

Cook . . . . over boiling water until smooth, stirring constantly.

Stir . . . . in milk gradually.

Cook . . . . until thick, stirring constantly.

Add . . . . cheese.

Cook . . . . until cheese melts, stirring frequently.

Layer . . . . . . potatoes, onion and cheese sauce alternately in buttered casserole until all ingredients are used.

Garnish . . . . . with parsley.

Bake . . . . at 350 degrees for 1 hour.

Yields . . . . . . 6 servings.

Approx Per Serv: Cal 420.1, Prot 16.6 g, T Fat 19.2 g, Chl 81.9 mg, Car 46.8 g, Sod 667.4 mg, Pot 1120.1 mg.

Karen Sattazahn, Berks

POTATO-CHEESE BALLS

2 c. mashed potatoes
2 tbsp. flour
1/4 c. finely chopped onion
2 tbsp. celery leaves, chopped
1 egg, slightly beaten
1/2 c. grated sharp cheese
1/2 tsp. (about) salt
Pepper to taste
Paprika

Combine . . . . all ingredients, except paprika, in bowl, mixing well.

Shape . . . . . . into 2-inch balls.

Place . . . . on greased baking sheet.

Sprinkle . . . . with paprika.

Bake . . . . at 350 degrees for 20 to 30 minutes or until lightly browned.

Yields . . . . . . 4 servings.

Approx Per Serv: Cal 194, Prot 7.9 g, T Fat 10.6 g, Chl 90.8 mg, Car 17.2 g, Sod 733.9 mg, Pot 322.8 mg.

Kelly and Amy Champluvier, Bradford

NINA'S SCALLOPED POTATOES

2 lb. potatoes, peeled, thinly sliced
1 sm. onion, grated
3 tbsp. flour
1/4 tsp. salt
Dash of pepper
1/4 c. margarine
1 c. evaporated milk

Layer . . . . . . potatoes, onion, flour, salt, pepper and margarine alternately in 2-quart casserole until all ingredients are used.

Combine . . . . evaporated milk with 1 1/2 cups water in saucepan.

Heat . . . . to scalding.

Pour . . . . over layers, adding more water if necessary to moisten.

Bake . . . . covered, at 350 degrees for 30 minutes.

Bake . . . . uncovered, for 60 to 70 minutes longer or until potatoes are tender.

Let . . . . stand for 5 to 10 minutes before serving.

Yields . . . . . . 4 servings.

Approx Per Serv: Cal 263, Prot 9.8 g, T Fat 6.3 g, Chl 21.3 mg, Car 42.7 g, Sod 225.6 mg, Pot 950.8 mg.

Nina Lonchar, Allegheny

MICROWAVE QUICK-BAKED POTATOES

    1/2 c. Parmesan cheese
    1 tbsp. paprika
    1 tsp. parsley flakes
    1/2 tsp. salt
    1/4 tsp. pepper
    4 med. potatoes, quartered
    2 tbsp. butter, melted

Combine .... first 5 ingredients in bowl, mixing well.
Dip .... potatoes into melted butter.
Coat .... with cheese mixture.
Arrange ..... in glass baking dish.
Microwave .. on High for 10 to 12 minutes or until tender.
Let .... stand for 5 minutes.
Yields ...... 4 servings.

Approx Per Serv: Cal 252, Prot 9.3 g, T Fat 9.8 g, Chl 31.9 mg, Car 32.5 g, Sod 450.9 mg, Pot 786.9 mg.

Carol Garling, Franklin

PARTY SCALLOPED POTATOES

    1 onion, chopped
    1/4 lb. bacon, crisp-cooked, crumbled
    12 c. thinly sliced peeled potatoes
    10 oz. extra sharp white cheese, sliced
    2 tbsp. margarine

Combine .... onion and bacon in small bowl, mixing well.
Alternate ... layers of potatoes, onion mixture and cheese in foil-lined 9 x 13-inch baking dish, ending with potatoes.
Dot .... with margarine.
Bake .... tightly sealed, at 400 degrees for 1 1/2 hours or until potatoes are tender.
Yields ...... 25 servings.

Approx Per Serv: Cal 125, Prot 5.1 g, T Fat 5.9 g, Chl 13.4 mg, Car 13.2 g, Sod 117.9 mg, Pot 318.9 mg.

Mildred S. Bleiler, Lehigh

CREAMY SCALLOPED POTATOES

    6 med. potatoes, sliced
    3 tbsp. margarine
    1 sm. onion, finely chopped
    1 tsp. salt
    1/4 tsp. pepper
    3 tbsp. flour
    2 1/2 c. milk

Layer ...... potatoes, margarine, onion, seasonings and flour alternately in baking dish until all ingredients are used.
Pour .... milk over layers.
Bake .... at 425 degrees for 1 hour or until potatoes are tender.
Yields ...... 12 servings.

Approx Per Serv: Cal 140, Prot 4.1 g, T Fat 4.8 g, Chl 7.1 mg, Car 20.6 g, Sod 241.7 mg, Pot 468.6 mg.

Karol Sherman, Amy Sherman, Adams

IMPOSSIBLE PATTY PAN PIES

    6 eggs
    1/4 c. margarine, softened
    3/4 c. sugar
    1/2 c. flour
    3 c. milk
    1 tsp. vanilla extract
    2 c. grated patty pan squash

Place .... all ingredients in blender container.
Process ..... for several seconds.
Pour .... into two 9-inch pie plates.
Bake .... at 350 degrees for 35 to 45 minutes or until golden.
Yields ...... 12 servings.

Approx Per Serv: Cal 186, Prot 6.1 g, T Fat 8.9 g, Chl 134.9 mg, Car 20.7 g, Sod 108 mg, Pot 170.4 mg.

Crossroads Community Center, Philadelphia

YUMMY SWEET POTATOES

    3 c. mashed sweet potatoes
    1/4 c. sugar
    1 tbsp. vanilla extract
    4 tbsp. melted butter
    2 eggs, beaten
    3/4 c. packed brown sugar
    1/3 c. flour
    4 tbsp. melted butter
    1 c. chopped pecans (opt.)

Combine .... first 5 ingredients in bowl, mixing well.
Spoon ...... into 1 1/2-quart baking dish.
Combine .... brown sugar, flour, butter and pecans in bowl, mixing well.

Sprinkle . . . . over casserole.
Bake . . . . at 350 degrees for 25 minutes.
Yields . . . . . . 6 servings.

Approx Per Serv: Cal 603, Prot 6.9 g, T Fat 31.8 g, Chl 107.9 mg, Car 76.4 g, Sod 228.3 mg, Pot 553.6 mg.

Hilda Lewis, Lackawanna

SQUASH-STUFFED TOMATOES

4 med. tomatoes
3/4 tsp. salt
2 zucchini, grated
1/3 c. chopped onion
1 c. grated Swiss cheese
1/4 tsp. each pepper, basil

Slice . . . . stem end from each tomato.
Scoop . . . . . . out centers with spoon, reserving pulp.
Sprinkle . . . . with 1/2 teaspoon salt.
Invert . . . . . . on paper towel and let stand for 30 minutes.
Pat . . . . dry and place on baking sheet.
Combine . . . . reserved tomato pulp, 1/4 teaspoon salt and remaining ingredients in bowl.
Spoon . . . . . . into tomato shells.
Bake . . . . at 350 degrees for 10 minutes. Do not overbake.
Yields . . . . . . 4 servings.

Photograph for this recipe on page 36.

PARMESAN ZUCCHINI

3 c. sliced zucchini
4 c. canned tomatoes
1 med. onion, sliced
1/2 tsp. each Italian seasoning, salt
Pepper to taste
1/4 c. Parmesan cheese

Layer . . . . . . zucchini, tomatoes and onion alternately in greased 2-quart casserole until all ingredients are used.
Sprinkle . . . . with seasonings.
Top . . . . with Parmesan cheese.
Bake . . . . at 350 degrees for 1 hour.
Yields . . . . . . 6 servings.

Approx Per Serv: Cal 72, Prot 4.5 g, T Fat 1.5 g, Chl 4.7 mg, Car 11.2 g, Sod 425.5 mg, Pot 520.7 mg.

Jill Prichard, Erie

CAROL'S ZUCCHINI CASSEROLE

2 c. coarsely chopped zucchini
1 sm. onion, grated
2 carrots, grated
1/2 c. sour cream
1 can cream of chicken soup
2 c. stuffing mix
1/3 c. melted butter

Cook . . . . zucchini in water in saucepan until just tender; drain.
Add . . . . next 4 ingredients, mixing well.
Toss . . . . stuffing mix with butter in bowl.
Add . . . . 2/3 of the stuffing mixture to squash mixture, mixing well.
Spoon . . . . . . into 2-quart casserole.
Top . . . . with remaining stuffing mixture.
Bake . . . . at 350 degrees for 30 minutes.
Yields . . . . . . 8 servings.

Approx Per Serv: Cal 248, Prot 5.8 g, T Fat 13.6 g, Chl 34 mg, Car 27.1 g, Sod 787.3 mg, Pot 225.5 mg.

Carol Kaufman, Lawrence

SLICED ZUCCHINI CASSEROLE

4 med. zucchini, sliced 1/2 in. thick
1/2 tsp. salt
2 1/4 c. herb and cheese croutons
6 tbsp. melted butter
3/4 c. shredded carrots
1/2 c. chopped onion
1 can cream of chicken soup
1/2 c. sour cream

Cook . . . . zucchini in lightly salted water in saucepan until just tender; drain.
Toss . . . . croutons with 4 tablespoons butter in small bowl.
Combine . . . . carrots, onion, and half the croutons in bowl.
Stir . . . . in soup and sour cream.
Add . . . . zucchini, stirring gently.
Spoon . . . . . . into greased casserole.
Top . . . . with reserved croutons tossed with remaining 2 tablespoons butter.
Bake . . . . at 350 degrees for 30 to 40 minutes or until bubbly.
Yields . . . . . . 6 servings.

Approx Per Serv: Cal 264, Prot 5.8 g, T Fat 18.6 g, Chl 48.4 mg, Car 21.2 g, Sod 889.1 mg, Pot 502.3 mg.

Katrina Harbach, Clinton

STEAMED SUMMER VEGETABLES TWO WAYS

1/2 tsp. salt
3 med. potatoes, pared, sliced
1/2 lb. fresh green beans, cut
*   in 1-in. pieces*
1 lg. onion, sliced
2 zucchini, sliced
2 c. sliced yellow squash
Lemon Herb Butter
Zesty Marinade

Bring . . . . 1 1/2 cups water and salt to a boil in large skillet; reduce heat.
Place . . . . steamer in skillet.
Layer . . . . . . potatoes and green beans in steamer.
Simmer . . . . . covered, for 5 minutes.
Add . . . . remaining vegetables.
Simmer . . . . . for 5 minutes or until tender-crisp.
Toss . . . . half the vegetables with Lemon Herb Butter, serving hot.
Toss . . . . remaining vegetables with Zesty Marinade.
Chill . . . . covered, overnight.

Lemon Herb Butter

1/3 c. butter
1 tbsp. lemon juice
1/2 tsp. salt
Dash of pepper

Melt . . . . butter in small saucepan.
Stir . . . . in remaining ingredients.

Zesty Marinade

1/3 c. oil
1 tbsp. wine vinegar
2 tbsp. lemon juice
1 tsp. chopped fresh parsley
1/2 tsp. salt
1/2 tsp. dried leaf basil, crumbled

Combine . . . . all ingredients in jar.
Shake . . . . . . covered, to blend well.

Photograph for this recipe on page 36.

VEGETABLES A LA ESPANA

1 can chicken broth
2 tbsp. lemon juice

1/3 c. olive oil
1/4 tsp. pepper
1 clove of garlic, crushed
1 tsp. oregano
4 med. carrots, cut into 1/2-in. slices
1 c. 1-inch celery slices
1 lg. green pepper, cut into 1-in. pieces
2 10-oz. packages frozen cauliflower
1 lb. zucchini, cut into 3/4-in. slices
1 c. sliced lg. pimento-stuffed olives

Combine . . . . first 6 ingredients in large saucepan.
Bring . . . . to a boil.
Add . . . . carrots, celery, green pepper, cauliflower and zucchini.
Simmer . . . . . covered, for 10 minutes or until vegetables are tender; drain.
Stir . . . . in olives.
Serve . . . . hot or cold.
Yields . . . . . . 8-10 servings.

Photograph for this recipe on page 6.

FRESH STIR-FRY MELANGE

3 1/2 c. each green pepper, red pepper
*   strips*
2 1/2 c. sliced mushrooms
1 c. sliced celery
2 tbsp. chopped onion
1/2 clove of garlic, crushed
1/2 tsp. sugar
1/4 tsp. oregano
3/4 tsp. salt
Dash of pepper
1/4 c. olive oil
1 tsp. wine vinegar
2 tomatoes, cut in wedges

Stir-fry . . . . . first 10 ingredients in hot olive oil in skillet over medium-high heat until peppers are tender-crisp.
Add . . . . vinegar and tomatoes.
Cook . . . . until heated through.
Yields . . . . . . 6 servings.

Photograph for this recipe on page 36.

BAKED APPLES

6 baking apples, cored
6 tsp. butter
3/4 tsp. cinnamon

Peel . . . . top half of each apple.
Place . . . . in water 1/4 inch deep in baking dish.
Place . . . . 1 teaspoon butter and 1/8 teaspoon cinnamon in center of each apple.
Bake . . . . at 375 degrees for 45 minutes or until tender, basting occasionally.
Yields . . . . . . 6 servings.

Approx Per Serv: Cal 157, Prot .5 g, T Fat 5.1 g, Chl 11.8 mg, Car 30.7 g, Sod 48.8 mg, Pot 233.8 mg.

Tina Duke, Union

SCALLOPED PINEAPPLE

4 c. bread cubes
1 c. melted margarine
3 eggs, beaten
2 c. sugar
1/2 c. evaporated milk
1 can pineapple, drained

Combine . . . . all ingredients in bowl, mixing well.
Spoon . . . . . . into casserole.
Bake . . . . at 350 degrees for 35 to 40 minutes or until set.
Yields . . . . . . 8 servings.

Approx Per Serv: Cal 691, Prot 10.2 g, T Fat 28.8 g, Chl 173.2 mg, Car 100 g, Sod 691 mg, Pot 217.2 mg.

Nadine Long, Cambria

SCRAMBLED EGGS

8 eggs, slightly beaten
1/2 c. milk
1/4 c. grated Cheddar cheese
1/4 tsp. garlic salt
Pepper to taste
4 slices crisp-cooked bacon, crumbled
1 tbsp. parsley flakes
4 tsp. bacon drippings

Combine . . . . first 7 ingredients in bowl, mixing well.
Pour . . . . into bacon drippings in large skillet.

Cook . . . . until set, stirring constantly.
Yields . . . . . . 8 servings.

Approx Per Serv: Cal 131, Prot 9.1 g, T Fat 9.4 g, Chl 261.8 mg, Car 2 g, Sod 201.8 mg, Pot 152.9 mg.

Connie Homan, Westmoreland

EASY DUMPLINGS

1 c. sifted flour
2 tsp. baking powder
1/2 tsp. salt
1 sprig of parsley, minced
1/2 c. milk
Chicken broth

Combine . . . . first 5 ingredients in bowl, mixing well.
Drop . . . . by spoonfuls into boiling chicken broth in saucepan.
Cook . . . . covered, for 20 minutes.
Yields . . . . . . 6 servings.

Approx Per Serv: Cal 94.7, Prot 3.3 g, T Fat 1 g, Chl 2.8 mg, Car 18 g, Sod 302.3 mg, Pot 123.3 mg.

Nutritional information does not include chicken broth.

Michele Hollenbach, Union

NOODLE PIZZA

1 8-oz. package fine egg noodles, cooked
3 eggs, beaten
2 c. shredded mozzarella cheese
1 tsp. salt
1 15 1/2-oz. jar pizza sauce

Combine . . . . first 4 ingredients in bowl, mixing well.
Press . . . . into greased 12-inch pizza pan.
Bake . . . . at 350 degrees for 20 minutes or until lightly browned.
Spread . . . . . sauce over crust.
Garnish . . . . . with pepperoni, cooked sausage or ground beef, sliced green pepper, onion and tomato as desired.
Bake . . . . for 10 minutes longer.
Yields . . . . . . 8 servings.

Approx Per Serv: Cal 230, Prot 13 g, T Fat 10.5 g, Chl 146.4 mg, Car 26.2 g, Sod 735 mg, Pot 315.4 mg.

Sherry Fike, Blair

SPAGHETTI PIZZA

1 lb. spaghetti, cooked
1 egg, beaten
1/3 c. milk
1/2 stick butter, melted
2 1/2 c. (or more) shredded mozzarella
* cheese*
Spaghetti sauce
1/4 c. Parmesan cheese
Pepperoni

Combine . . . . first 4 ingredients with 1/2 cup mozzarella cheese in bowl, mixing well.
Place . . . . on greased 10 1/2 x 15-inch baking sheet.
Spread . . . . . sauce over top.
Top . . . . with Parmesan cheese, remaining mozzarella cheese and pepperoni.
Bake . . . . at 350 degrees for 35 to 40 minutes or until bubbly.
Yields . . . . . . 10 servings.

Approx Per Serv: Cal 363, Prot 13.8 g, T Fat 18.3 g, Chl 82.6 mg, Car 35.4 g, Sod 261.1 mg, Pot 135.5 mg.

Nutritional information does not include spaghetti sauce and pepperoni.

Carol Pifer, Jefferson

MACARONI IN CHEESE SAUCE

1 8-oz. package macaroni
2 tbsp. oil
3 tbsp. margarine
3 tbsp. flour
1 1/2 c. milk
4 tsp. salt
1/4 tsp. pepper
1/2 c. grated cheese
1/4 c. bread crumbs

Cook . . . . macaroni in boiling water with oil for 10 minutes; drain.
Melt . . . . margarine in 1-quart saucepan; remove from heat.
Blend . . . . . . in flour.
Stir . . . . in 1/2 cup milk until smooth.
Stir . . . . in remaining milk gradually.
Cook . . . . over medium heat until thick, stirring constantly.
Add . . . . salt, pepper and cheese.

Cook . . . . until cheese melts, stirring constantly.
Combine . . . . macaroni and cheese sauce in greased baking dish, mixing well.
Top . . . . with bread crumbs.
Bake . . . . at 350 degrees for 30 minutes.
Yields . . . . . . 6 servings.

Approx Per Serv: Cal 329, Prot 9.9 g, T Fat 16 g, Chl 17.9 mg, Car 35.8 g, Sod 1600.4 mg, Pot 178.1 mg.

Wendy Newhard, Lehigh

EASY MACARONI AND CHEESE

4 c. cooked macaroni, drained
1 c. grated sharp cheese
1 tsp. salt
1/8 tsp. pepper
3 1/2 c. milk
1/2 c. (or more) Parmesan cheese

Mix . . . . first 4 ingredients in casserole.
Stir . . . . in milk.
Sprinkle . . . . with Parmesan cheese.
Bake . . . . at 350 degrees for 1 hour.
Yields . . . . . . 4 servings.

Approx Per Serv: Cal 465, Prot 24.6 g, T Fat 21 g, Chl 57.9 mg, Car 43.7 g, Sod 947.6 mg, Pot 438.1 mg.

Linda Buffington, Dauphin

BAKED STUFFING BALLS

1 loaf bread, crumbled
1 onion, finely chopped
1/2 c. finely chopped celery
2 tbsp. parsley flakes
1 tsp. (about) salt
Pepper to taste
1 or 2 eggs, beaten
1 can tomatoes, chopped
4 to 6 slices bacon

Combine . . . . first 7 ingredients in bowl, mixing well.
Shape . . . . . . into 2-inch balls.
Place . . . . in casserole.
Top . . . . with tomatoes and bacon.
Bake . . . . at 350 degrees for 1 hour.
Yields . . . . . . 8 servings.

Approx Per Serv: Cal 267, Prot 10.2 g, T Fat 6.8 g, Chl 70.3 mg, Car 40.7 g, Sod 82.7 mg, Pot 128.5 mg.

Helen Caswell, Blair

Breads

MAPLE WALNUT LOAF, recipe on page 84.

BISCUITS SUPREME

2 c. sifted flour
4 tsp. baking powder
1/2 tsp. each salt, cream of tartar
2 tsp. sugar
1/2 c. shortening
2/3 c. milk

Sift .... first 5 ingredients into bowl.
Cut .... in shortening until crumbly.
Add .... milk, stirring until dough leaves side of bowl.
Knead ...... for 30 seconds on floured surface.
Roll .... out 1/2 inch thick.
Cut .... with biscuit cutter.
Place .... on baking sheet.
Bake .... at 450 degrees for 10 to 12 minutes.
Yields ...... 12 servings.

Approx Per Serv: Cal 165, Prot 2.5 g, T Fat 10 g, Chl 1.9 mg, Car 16.3 g, Sod 214.1 mg, Pot 43.8 mg.

Joanne Hash, Tioga

QUICK BAKING POWDER BISCUITS

1 c. flour
1/4 tsp. salt
1 tsp. baking powder
1 tbsp. shortening
Milk

Combine .... dry ingredients in bowl, mixing well.
Cut .... in shortening until crumbly.
Add .... enough milk to moisten, mixing well.
Drop .... by spoonfuls into greased muffin cups.
Bake .... at 400 degrees for 12 minutes.
Yields ...... 6 servings.

Approx Per Serv: Cal 97, Prot 2.2 g, T Fat 2.5 g, Chl 0 mg, Car 16 g, Sod 144 mg, Pot 20.6 mg.

Nutritional information does not include milk.

Nancy Myers, Columbia

SKY-HIGH BISCUITS

2 c. flour
1 c. whole wheat flour
4 1/2 tsp. baking powder

2 tbsp. sugar
1/2 tsp. salt
3/4 tsp. cream of tartar
3/4 c. butter
1 egg, beaten
1 c. milk

Combine .... dry ingredients in bowl, mixing well.
Cut .... in butter until crumbly.
Stir .... in egg and milk until just mixed.
Knead ...... lightly on floured surface.
Roll .... to 1-inch thickness.
Cut .... with biscuit cutter.
Place .... on greased baking sheet.
Bake .... at 450 degrees for 12 to 15 minutes or until golden brown.
Yields ...... 15 servings.

Approx Per Serv: Cal 192, Prot 3.9 g, T Fat 10.5 g, Chl 47.5 mg, Car 21.1 g, Sod 304.8 mg, Pot 82.5 mg.

Lee Ann Eicholtz, Adams

CORN FRITTERS

1 egg, beaten
1/3 c. milk
1 c. flour
1 1/2 tsp. baking powder
2 tbsp. sugar
1 tsp. salt
1 tbsp. shortening, melted
2 c. corn

Mix .... egg and milk together in large bowl.
Add .... remaining ingredients, mixing well.
Drop .... by spoonfuls into hot greased skillet.
Cook .... until brown, turning once.
Yields ...... 12 servings.

Approx Per Serv: Cal 91, Prot 2.6 g, T Fat 2.2 g, Chl 22 mg, Car 15.9 g, Sod 292.3 mg, Pot 52.3 mg.

Betsy Geise, Northumberland

SUNDAY CORN BREAD

1 c. yellow cornmeal
3/4 c. flour
2 eggs
1/2 tsp. salt

2 tbsp. baking powder
1 c. milk

Combine . . . . all ingredients in medium bowl, mixing well.
Pour . . . . into greased 9 x 9-inch baking pan.
Bake . . . . at 400 degrees for 1/2 hour or until golden brown.
Yields . . . . . . 6 servings.

Approx Per Serv: Cal 198, Prot 7 g, T Fat 3.8 g, Chl 90 mg, Car 33 g, Sod 547.5 mg, Pot 127.1 mg.

Marvin Jones, Erie

FUNNEL CAKES

3 eggs, beaten
1/2 c. sugar
2 c. milk
2 tsp. baking powder
1/2 tsp. salt
3 to 4 c. flour
Oil for deep frying

Mix . . . . eggs, sugar and milk together in large bowl.
Sift . . . . baking powder, salt and half the flour together.
Add . . . . to egg mixture.
Beat . . . . until smooth.
Mix . . . . in enough remaining flour to make thin batter.
Drop . . . . from funnel into deep 375-degree oil.
Fry . . . . until light brown; drain on paper towel.
Garnish . . . . . with confectioners' sugar.
Yields . . . . . . 12 servings.

Approx Per Serv: Cal 231, Prot 7.4 g, T Fat 3.3 g, Chl 68.9 mg, Car 42.3 g, Sod 180.1 mg, Pot 115.3 mg.

Nutritional information does not include oil.

Edward Transue, Monroe

GOLDEN PUFFS

2 c. flour
3/4 c. sugar
3 tsp. baking powder
1 tsp. salt
1 tsp. nutmeg
1/4 c. oil
3/4 c. milk

1 egg
Oil for deep frying
1 tsp. cinnamon

Combine . . . . flour, 1/4 cup sugar, baking powder, salt and nutmeg in bowl, mixing well.
Add . . . . oil, milk and egg.
Beat . . . . until smooth.
Drop . . . . by teaspoonfuls into deep 375-degree oil.
Fry . . . . several at a time for 3 minutes or until golden brown; drain on paper towel.
Mix . . . . cinnamon and remaining 1/2 cup sugar in bowl.
Roll . . . . warm puffs in cinnamon sugar.
Yields . . . . . . 30 servings.

Approx Per Serv: Cal 73, Prot 1.3 g, T Fat 2.3 g, Chl 9.3 mg, Car 11.7 g, Sod 109.2 mg, Pot 19.5 mg.

Nutritional information does not include oil.

Vida Grace Brown, Allegheny

SURPRISE DOUGHNUT HOLES

2 c. flour
1 tbsp. baking powder
1/2 tsp. salt
1/3 c. shortening
3/4 c. milk
Raisins
Nuts
Chocolate chips
Oil for deep frying
Cinnamon

Mix . . . . flour, baking powder and salt in bowl.
Cut . . . . in shortening until crumbly.
Stir . . . . in milk until just mixed.
Knead . . . . . . 10 to 12 times on floured surface.
Roll . . . . to 1/2-inch thickness.
Cut . . . . into small circles.
Place . . . . raisins, nuts and chocolate chips in center.
Pull . . . . up dough to enclose filling.
Fry . . . . in deep hot oil until golden brown.
Roll . . . . in cinnamon.
Serve . . . . hot.

Karan Heffelfinger, Carbon

BLUEBERRY MUFFINS

1/2 c. butter, softened
1 1/4 c. sugar
1 egg
Flour
2 tsp. baking powder
1/2 tsp. salt
1/2 c. milk
2 c. blueberries
1/2 tsp. cinnamon

Cream ...... 1/4 cup butter and 3/4 cup sugar in bowl.
Beat .... in egg.
Mix .... 2 cups sifted flour, baking powder and salt in bowl.
Add .... to creamed mixture alternately with milk, beating well after each addition.
Fold .... in blueberries.
Fill .... oiled muffin cups 2/3 full.
Combine .... remaining 1/4 cup butter, 1/2 cup sugar, 1/3 cup flour and cinnamon in bowl, mixing well.
Sprinkle .... into muffin cups.
Bake .... at 400 degrees for 20 to 25 minutes or until golden brown.
Yields ...... 18 servings.

Approx Per Serv: Cal 177, Prot 2.4 g, T Fat 5.9 g, Chl 30.8 mg, Car 29.1 g, Sod 165.4 mg, Pot 44.2 mg.

Nancy Honeywell, Luzerne

HONEY-OATMEAL MUFFINS

2/3 c. milk
1/3 c. oil
1 egg, beaten
1/4 c. honey
1/3 c. packed brown sugar
1 1/2 c. oats
1 c. flour
1 tbsp. baking powder
3/4 tsp. salt
1/2 c. raisins
1/2 c. chopped nuts

Mix .... milk, oil, egg and honey in large bowl.
Combine .... remaining 7 ingredients in bowl, mixing well.
Add .... to milk mixture, stirring until just moistened.
Fill .... greased muffin cups 2/3 full.

Bake .... at 400 degrees for 15 to 18 minutes or until golden brown.
Yields ...... 1 dozen.

Photograph for this recipe on page 104.

TEA MUFFINS

4 c. flour
1 tsp. soda
1 tbsp. baking powder
1 tsp. salt
Sugar
1 c. margarine
2 c. buttermilk
1 c. blueberries
Cinnamon-sugar

Combine .... first 4 dry ingredients and 1 cup plus 2 tablespoons sugar in bowl.
Cut .... in margarine until crumbly.
Add .... buttermilk and blueberries, stirring until moistened.
Fill .... paper-lined muffin cups 3/4 full.
Sprinkle .... cinnamon-sugar over muffins.
Bake .... in moderately hot oven until golden brown.
Yields ...... 24 servings.

Approx Per Serv: Cal 198, Prot 3 g, T Fat 8.6 g, Chl 2.8 mg, Car 27.3 g, Sod 268.3 mg, Pot 57 mg.

Nutritional information does not include cinnamon-sugar.

Gina Bittner, Lehigh

EASY PANCAKES

2 c. flour
2 tsp. baking powder
2 tsp. sugar
3/4 tsp. salt
1 egg
2 tbsp. melted shortening
1 1/2 c. milk

Mix .... dry ingredients in bowl.
Add .... egg, shortening and milk, stirring until just moistened.
Bake .... on hot greased griddle until golden brown, turning once.
Yields ...... 5 servings.

Approx Per Serv: Cal 304, Prot 9.1 g, T Fat 9.8 g, Chl 60.8 mg, Car 43.9 g, Sod 581.3 mg, Pot 167.7 mg.

Nancy Myers, Columbia

OAT SCONES

1 1/2 c. flour
1 1/4 c. quick oats
1/4 c. sugar
1 tbsp. baking powder
1 tsp. cream of tartar
1/2 tsp. salt
2/3 c. melted butter
1/3 c. milk
1 egg, beaten
1/2 c. raisins

Combine .... first 6 ingredients in large bowl, mixing well.
Mix .... butter, milk and egg in bowl.
Add .... to dry ingredients, stirring until moistened.
Stir .... in raisins.
Shape ...... dough into ball.
Pat .... into 8-inch circle on lightly floured surface.
Cut .... into 8 to 12 wedges.
Place .... on greased baking sheet.
Bake .... at 425 degrees for 12 to 15 minutes or until golden brown.
Serve .... with preserves.
Yields ...... 8-12 servings.

Photograph for this recipe on page 104.

EASY TORTILLAS

2 c. flour
1 c. masa harina corn flour
1/2 tsp. (or more) salt

Combine .... all ingredients in bowl, mixing well.
Add .... enough water to make stiff dough.
Knead ...... on floured surface until smooth.
Shape ...... into 2-inch balls.
Roll .... into thin circles on floured surface.
Bake .... 1 at a time, on hot ungreased griddle until edges begin to curl; turn.
Cook .... until puffy.
Wrap .... in dampened cloth and foil.
Place .... in warm oven until serving time.
Yields ...... 12 servings.

Approx Per Serv: Cal 112, Prot 2.9 g, T Fat .5 g, Chl 0 mg, Car 23.3 g, Sod 89.3 mg, Pot 42.3 mg.

Tish Avery, Wayne

APRIL'S APPLE BREAD

2 c. sugar
1 1/4 c. shortening
3 eggs
2 tsp. vanilla extract
3 c. flour
1 1/2 tsp. soda
1 tsp. each cinnamon, salt
3 c. sliced apples

Cream ...... sugar, shortening, eggs and vanilla in large bowl.
Mix .... dry ingredients in bowl.
Add .... to creamed mixture alternately with apples, mixing well after each addition.
Spoon ...... into greased and floured loaf pan.
Bake .... at 350 degrees for 1 hour.
Yields ...... 12 servings.

Approx Per Serv: Cal 487, Prot 5 g, T Fat 25.3 g, Chl 63.2 mg, Car 61.6 g, Sod 296.8 mg, Pot 81.3 mg.

April Reasinger, Tioga

BANANA-PECAN BREAD

1/4 c. shortening
3/4 c. sugar
1 egg
2/3 c. mashed bananas
2 c. flour
1/2 tsp. each baking powder, soda, salt
3 tbsp. sour milk
1/2 c. chopped pecans

Cream ...... shortening and sugar in bowl.
Add .... egg and bananas, mixing well.
Sift .... dry ingredients together.
Mix .... into banana mixture.
Add .... sour milk and pecans, mixing well.
Spoon ...... into greased loaf pan.
Bake .... at 350 degrees for 50 to 60 minutes or until bread tests done.
Yields ...... 12 servings.

Approx Per Serv: Cal 219, Prot 3.4 g, T Fat 9 g, Chl 21.6 mg, Car 32.1 g, Sod 144.3 mg, Pot 107.2 mg.

Tish Avery, Wayne

BLUEBERRY BREAD

1 egg, beaten
1 c. sugar
2 tbsp. oil
2/3 c. orange juice
2 c. flour
1 1/2 tsp. soda
1/4 tsp. salt
3/4 c. chopped pecans
1 c. blueberries

Mix . . . . first 4 ingredients in bowl.
Combine . . . . flour, soda and salt in large bowl, mixing well.
Add . . . . pecans and blueberries, stirring to coat.
Stir . . . . in egg mixture.
Spoon . . . . . . into loaf pan.
Bake . . . . at 350 degrees for 1 hour.
Yields . . . . . . 12 servings.

Approx Per Serv: Cal 231, Prot 3.6 g, T Fat 8.3 g, Chl 21.1 mg, Car 36.8 g, Sod 153 mg, Pot 107.6 mg.

Darlene Ogden, Tioga

BROWN BREAD

1 c. flour
3 c. graham flour
1 tsp. (heaping) soda
1/4 tsp. salt
2 c. sour milk
2 eggs, beaten
1 c. molasses
3/4 c. packed brown sugar
2 tbsp. shortening, melted

Combine . . . . dry ingredients in large bowl.
Mix . . . . sour milk, eggs, molasses, brown sugar and shortening in bowl.
Add . . . . to dry ingredients, mixing well.
Spoon . . . . . . into 2 greased loaf pans.
Bake . . . . at 350 degrees for 45 minutes or until bread tests done.
Yields . . . . . . 24 servings.

Approx Per Serv: Cal 159, Prot 3.8 g, T Fat 2.7 g, Chl 23.9 mg, Car 31.2 g, Sod 76.3 mg, Pot 244.1 mg.

Evelyn Brower, Lackawanna

ORANGE BREAD

2 tbsp. butter
3/4 c. sugar
1 egg, beaten

2 c. flour
2 tsp. baking powder
1/2 c. milk
Juice of 1 orange
Grated rind of 1 orange

Cream . . . . . . butter and sugar in large bowl.
Add . . . . egg and sifted dry ingredients, mixing well.
Add . . . . enough milk to orange juice and rind to measure 3/4 cup.
Stir . . . . into flour mixture.
Spoon . . . . . . into well-greased loaf pan.
Bake . . . . at 375 degrees for 45 minutes.
Yields . . . . . . 12 servings.

Approx Per Serv: Cal 158, Prot 3.1 g, T Fat 3 g, Chl 28.4 mg, Car 29.7 g, Sod 88.9 mg, Pot 55.5 mg.

Diane Kripp, Schuylkill

FRESH STRAWBERRY BREAD

2 eggs
2/3 c. sugar
1/3 c. oil
1 tsp. vanilla extract
1 c. flour
1 tsp. cinnamon
1/2 tsp. each soda, salt
2/3 c. crushed strawberries

Combine . . . . eggs, sugar, oil and vanilla in large mixer bowl.
Beat . . . . until light and fluffy.
Add . . . . dry ingredients, beating well.
Stir . . . . in strawberries.
Pour . . . . into greased loaf pan.
Bake . . . . at 350 degrees for 55 to 60 minutes or until bread tests done.
Cool . . . . on wire rack before removing from pan.
Yields . . . . . . 12 servings.

Approx Per Serv: Cal 155, Prot 2.3 g, T Fat 7.5 g, Chl 42.1 mg, Car 20.2 g, Sod 133.7 mg, Pot 41.4 mg.

Lois Murray, Delaware

MAPLE WALNUT LOAF

3/4 c. shortening
1 c. packed brown sugar
1/2 c. sugar
3 eggs
1 tsp. maple flavoring
2 tsp. grated orange rind

2 c. sifted flour
1 tsp. each salt, soda, baking powder
1/2 c. milk
1 1/2 c. chopped dates
1 c. chopped walnuts

Cream . . . . . . shortening and sugars together in bowl.
Add . . . . eggs, maple flavoring and orange rind, beating until light and fluffy.
Sift . . . . flour, salt, soda and baking powder together.
Add . . . . milk and dry ingredients alternately to creamed mixture, beating well after each addition.
Stir . . . . in dates and walnuts.
Pour . . . . into greased and floured 5 x 9-inch loaf pan.
Bake . . . . at 350 degrees for 1 hour or until bread tests done.

Photograph for this recipe on page 79.

DELICIOUS ZUCCHINI BREAD

2 eggs, beaten
1 c. oil
2 c. sugar
2 c. grated zucchini
1 tbsp. vanilla extract
3 c. flour
1 tsp. each salt, soda
1 tbsp. cinnamon
1/4 tsp. baking powder
1/2 c. coconut (opt.)
1/2 c. chopped pecans (opt.)

Mix . . . . eggs, oil, sugar, zucchini and vanilla in bowl.
Add . . . . remaining ingredients, mixing well.
Pour . . . . into 2 prepared loaf pans.
Bake . . . . at 350 degrees until bread tests done.
Yields . . . . . . 24 servings.

Approx Per Serv: Cal 235, Prot 2.6 g, T Fat 12 g, Chl 21.1 mg, Car 29.9 g, Sod 135.8 mg, Pot 63.1 mg.

Sheila Hurlburt, Tioga

ENGLISH BRAN MUFFIN BREAD

4 1/4 c. flour
1 c. wheat bran cereal

2 pkg. dry yeast
1 tbsp. sugar
2 tsp. salt
1/4 tsp. soda
2 c. milk
Cornmeal

Combine . . . . 2 1/2 cups flour and next 5 ingredients in large bowl.
Heat . . . . milk and 1/2 cup water in saucepan to 130 degrees.
Add . . . . to dry ingredients, beating well.
Stir . . . . in enough remaining flour to make stiff batter.
Sprinkle . . . . 2 greased 4 x 8-inch microwave-proof loaf pans with cornmeal.
Spoon . . . . . . batter into prepared loaf pans.
Sprinkle . . . . with additional cornmeal.
Let . . . . rise, covered, in warm place for 45 minutes.
Microwave . . each loaf on High for 6 1/2 minutes.
Let . . . . stand for 5 minutes.
Slice . . . . and toast.
Yields . . . . . . 2 loaves.

Photograph for this recipe on page 70.

SAUSAGE ROLL

1 lb. sausage
1 tsp. olive oil
1 lg. egg
1 recipe basic white bread dough
1/2 c. (or more) mozzarella cheese
2 tsp. grated Italian cheese
1/4 tsp. each salt, pepper, garlic powder
1 egg yolk, beaten

Brown . . . . . . sausage in olive oil in skillet, stirring until crumbly; cool.
Mix . . . . in egg.
Roll . . . . dough into rectangle on floured surface.
Top . . . . with sausage mixture, cheeses and seasonings.
Roll . . . . as for jelly roll.
Brush . . . . . . with egg yolk.
Place . . . . on baking sheet.
Bake . . . . at 350 degrees for 45 minutes.
Yields . . . . . . 10 servings.

Approx Per Serv: Cal 301, Prot 11.4 g, T Fat 18.3 g, Chl 53.9 mg, Car 21.5 g, Sod 607.7 mg, Pot 144.9 mg.

Carmen M. Fluhr, Pike

HERB BREAD

1 pkg. dry yeast
2 tbsp. sugar
1 1/2 tsp. salt
2 tbsp. shortening
3/4 c. milk, scalded
3 to 3 1/2 c. flour
1/2 tsp. nutmeg
1 tsp. sage
2 tsp. celery seed
1 egg, slightly beaten

Dissolve .... yeast in 1/4 cup warm water.
Combine .... next 4 ingredients in large bowl, mixing well; cool to lukewarm.
Add .... half the flour, yeast mixture, nutmeg, sage, celery seed and egg, mixing well after each addition.
Mix .... in enough remaining flour to make soft dough.
Knead ...... on lightly floured surface for 8 minutes or until smooth.
Place .... in lightly greased bowl, turning once to coat surface.
Let .... rise, covered, for 1 1/2 hours or until doubled in bulk.
Punch ...... dough down.
Let .... rest, covered, for 10 to 15 minutes.
Shape ...... into round loaf in 9-inch pie plate.
Let .... rise, covered, for 45 to 60 minutes or until doubled in bulk.
Bake .... at 400 degrees for 35 minutes or until golden brown.
Yields ...... 6 servings.

Approx Per Serv: Cal 259, Prot 10.2 g, T Fat 7.4 g, Chl 46.4 mg, Car 61.5 g, Sod 560.5 mg, Pot 147.5 mg.

Gail L. Reed, Lancaster

TOOFER BREAD

2 pkg. dry yeast
2 tbsp. sugar
2 tbsp. butter, melted
2 tsp. salt
6 c. flour

Dissolve .... yeast in 2 cups warm water in large bowl.
Stir .... in sugar, butter, salt, yeast and 2 cups flour.

Add .... 2 cups flour, mixing well.
Add .... remaining 2 cups flour, mixing well.
Knead ...... on floured surface until smooth and elastic.
Shape ...... into ball.
Let .... rise in warm place until doubled in bulk.
Punch ...... dough down.
Let .... rise until doubled in bulk.
Place .... into two 5 x 9-inch loaf pans.
Let .... rise until doubled in bulk.
Bake .... at 350 degrees for 45 minutes or until bread tests done.
Yields ...... 12 servings.

Approx Per Serv: Cal 255, Prot 7 g, T Fat 2.6 g, Chl 5.9 mg, Car 50 g, Sod 380.5 mg, Pot 83.3 mg.

Brett Snyder, Venango

RICH WHITE BATTER BREAD

1 pkg. dry yeast
1/8 tsp. ginger
3 tbsp. sugar
1 lg. can evaporated milk
1 tsp. salt
2 tbsp. oil
4 to 4 1/2 c. flour
Butter, melted

Dissolve .... yeast in 1/2 cup warm water in large bowl.
Stir .... in ginger and 1 tablespoon sugar.
Let .... stand for 15 minutes or until bubbly.
Mix .... in remaining sugar and next 3 ingredients.
Add .... flour, 1 cup at a time, mixing well after each addition.
Place .... in 2 well-greased 1-pound coffee cans.
Cover ...... with greased plastic lids.
Let .... rise in warm place for 45 to 60 minutes or until lids pop off.
Bake .... at 350 degrees for 45 minutes.
Brush ...... with butter.
Let .... stand for 10 minutes before removing from cans.
Yields ...... 24 servings.

Approx Per Serv: Cal 126, Prot 3.7 g, T Fat 2.7 g, Chl 2.2 mg, Car 20.2 g, Sod 110.2 mg, Pot 81.3 mg.

Siemon Family, Allegheny

WHOLE WHEAT BRAID

2 pkg. dry yeast
1 c. nonfat dry milk
1 tbsp. salt
1 c. quick oats
1/2 c. margarine, melted
1/2 c. honey
3 eggs, slightly beaten
4 c. whole wheat flour
5 1/2 to 6 c. all-purpose flour
4 c. peanut butter chips
3/4 c. milk
3/4 c. strawberry preserves

Combine .... yeast, nonfat dry milk, salt and oats in large bowl, mixing well.
Add .... 2 cups warm water, stirring until yeast dissolves.
Add .... next 4 ingredients and 1 1/2 cups warm water, beating well.
Stir .... in 4 cups all-purpose flour.
Knead ...... in remaining flour on floured surface until smooth and elastic.
Shape ...... into ball.
Let .... stand, covered with damp towel, for 15 minutes.
Melt .... peanut butter chips in milk in saucepan over medium heat, stirring constantly until smooth.
Divide ...... dough into 4 portions.
Roll .... into 12 x 14-inch rectangles on floured surface.
Cut .... into 4 x 14-inch strips.
Spread ..... each strip to within 1/2 inch of edges with preserves and peanut butter mixture.
Fold .... lengthwise to enclose filling, sealing ends and edges.
Braid .... 3 strips together, sealing and folding ends under.
Place .... in 4 greased 5 x 9-inch loaf pans.
Let .... rise, covered, until doubled in bulk.
Bake .... at 350 degrees for 20 to 25 minutes or until golden brown.
Remove .... from pans immediately.
Cool .... on wire racks.
Yields ...... 20 servings.

Approx Per Serv: Cal 375, Prot 10.6 g, T Fat 9.8 g, Chl 39 mg, Car 63.8 g, Sod 406.7 mg, Pot 259.1 mg.

Pam Ross, Indiana

PIZZA CRUST

1 pkg. dry yeast
2 tbsp. oil
1 tsp. sugar
1 tsp. salt
2 1/2 c. flour

Dissolve .... yeast in 1 cup warm water in bowl.
Add .... remaining ingredients in order given, mixing well after each addition.
Let .... rise in warm place for 30 minutes.
Spread ..... on greased cookie sheet.
Let .... rise for 15 to 20 minutes.
Bake .... at 400 degrees for 10 minutes.
Top .... with pizza sauce, cheese and desired toppings.
Bake .... for 15 to 20 minutes longer or until cheese is melted.
Yields ...... 4 servings.

Approx Per Serv: Cal 353, Prot 8.8 g, T Fat 7.6 g, Chl 0 mg, Car 61.1 g, Sod 535.4 mg, Pot 109.3 mg.

Nutritional information does not include pizza sauce, cheese and toppings.

Christopher Norman, Tioga

EASY PIZZA DOUGH

1 tbsp. yeast
2 tsp. sugar
4 1/2 c. flour

Dissolve .... yeast in 1 1/2 cups warm water in bowl.
Mix .... in sugar and flour.
Let .... rise for 1 hour.
Knead ...... on floured surface.
Press .... into pizza pan.
Let .... rise for 1/2 hour.
Bake .... at 350 degrees for 10 minutes.
Top .... with pizza sauce and cheese.
Bake .... for 15 minutes longer or until cheese is melted.
Yields ...... 8 servings.

Approx Per Serv: Cal 270, Prot 7.7 g, T Fat .7 g, Chl 0 mg, Car 56.8 g, Sod 1.9 mg, Pot 84.4 mg.

Nutritional information does not include pizza sauce and cheese.

Cynthia L. Breiner, Schuylkill

REFRIGERATOR DOUGHNUTS

3 pkg. dry yeast
1 1/8 c. sugar
1 1/8 c. shortening, melted
12 3/4 c. flour
3 eggs, well beaten
3 3/4 tsp. salt
Oil for deep frying

Dissolve .... yeast in 3 3/4 cups warm water in large bowl.
Add .... sugar, shortening and 4 cups flour, beating well.
Mix .... in eggs and salt until smooth.
Stir .... in remaining flour.
Place .... in greased bowl.
Chill .... covered, overnight.
Roll .... on floured surface.
Cut .... with doughnut cutter.
Let .... rise until doubled in bulk.
Fry .... in deep 375-degree oil until browned on both sides.
Yields ...... 60 servings.

Approx Per Serv: Cal 139, Prot 3.2 g, T Fat 4.8 g, Chl 12.6 mg, Car 24.1 g, Sod 137 mg, Pot 35.5 mg.

Nutritional information does not include oil for deep frying.

Mrs. Bessie Hutschenreuter, York

COFFEE RING

3 tsp. dry yeast
1 c. warm milk
2 tbsp. shortening
1/3 c. sugar
1 egg, beaten
3 to 3 1/2 c. flour
3 tbsp. (about) butter, softened
1/4 c. packed brown sugar
1 tsp. (about) cinnamon

Dissolve .... yeast in a small amount of warm milk in small bowl.
Add .... shortening and sugar to remaining milk.
Combine .... sugar mixture, yeast mixture, egg and enough flour to make stiff dough in large bowl, mixing well.
Knead ...... on floured surface for 5 to 6 minutes.

Place .... in lightly greased bowl, turning to coat surface.
Let .... rise, covered, until doubled in bulk.
Roll .... into 12 x 15-inch rectangle on floured surface.
Spread ..... with butter.
Sprinkle .... with brown sugar and cinnamon.
Roll .... as for jelly roll from long side.
Shape ...... into ring on 12-inch round baking pan, sealing ends together.
Cut .... 3/4 through from outer edge every inch.
Separate .... slices slightly.
Let .... rise for 20 minutes.
Bake .... at 350 degrees for 30 minutes.
Yields ...... 15 servings.

Approx Per Serv: Cal 191, Prot 4.2 g, T Fat 5.4 g, Chl 26.2 mg, Car 31.1 g, Sod 42.2 mg Pot 75.8 mg.

Jennifer Stethers, Bradford

CHERRY COFFEE CAKE

4 1/2 c. flour
1/2 c. sugar
1 tsp. salt
1 pkg. yeast
1 c. milk
1/2 c. butter, melted
1 egg
1 20-oz. can cherry pie filling

Combine .... 1 1/4 cups flour, sugar, salt and yeast in large mixer bowl, mixing well.
Combine .... milk, 1/4 cup water and butter in saucepan.
Heat .... to lukewarm.
Stir .... into dry ingredients gradually.
Beat .... at medium speed for 2 minutes.
Add .... egg and 3 cups flour.
Beat .... at high speed for 2 minutes.
Add .... remaining 1/4 cup flour, mixing well.
Pour .... into warm greased bowl.
Let .... rise, covered, in warm place for 1 hour or until doubled in bulk.
Punch ...... dough down.
Spread ..... in greased 10 x 15-inch baking pan.
Top .... with pie filling.

Bake .... at 350 degrees for 30 to 35 minutes or until golden brown.
Yields ...... 10 servings.

Approx Per Serv: Cal 417, Prot 7.8 g, T Fat 11.2 g, Chl 57.1 mg, Car 70.6 g, Sod 345.2 mg, Pot 112 mg.

Edith A. Riker, Allegheny

GARY'S ROLLS

1 pkg. dry yeast
1 egg, beaten
1 tsp. salt
2 tbsp. sugar
2 tbsp. shortening, melted
3 1/2 c. flour

Dissolve .... yeast in 1 cup warm water in bowl.
Combine .... with remaining ingredients, except flour, in medium mixer bowl, beating well.
Add .... flour gradually, mixing well.
Knead ...... dough on floured surface until smooth and elastic.
Place .... in greased bowl.
Let .... rise, covered, for 2 hours or until doubled in bulk.
Shape ...... into rolls.
Place .... in greased baking pan.
Let .... rise for 2 hours.
Bake .... at 350 degrees for 15 minutes or until golden brown.
Yields ...... 12 servings.

Approx Per Serv: Cal 170, Prot 4.6 g, T Fat 3.2 g, Chl 42.1 mg, Car 30 g, Sod 189 mg, Pot 52 mg.

Gary Fink, Westmoreland

CRESCENT ROLLS

1/2 cake yeast
1 c. sugar
4 tsp. salt
6 c. (or more) flour
2 eggs
1/2 c. shortening

Dissolve .... yeast in 4 cups warm water in bowl.
Add .... sugar, salt and 3 cups flour, mixing well.

Beat .... for 2 minutes.
Add .... eggs and shortening, mixing well.
Knead ...... in remaining 3 cups flour until smooth.
Let .... rise, covered with damp cloth, in refrigerator.
Punch ...... dough down.
Roll .... into circle.
Brush ...... with oil.
Cut .... into wedges.
Roll .... up from wide end.
Arrange ..... 1 inch apart on greased baking sheet.
Let .... rise until doubled in bulk.
Bake .... at 375 degrees for 12 to 15 minutes or until golden brown.
Yields ...... 24 servings.

Approx Per Serv: Cal 194, Prot 3.9 g, T Fat 5.5 g, Chl 21.5 mg, Car 32.2 g, Sod 361.2 mg, Pot 38.3 mg.

Judy Love, Blair

POTATO ROLLS

1 pkg. dry yeast
2/3 c. shortening
1 c. mashed potatoes
1/2 c. sugar
1 c. milk, scalded, cooled to lukewarm
1 1/2 tsp. salt
2 eggs, well beaten
6 c. flour

Dissolve .... yeast in 1 cup warm water in large bowl.
Mix .... in remaining ingredients, except flour.
Add .... enough flour to make stiff dough, mixing well.
Let .... rise, covered, until doubled in bulk.
Punch ...... dough down.
Knead ...... until smooth and elastic.
Shape ...... into rolls.
Place .... on baking sheet.
Let .... rise until doubled in bulk.
Bake .... at 350 degrees for 20 minutes or until golden brown.
Yields ...... 30 servings.

Approx Per Serv: Cal 166, Prot 3.6 g, T Fat 6.2 g, Chl 18.9 mg, Car 23.7 g, Sod 138.6 mg, Pot 62 mg.

Katrina Harbach, Clinton

NO-KNEAD CINNAMON ROLLS

1 env. dry yeast
1/2 c. scalded milk
3 tbsp. shortening
3 tbsp. sugar
1 1/2 tsp. salt
1 egg
3 1/4 c. flour
1/2 c. packed brown sugar
1 tsp. cinnamon
2 tbsp. butter, softened

Dissolve .... yeast in 1/4 cup warm water in large bowl.
Combine .... milk with next 3 ingredients and 1/4 cup cold water.
Stir .... milk mixture and egg into yeast.
Add .... flour gradually, mixing well.
Let .... rise, covered, for 15 minutes.
Mix .... brown sugar with cinnamon in bowl.
Roll .... dough into 12 x 18-inch rectangle.
Spread ..... with butter.
Sprinkle .... with brown sugar mixture.
Roll .... as for jelly roll.
Cut .... into 1-inch slices.
Place .... in greased baking pan.
Let .... rise for 1 hour or until doubled in bulk.
Bake .... at 375 degrees for 20 to 25 minutes or until golden brown.
Garnish ..... with confectioners' sugar glaze.
Yields ...... 18 servings.

Approx Per Serv: Cal 155, Prot 3.1 g, T Fat 4.4 g, Chl 18.9 mg, Car 25.6 g, Sod 202.5 mg, Pot 64 mg.

Kathy Hurlburt, Tioga

ICEBOX BUTTER BUNS

1 pkg. dry yeast
1/2 c. sugar
2 c. warm milk
1 egg, beaten
1 tsp. salt
6 c. flour, sifted
3/4 c. shortening, melted

Combine .... yeast, sugar and 2 tablespoons lukewarm water in large bowl, stirring until yeast dissolves.
Add .... milk, egg, salt and half the flour, mixing well after each addition.

Mix .... in shortening.
Add .... remaining flour, mixing until smooth. Do not knead.
Chill .... covered, overnight.
Divide ...... dough into 3 equal portions.
Roll .... into circles.
Cut .... each into 12 wedges.
Roll .... as for crescent rolls.
Place .... on baking sheet.
Let .... rise for 3 hours.
Bake .... at 350 degrees for 15 to 20 minutes or until golden.
Yields ...... 36 servings.

Approx Per Serv: Cal 101, Prot 2.9 g, T Fat 1.1 g, Chl 8.9 mg, Car 19.4 g, Sod 68.2 mg, Pot 45.1 mg.

Charlene Wood, Indiana

QUICKY STICKY BUNS

3/4 c. milk
1/4 c. margarine
1/4 c. sugar
1 tsp. salt
2 tbsp. dry yeast
3 1/4 c. flour
1 egg, beaten
3/4 c. butter
1 c. packed brown sugar
1 tsp. cinnamon
3/4 c. chopped walnuts
1 tbsp. corn syrup

Combine .... milk, 1/2 cup water, margarine, sugar and salt in large saucepan.
Heat .... to lukewarm.
Add .... to yeast and 1 1/2 cups flour in bowl, mixing well.
Mix .... in egg.
Stir .... in remaining 1 3/4 cups flour.
Let .... rise, covered, for 30 minutes.
Combine .... remaining 5 ingredients with 1 tablespoon water in saucepan.
Cook .... until butter melts, stirring constantly.
Pour .... into 9 x 13-inch baking pan.
Stir .... dough down.
Drop .... by large spoonfuls into baking pan.
Bake .... at 375 degrees for 15 minutes.
Yields ...... 16 servings.

Approx Per Serv: Cal 276, Prot 3.9 g, T Fat 12.6 g, Chl 44.1 mg, Car 37.7 g, Sod 288.9 mg, Pot 112.9 mg.

Michele Rohrer, Lancaster

Desserts

SAUCY PEAR SNOW, recipe on page 94.

FRENCH APPLE COBBLER

5 c. peeled sliced tart apples
1 1/4 c. sugar
Sifted flour
1/2 tsp. salt
1/2 tsp. cinnamon
1 tsp. vanilla extract
3 tbsp. butter, softened
1/2 tsp. baking powder
1 egg, slightly beaten

Combine .... apples, 3/4 cup sugar, 2 tablespoons flour, 1/4 teaspoon salt,
cinnamon, vanilla and 1/4 cup
water in bowl, mixing well.
Spoon ...... into 9 x 13-inch baking pan.
Dot .... with 1 tablespoon butter.
Combine .... 1/2 cup flour, 1/2 cup sugar,
baking powder, 1/4 teaspoon
salt, 2 tablespoons butter and
egg in bowl, beating well.
Drop .... by 9 large spoonfuls over apples.
Bake .... at 375 degrees for 35 to 40 minutes or until golden brown.
Yields ...... 8 servings.

Approx Per Serv: Cal 266, Prot 3.6 g, T Fat 5.3 g, Chl
44.9 mg, Car 51.6 g, Sod 214.8 mg, Pot 35.9 mg.

Alberta Jordan, Delaware

HEIDI'S APPLE CRISP

1 c. oats
1/2 c. sifted flour
1/2 c. packed brown sugar
1/4 tsp. salt
1 tsp. cinnamon
1/2 c. butter, softened
4 c. peeled sliced tart apples

Combine .... first 5 ingredients in bowl, mix-
ing well.
Cut .... in butter until crumbly.
Layer ...... apples and oat mixture in but-
tered 8-inch square baking pan,
pressing gently.
Bake .... at 350 degrees for 30 minutes or
until apples are tender.
Serve .... warm or cold with cream.
Yields ...... 10 servings.

Approx Per Serv: Cal 129, Prot 1.9 g, T Fat 1.5 g, Chl
1.8 mg, Car 28.1 g, Sod 64.4 mg, Pot 127.1 mg.

Heidi Kaniper, Northampton

FAVORITE APPLE CRISP

1/2 c. butter, softened
1 c. sugar
1/8 tsp. salt
3/4 c. flour
4 c. peeled sliced apples
1/2 tsp. cinnamon

Mix .... butter, sugar, salt and flour in
bowl until crumbly.
Place .... apples in oiled baking dish.
Sprinkle .... with 2 tablespoons water and
cinnamon.
Sprinkle .... with flour mixture.
Bake .... at 350 degrees for 30 to 60 min-
utes or until apples are tender.
Yields ...... 4 servings.

Approx Per Serv: Cal 363, Prot 2.7 g, T Fat 2.4 g, Chl
4.4 mg, Car 85.7 g, Sod 86.4 mg, Pot 161.7 mg.

Kerry Freisen, Dauphin

DELICIOUS APPLE DESSERT

1 tsp. salt
Flour
1 c. sugar
1 egg yolk
1 tsp. vanilla extract
1/2 c. packed light brown sugar
1/2 c. shortening (part butter)
4 apples, peeled, sliced

Combine .... 1/2 teaspoon salt, 3 tablespoons
flour, sugar, egg yolk, vanilla and
1 cup water in saucepan, mixing
well.
Cook .... over low heat until thick, stirring
constantly.
Mix .... 2 cups flour, brown sugar and
1/2 teaspoon salt in bowl.
Cut .... in shortening until crumbly.
Press .... over bottom of greased and
floured 9 x 9-inch baking pan,
reserving 1 cup for topping.
Layer ...... apple slices, cooked mixture and
reserved brown sugar mixture
over prepared crust.
Bake .... at 350 degrees for 30 to 45 minutes or until apples are tender.
Yields ...... 10 servings.

Approx Per Serv: Cal 366, Prot 3.3 g, T Fat 12.3 g,
Chl 25.2 mg, Car 62.5 g, Sod 218.9 mg, Pot 153.3 mg.

Edna Minich, Clarion

BANANA PRALINE SUNDAES

3 tbsp. butter
1/3 c. packed brown sugar
1/4 c. golden raisins
2 med. bananas, sliced
1 pt. vanilla ice cream, softened
1/3 c. chopped pecans

Melt .... butter and brown sugar in skillet over low heat, stirring frequently.
Add .... raisins and bananas.
Cook .... for 5 minutes or until heated through, stirring gently.
Spoon ...... ice cream into 4 serving dishes.
Top .... with fruit mixture.
Sprinkle .... with pecans.
Yields ...... 4 servings.

Approx Per Serv: Cal 442, Prot 3.6 g, T Fat 27.6 g, Chl 68.8 mg, Car 49.9 g, Sod 137.9 mg, Pot 439.2 mg.

Kenny Singer, Huntingdon

BANANA SPLIT CAKE

2 c. graham cracker crumbs
6 tbsp. melted butter
2 c. confectioners' sugar
1 stick margarine
2 eggs
1 tsp. vanilla extract
3 bananas, sliced
1 29-oz. can crushed pineapple, drained
1 8-oz carton whipped topping
1/4 c. ground pecans

Combine .... graham cracker crumbs and butter in bowl, mixing well.
Press .... into 9 x 13-inch serving dish.
Cream ...... confectioners' sugar and margarine in bowl.
Beat .... in eggs until light and fluffy.
Mix .... in vanilla.
Spread ..... over crust.
Layer ...... bananas, pineapple and whipped topping over top.
Sprinkle .... with pecans.
Garnish ..... with maraschino cherries.
Chill .... overnight.
Yields ...... 8 servings.

Approx Per Serv: Cal 626, Prot 5.3 g, T Fat 33.9 g, Chl 89.8 mg, Car 81.5 g, Sod 445.2 mg, Pot 393 mg.

Nancy Colegrove, Tioga

BLUEBERRY DESSERT DELUXE

2 c. sugar
1 tsp. cream of tartar
1 tsp. vanilla extract
2 c. crushed saltines
3/4 c. chopped walnuts
6 egg whites, stiffly beaten
2 c. blueberry pie filling
2 c. whipped topping

Combine .... first 5 ingredients in bowl, mixing well.
Fold .... in egg whites.
Spoon ...... into greased 9 x 12-inch baking pan.
Bake .... at 325 degrees for 25 minutes; cool to room temperature.
Spread ..... pie filling over top.
Top .... with whipped topping.
Yields ...... 12 servings.

Approx Per Serv: Cal 311, Prot 4.1 g, T Fat 7.2 g, Chl 0 mg, Car 58.9 g, Sod 170.9 mg, Pot 81.3 mg.

Mary T. Hosterman, Centre

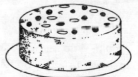

FROZEN FRUIT DESSERT

1/2 c. sugar
1 8-oz. package cream cheese, softened
1 16-oz. can crushed pineapple
1 10-oz. package frozen sliced strawberries, partially thawed
1 c. frozen blueberries
1 3-oz. package vanilla instant pudding mix
3 bananas, sliced
1 12-oz. container whipped topping

Cream ...... sugar and cream cheese together in bowl.
Add .... remaining ingredients, stirring until well blended.
Spoon ...... into 9 x 13-inch serving dish.
Freeze ...... until firm.
Thaw ...... in refrigerator for 2 hours before serving.
Yields ...... 16 servings.

Approx Per Serv: Cal 236, Prot 2.1 g, T Fat 10.9 g, Chl 15.7 mg, Car 35.1 g, Sod 73.8 mg, Pot 146.1 mg.

Lyn Horning, Centre

SAUCY PEAR SNOW

4 fresh Bartlett pears, peeled
1/4 c. lemon juice
1/4 tsp. salt
1/2 c. sugar
1 env. unflavored gelatin
1/2 tsp. vanilla extract
2 egg whites, stiffly beaten
1 10-oz. package frozen sliced
strawberries, thawed

Mash . . . . 2 pears.
Combine . . . . with lemon juice, salt and sugar in bowl, mixing well.
Soften . . . . . . gelatin in 1/4 cup cold water in bowl.
Add . . . . 1/2 cup boiling water, stirring until dissolved.
Stir . . . . in pear mixture and vanilla.
Chill . . . . until slightly thickened.
Fold . . . . in egg whites.
Spoon . . . . . . into 8 molds.
Chill . . . . until firm.
Slice . . . . remaining 2 pears.
Combine . . . . with strawberries in bowl, mixing well.
Invert . . . . . . molds onto serving dishes.
Top . . . . with strawberry mixture.
Garnish . . . . with slivered almonds.
Yields . . . . . . 8 servings.

Photograph for this recipe on page 91.

GOAT'S MILK ORANGE SHERBET

1 1/4 c. sugar
1 lg. package orange gelatin
1 1/2 c. orange juice
1/3 c. lemon juice
2 c. goat's milk

Heat . . . . sugar in 1 cup water in saucepan until dissolved.
Mix . . . . in gelatin until dissolved.
Blend . . . . . . in remaining 3 ingredients.
Freeze . . . . . . until nearly firm.
Beat . . . . with electric mixer.
Freeze . . . . . . until firm.
Yields . . . . . . 16 servings.

Approx Per Serv: Cal 132, Prot 2.2 g, T Fat 1.3 g, Chl 4.3 mg, Car 29.1 g, Sod 44.6 mg, Pot 131.3 mg.

Leslie K. Bowen, Juniata

PEACH CRISP

2 29-oz. cans sliced peaches, drained
1/4 tsp. each nutmeg, cinnamon
1/3 c. flour
1/2 c. packed brown sugar
1 c. oats
1/3 c. melted butter

Arrange . . . . . peaches in bottom of casserole.
Sprinkle . . . . with nutmeg and cinnamon.
Combine . . . . remaining 4 ingredients in bowl, mixing until crumbly.
Sprinkle . . . . over peaches.
Bake . . . . at 375 degrees for 30 minutes.
Yields . . . . . . 6 servings.

Approx Per Serv: Cal 369, Prot 3.4 g, T Fat 11.4 g, Chl 31.5 mg, Car 66.4 g, Sod 133.8 mg, Pot 341.3 mg.

Jacqueline Conklin, Snyder

PEACH GELATIN DESSERT

2 tbsp. cornstarch
3/4 c. sugar
1 3-oz. package peach gelatin
2 c. sliced peaches

Combine . . . . cornstarch, 1 1/2 cups water and sugar in saucepan.
Cook . . . . over medium heat until thick, stirring constantly.
Stir . . . . in gelatin until dissolved.
Spoon . . . . . . peaches into 9 x 9-inch serving dish.
Pour . . . . hot gelatin sauce over peaches, stirring to coat.
Garnish . . . . . with whipped topping.
Yields . . . . . . 9 servings.

Approx Per Serv: Cal 120, Prot 1.1 g, T Fat 0 g, Chl 0 mg, Car 30.1 g, Sod 30.6 mg, Pot 96.6 mg.

Jacki Sterner, Adams

DELICIOUS STRAWBERRY DESSERT

1 lg. package strawberry gelatin
1 lg. package vanilla instant pudding mix
1 8-oz. carton whipped topping
2 c. strawberries

Combine . . . . gelatin and pudding mix in 4-quart bowl.
Add . . . . 5 cups boiling water gradually, stirring until gelatin is dissolved.

Chill .... until partially set.
Fold .... in whipped topping and strawberries.
Yields ...... 20 servings.

Approx Per Serv: 107, Prot 1.3 g, T Fat 3.1 g, Chl 0 mg, Car 20 g, Sod 68.6 mg, Pot 52.4 mg.

Lila M. Newḥard, Berks

EASY APPLE CAKE

1 1/2 c. sugar
4 c. diced apples
2 c. flour
1 1/2 tsp. soda
1 tsp. each cinnamon, salt
2 eggs
3/4 c. oil
1 c. chopped walnuts
Vanilla extract to taste

Combine .... sugar and apples in large bowl.
Let .... stand for 5 to 10 minutes, stirring occasionally.
Sift .... flour, soda, cinnamon and salt together.
Add .... flour mixture and remaining 4 ingredients to apples, mixing well.
Spoon ...... into greased and floured 9-inch square baking pan.
Bake .... at 350 degrees for 45 to 50 minutes or until cake tests done.
Serve .... with ice cream.
Yields ...... 12 servings.

Approx Per Serv: Cal 278, Prot 4.8 g, T Fat 8.5 g, Chl 42.1 mg, Car 47.6 g, Sod 291.7 mg, Pot 116.7 mg.

Sandra Kokinda, Carbon

JOAN'S APPLESAUCE CAKE

2 c. sifted flour
1 c. sugar
1 tsp. each salt, cinnamon
1/2 tsp. each nutmeg, cloves
2 tsp. soda
1 c. raisins
1 c. chopped walnuts
1/2 c. melted butter
2 c. applesauce

Sift .... dry ingredients together into large bowl.

Add .... raisins, walnuts, butter and applesauce, mixing well.
Beat .... until well blended.
Pour .... into greased 9 x 9-inch cake pan.
Bake .... at 350 degrees for 45 to 50 minutes or until cake tests done.
Yields ...... 16 servings.

Approx Per Serv: Cal 212, Prot 3.5 g, T Fat 5.2 g, Chl 1.1 mg, Car 40.1 g, Sod 244 mg, Pot 141.1 mg.

Joan Marie Gagliardi, Philadelphia

WHITE BUTTERMILK CAKE

Flour
1/2 tsp. soda
1 1/2 tsp. baking powder
1 tsp. salt
2 2/3 c. sugar
1 3/4 c. butter, softened
3/4 c. buttermilk
2 tsp. vanilla extract
3 eggs
1 c. milk

Combine .... 2 1/2 cups sifted flour, soda, baking powder, salt and 1 2/3 cups sugar in bowl, mixing well.
Add .... 3/4 cup butter, buttermilk and 1 teaspoon vanilla, mixing until just moistened.
Beat .... for 2 minutes.
Add .... eggs.
Beat .... for 1 minute longer.
Pour .... into 2 waxed paper-lined 9-inch layer pans.
Bake .... at 350 degrees for 30 to 35 minutes or until cake tests done.
Blend ...... 5 tablespoons flour with milk in saucepan.
Cook .... over low heat until thick, stirring constantly.
Let .... stand for several hours.
Beat .... remaining 1 cup butter with 1 cup sugar and 1 teaspoon vanilla in bowl until creamy.
Add .... milk mixture, beating until fluffy.
Spread ..... between layers and over top and side of cake.
Yields ...... 12 servings.

Approx Per Serv: Cal 325, Prot 5.7 g, T Fat 4.1 g, Chl 71.5 mg, Car 67 g, Sod 319.7 mg, Pot 95.1 mg.

Stacy Nestleroth, Lancaster

MOIST BANANA CAKE

1 1/2 c. sugar
1/2 c. shortening
2 eggs
1 tsp. soda
1 c. buttermilk
1 tsp. vanilla extract
1 3/4 c. flour
1 tsp. baking powder
1/4 tsp. salt
1 c. mashed bananas

Cream . . . . . . sugar and shortening together in bowl.
Add . . . . eggs, beating well.
Combine . . . . soda, buttermilk and vanilla in small bowl.
Add . . . . sifted dry ingredients and butter-milk mixture alternately to creamed mixture, beating well after each addition.
Stir . . . . in bananas.
Pour . . . . into 2 prepared cake pans.
Bake . . . . at 375 degrees for 30 minutes.
Yields . . . . . . 12 servings.

Approx Per Serv: Cal 283, Prot 3.9 g, T Fat 10.5 g, Chl 42.5 mg, Car 44.1 g, Sod 177.8 mg, Pot 127.2 mg.

Louise Mengel, Lehigh

CHOCOLATE ZUCCHINI CAKE

1 c. packed brown sugar
1/2 c. sugar
1/2 c. margarine
1/2 c. oil
2 c. grated zucchini
3 eggs
1 tsp. vanilla extract
1/2 c. buttermilk
2 1/2 c. sifted flour
1/2 tsp. cinnamon
1/2 tsp. salt
2 tsp. soda
4 tbsp. cocoa
1/2 to 1 c. chocolate chips

Cream . . . . . . first 4 ingredients together in large bowl.
Add . . . . zucchini, eggs, vanilla and buttermilk, mixing well.
Combine . . . . next 5 ingredients in small bowl, blending well.
Mix . . . . into zucchini mixture.

Pour . . . . into greased and floured 9 x 13-inch baking pan.
Sprinkle . . . . with chocolate chips.
Bake . . . . at 325 degrees for 45 minutes.
Yields . . . . . . 24 servings.

Approx Per Serv: Cal 221, Prot 2.9 g, T Fat 11.9 g, Chl 31.7 mg, Car 27.4 g, Sod 136.1 mg, Pot 118.4 mg.

Alinda L. Kantz, Snyder

DUMP CAKE

1 box white cake mix
1/2 c. chopped walnuts
1/2 c. coconut
1 can cherry pie filling
1 lg. can crushed pineapple
1 stick margarine, melted

Combine . . . . cake mix, walnuts and coconut in bowl, mixing well.
Layer . . . . . . pie filling, pineapple and coco-nut mixture in baking pan.
Drizzle . . . . . margarine over top.
Bake . . . . at 350 degrees for 50 minutes or until golden brown.
Yields . . . . . . 10 servings.

Approx Per Serv: Cal 489, Prot 3.8 g, T Fat 18 g, Chl 0 mg, Car 78.7 g, Sod 606.7 mg, Pot 131.2 mg.

Melanie Gold, Northampton

OATMEAL SPICE CAKE

1 c. quick-cooking oats
1/2 c. margarine
2 eggs
1 1/2 c. flour
1 c. sugar
1 tsp. soda
1/2 tsp. salt
1 tsp. cinnamon
1/2 tsp. each allspice, nutmeg
2 c. packed brown sugar
1 c. coconut
1 c. chopped walnuts
1/3 c. milk

Combine . . . . oats, margarine and 1 1/2 cups boiling water in bowl, mixing well; cool.
Mix . . . . in eggs.
Add . . . . next 7 sifted dry ingredients and 1 cup brown sugar.

Beat .... for 2 minutes.
Pour .... into prepared 9 x 13-inch baking pan.
Bake .... in moderate oven for 30 minutes.
Mix .... remaining 1 cup brown sugar, coconut, walnuts and milk in bowl.
Spread ..... over cake.
Broil .... for 2 to 3 minutes or until lightly browned.
Yields ...... 15 servings.

Approx Per Serv: Cal 372, Prot 4.5 g, T Fat 14.4 g, Chl 34.5 mg, Car 58.4 g, Sod 232.6 mg, Pot 203.9 mg.

Ann Hutschenreuter, York

PUMPKIN CAKE ROLL

3 eggs
1 c. sugar
2/3 c. cooked pumpkin
1 tsp. lemon juice
3/4 c. flour
1 tsp. baking powder
2 tsp. cinnamon
1 tsp. ginger
1/2 tsp. nutmeg
1/8 tsp. (about) salt
1 c. finely chopped walnuts
1 1/2 c. (about) confectioners' sugar
2 3-oz. packages cream cheese, softened
4 tbsp. butter, softened
1/2 tsp. vanilla extract

Beat .... eggs in large mixer bowl at high speed for 5 minutes.
Add .... sugar gradually, beating constantly.
Stir .... in pumpkin and lemon juice.
Fold .... in next 6 sifted dry ingredients.
Spread ..... in greased and floured 10 x 15-inch baking pan.
Sprinkle .... walnuts over top.
Bake .... at 375 degrees for 15 minutes.
Invert ...... onto towel sprinkled with 1/2 cup confectioners' sugar.
Roll .... with towel as for jelly roll; cool.
Combine .... remaining 1 cup confectioners' sugar, cream cheese, butter and vanilla in bowl, mixing well.
Unroll ...... cake, removing towel.
Spread ..... with cream cheese mixture; reroll.

Chill .... until serving time.
Yields ...... 10 servings.

Approx Per Serv: Cal 382, Prot 6.3 g, T Fat 20.6 g, Chl 108.9 mg, Car 45.8 g, Sod 216 mg, Pot 137.8 mg.

Leanne Biddle, Blair

RAISIN CAKE

1 16-oz. box raisins
1/2 c. shortening
2 c. sugar
4 c. flour
2 tsp. soda
1 tsp. each cloves, cinnamon

Boil .... raisins in 2 cups water in large saucepan for 5 minutes.
Add .... 1 cup cold water, shortening and sugar, mixing well.
Stir .... in remaining 4 ingredients.
Spoon ...... into greased loaf pan.
Bake .... at 350 degrees for 45 minutes or until cake tests done.
Yields ...... 12 servings.

Approx Per Serv: Cal 433, Prot 5 g, T Fat 9.8 g, Chl 0 mg, Car 83.5 g, Sod 144.5 mg, Pot 225 mg.

Nancy Myers, Columbia

GINGERBREAD

3 eggs
1 c. sugar
1 c. oil
1 c. molasses
1 tsp. each ground cloves, ginger, cinnamon
2 tsp. baking soda
2 c. flour

Combine .... first 7 ingredients in bowl, mixing well.
Dissolve .... soda in 2 tablespoons hot water.
Stir .... into molasses mixture.
Add .... flour, mixing well.
Mix .... in 1 cup boiling water.
Pour .... into prepared 9 x 11-inch baking pan.
Bake .... at 350 degrees for 45 minutes.
Yields ...... 6 servings.

Approx Per Serv: Cal 129.8, Prog 1 g, T Fat 6.6 g, Car 16.8 g, Sod 123.2 mg, Pot 95.8 mg.

Jackie Heald, Chester

RHUBARB CAKE

1/2 c. shortening
1 1/2 c. sugar
3 eggs, beaten
2 c. flour
1 tsp. each salt, soda, allspice,
  cinnamon
1/2 c. milk
1 tsp. vanilla extract
2 1/2 c. chopped fresh rhubarb
1/2 c. packed brown sugar
Cinnamon to taste

Combine .... shortening, sugar and eggs in bowl, mixing well.
Add .... next 5 combined ingredients alternately with milk and vanilla, mixing well after each addition.
Mix .... in rhubarb.
Spoon ...... into prepared 9 x 13-inch baking pan.
Sprinkle .... brown sugar and cinnamon over top.
Bake .... at 350 degrees for 38 minutes.
Yields ...... 8 servings.

Approx Per Serv: Cal 364, Prot 6.5 g, T Fat 3.9 g, Chl 96.9 mg, Car 76.7 g, Sod 302.9 mg, Pot 220.1 mg.

Lucille A. Dashem, Centre

STRAWBERRY FUNNY CAKE

1 tbsp. cornstarch
1 c. sugar
3/4 tsp. salt
2 to 3 c. sliced sweetened strawberries
Butter
1 1/4 c. sifted cake flour
1 tsp. baking powder
1/2 c. milk
1 tsp. vanilla extract
1 egg
1 unbaked 10-in. deep-dish pie shell

Blend ...... cornstarch, 1/4 cup sugar and 1/4 teaspoon salt with 1/4 cup water in saucepan.
Cook .... until thick, stirring constantly.
Add .... strawberries and 2 tablespoons butter.
Bring .... to a boil, stirring constantly; cool to lukewarm.
Sift .... 3/4 cup sugar, 1/2 teaspoon salt, flour and baking powder into mixer bowl.

Add .... 1/4 cup softened butter and milk.
Beat .... for 2 minutes.
Add .... vanilla and egg.
Beat .... for 1 minute.
Pour .... into pie shell.
Drizzle ..... strawberry mixture over cake batter.
Bake .... at 350 degrees for 50 to 55 minutes.
Yields ...... 12 servings.

Approx Per Serv: Cal 290, Prot 3 g, T Fat 8.4 g, Chl 8.5 mg, Car 51.8 g, Sod 291.7 mg, Pot 112.1 mg.

Connie and Sandy Smoyer, Lehigh

TANDY CAKE

4 eggs, beaten
2 c. sugar
1 tbsp. vanilla extract
2 c. flour
2 tsp. baking powder
1/4 tsp. salt
1 c. milk
1 1/2 c. (or more) peanut butter
1   12-oz. chocolate bar, melted

Beat .... eggs, sugar and vanilla in bowl.
Add .... sifted dry ingredients alternately with milk, beating well after each addition.
Pour .... into greased 10 x 15-inch baking pan.
Bake .... at 350 degrees for 12 to 15 minutes or until cake tests done.
Spread ..... peanut butter generously over warm cake; cool.
Drizzle ..... chocolate over top.
Yields ...... 12 servings.

Approx Per Serv: Cal 581, Prot 15.3 g, T Fat 28.2 g, Chl 92.8 mg, Car 72.5 g, Sod 350.7 mg, Pot 381.9 mg.

Sylvania Negley, Cumberland

WONDER CAKE

1 1/2 c. flour
1 c. sugar
1 1/2 tsp. soda
1 tsp. salt
3 tbsp. (heaping) cocoa
6 tbsp. oil

1 tsp. vinegar
2 tsp. vanilla extract
1 1/2 c. confectioners' sugar
1/4 c. butter, softened
3 tbsp. milk
1/4 c. peanut butter

Combine .... first 5 ingredients in bowl.
Blend ...... oil, vinegar, 1 teaspoon vanilla and 1 cup water in small bowl.
Add .... to flour mixture, mixing well.
Pour .... into prepared 9-inch baking pan.
Bake .... at 350 degrees for 30 to 40 minutes or until cake tests done.
Combine .... remaining 4 ingredients and 1 teaspoon vanilla in bowl, blending well.
Spread ..... over cake.
Yields ...... 9 servings.

Approx Per Serv: Cal 401, Prot 4.5 g, T Fat 18.5 g, Chl 16.5 mg, Car 57.1 g, Sod 482.4 mg, Pot 102 mg.

Georgina Messinger, Fulton

YUM-YUM CAKE

2 eggs
2 c. sugar
2 c. flour
1 20-oz. can crushed pineapple
2 tsp. soda
2 1/2 tsp. vanilla extract
2 c. chopped walnuts
1 8-oz. package cream cheese, softened
1 stick butter, softened
1 1/2 c. confectioners' sugar

Combine .... first 5 ingredients, 1 1/2 teaspoons vanilla and 1 cup walnuts in bowl, mixing well.
Spoon ...... into rectangular baking pan.
Bake .... at 350 degrees for 35 to 40 minutes or until cake tests done.
Combine .... cream cheese, butter, confectioners' sugar and 1 teaspoon vanilla in mixer bowl, beating until smooth.
Spread ..... over warm cake.
Sprinkle .... remaining 1 cup walnuts over top.
Yields ...... 12 servings.

Approx Per Serv: Cal 576, Prot 7.4 g, T Fat 29.4 g, Chl 86.8 mg, Car 75.3 g, Sod 289.3 mg, Car 203.4 mg.

Lisa Romberger, Dauphin

BAKED CHEESECAKE

1 1/4 c. sugar
2 1/4 c. flour
3/4 c. butter, softened
6 eggs, separated
2 8-oz. packages cream cheese, softened
1 tsp. vanilla extract
3 c. milk
Cinnamon to taste

Mix .... 1/4 cup sugar and 2 cups flour in bowl.
Cut .... in butter until crumbly.
Mix .... in 2 egg yolks.
Press .... over bottom and 2 inches up sides of buttered 10 x 16-inch baking pan.
Bake .... at 300 degrees for 20 minutes.
Combine .... remaining 1/4 cup flour, 4 egg yolks, 1 cup sugar, cream cheese and vanilla in bowl, beating until smooth.
Add .... milk gradually, beating constantly.
Fold .... in stiffly beaten egg whites.
Pour .... into crust.
Sprinkle .... with cinnamon.
Bake .... at 325 degrees for 1 hour.
Yields ...... 15 servings.

Approx Per Serv: Cal 389, Prot 8.7 g, T Fat 24.6 g, Chl 169.4 mg, Car 34.1 g, Sod 235.3 mg, Pot 138.2 mg.

Janice Blose, Delaware

PUDDING CHEESECAKE

1 8-oz. package cream cheese, softened
2 c. milk
1 pkg. instant lemon pudding mix
1 9-in. graham cracker crust

Blend ...... cream cheese with 1/2 cup milk in bowl until smooth.
Stir .... in remaining milk and pudding mix.
Beat .... slowly for 1 minute.
Pour .... into crust.
Garnish ..... with graham cracker crumbs.
Chill .... until set.
Yields ...... 8 servings.

Approx Per Serv: Cal 309, Prot 5.7 g, T Fat 19.7 g, Chl 55.5 mg, Car 29.7 g, Sod 288.3 mg, Pot 160.3 mg.

Ronald Transue, Monroe

CHEESECAKE FREEZE

1 c. graham cracker crumbs
Sugar
3 tbsp. butter, melted
2 8-oz. packages cream cheese, softened
2 eggs, separated
2 tbsp. frozen orange juice concentrate,
   thawed
2 c. heavy cream, whipped
1 c. chopped M & M plain chocolate
   candies, frozen

Combine .... crumbs, 3 tablespoons sugar and butter in bowl, mixing well.
Press .... into 9-inch springform pan.
Bake .... at 350 degrees for 10 minutes; cool.
Beat .... cream cheese, 1 cup sugar, egg yolks and juice in bowl with electric mixer at medium speed until smooth.
Fold .... stiffly beaten egg whites and whipped cream into cream cheese mixture.
Stir .... in candies.
Spoon ...... over crust.
Freeze ...... until firm.
Thaw ...... for 10 minutes before serving.
Cut .... into wedges.

Photograph for this recipe on page 103.

JUMBO RAISIN COOKIES

2 c. raisins
2 c. sugar
1 c. shortening
3 eggs
1 tsp. vanilla extract
1 c. chopped pecans
4 c. flour
1 tsp. each baking powder, soda
2 tsp. salt
1 1/2 tsp. cinnamon
1/4 tsp. allspice

Boil .... raisins in 1 cup water in saucepan for 5 minutes; cool.
Cream ...... sugar and shortening in bowl.
Add .... eggs, beating well.
Stir .... in vanilla, raisin mixture and pecans.
Add .... sifted dry ingredients, mixing well.

Drop .... by teaspoonfuls onto greased cookie sheet.
Bake .... at 400 degrees for 12 to 15 minutes or until golden brown.
Yields ...... 48 servings.

Approx Per Serv: Cal 151, Prot 1.9 g, T Fat 6.9 g, Chl 15.8 mg, Car 21.3 g, Sod 74.1 mg, Pot 75.2 mg.

Carrie Cook, Forest

NATE'S NO-BAKES

2 c. sugar
6 tbsp. cocoa
1/2 c. milk
1 tbsp. butter
1/2 c. peanut butter
3 c. quick-cooking oats

Combine .... sugar, cocoa and milk in saucepan.
Bring .... to a boil over medium heat, stirring constantly; remove from heat.
Stir .... in remaining ingredients.
Drop .... by teaspoonfuls onto waxed paper.
Yields ...... 12 servings.

Approx Per Serv: Cal 291, Prot 6.4 g, T Fat 8.7 g, Chl 4.4 mg, Car 50.7 g, Sod 82.2 mg, Pot 194.3 mg.

Nathan Chase, Sullivan

NO-BAKE CAROB BALLS

1/4 c. margarine
1/2 c. honey
1/2 c. applesauce
2 tbsp. carob powder
1/4 tsp. salt
1 1/2 c. oats
1/2 c. chopped pecans
1/2 tsp. vanilla extract
2 c. coconut

Combine .... first 5 ingredients in saucepan, mixing well.
Boil .... for 1 minute; remove from heat.
Stir .... in oats, pecans and vanilla.
Drop .... by teaspoonfuls onto waxed paper.
Roll .... in coconut when cool.
Yields ...... 48 servings.

Approx Per Serv: Cal 56, Prot .6 g, T Fat 3.1 g, Chl 0 mg, Car 7 g, Sod 30.4 mg, Pot 31.2 mg.

Lois Murray, Delaware

CREAMY APPLE SQUARES

1 tsp. salt
2 c. flour
1/2 c. butter, softened
1/4 c. packed brown sugar
1 c. sour cream
1/2 tsp. cinnamon
1 tsp. soda
1/2 c. sugar
1 egg
2 apples, thinly sliced

Combine . . . . all ingredients in bowl, mixing well.
Spread . . . . . in 9 x 13-inch baking pan.
Bake . . . . at 350 degrees until apples are tender.
Cut . . . . into squares.
Yields . . . . . . 12 servings.

Approx Per Serv: Cal 251, Prot 3.4 g, T Fat 12.5 g, Chl 53.2 mg, Car 32 g, Sod 356.8 mg, Pot 90.4 mg.

Cheryl Partridge, Mercer

PORTABLE APPLE AND CHEESE PLEASERS

3/4 c. flour
2/3 c. butter, softened
1/3 c. packed brown sugar
1 egg
1 tsp. vanilla extract
1/2 tsp. each cinnamon, salt, baking powder
1 1/2 c. oats
1 c. shredded Cheddar cheese
3/4 c. raisins
1 c. chopped apple

Combine . . . . first 8 ingredients in large bowl, mixing well.
Stir . . . . in oats, cheese, raisins and apple.
Drop . . . . by tablespoonfuls onto cookie sheet.
Bake . . . . at 375 degrees for 15 minutes or until golden brown.
Yields . . . . . . 2 dozen.

Photograph for this recipe on page 104.

HONEY-CHOCOLATE-OATMEAL COOKIES

1 c. shortening
1 1/4 c. honey

2 eggs, beaten
2 oz. chocolate, melted
1 1/2 c. oats
2 1/2 c. cake flour
1 tsp. each baking powder, cinnamon
1/4 tsp. soda
1/2 tsp. salt
1 c. chopped pecans

Cream . . . . . . shortening and honey in bowl.
Add . . . . eggs, chocolate and oats, beating well after each addition.
Stir . . . . in sifted dry ingredients and pecans.
Drop . . . . by teaspoonfuls onto greased cookie sheet.
Bake . . . . at 325 degrees for 20 minutes.
Yields . . . . . . 66 servings.

Approx Per Serv: Cal 89, Prot 1 g, T Fat 5.5 g, Chl 7.7 mg, Car 9.9 g, Sod 26.6 mg, Pot 33 mg.

Sharon Handke, Westmoreland

OATMEAL COOKIES WITH CHOCOLATE CHIPS

1 c. shortening
2 c. sugar
2 eggs
2 c. sour milk
2 1/2 c. oats
3 1/2 c. flour
2 tsp. soda
1/4 tsp. salt
1 tsp. vanilla extract
1 6-oz. package chocolate chips

Cream . . . . . . shortening, sugar and eggs in large bowl.
Mix . . . . in sour milk and oats.
Add . . . . sifted dry ingredients and vanilla, mixing well.
Fold . . . . in chocolate chips.
Drop . . . . by teaspoonfuls onto greased cookie sheet.
Bake . . . . at 350 degrees for 8 to 10 minutes or until golden brown.
Yields . . . . . . 72 servings.

Approx Per Serv: Cal 101, Prot 1.5 g, T Fat 4.6 g, Chl 8 mg, Car 13.7 g, Sod 35.6 mg, Pot 35 mg.

Susan Zimmerman, Juniata

PEANUT BUTTER FINGERS

1/2 c. butter
1/2 c. sugar
1/2 c. packed brown sugar
1 egg
Peanut butter
1/2 tsp. vanilla extract
1 c. sifted flour
1/2 tsp. soda
1/4 tsp. salt
1 c. quick-cooking oats
1 6-oz. package semisweet
   chocolate chips
1/2 c. confectioners' sugar
2 to 4 tbsp. milk

Cream . . . . . . butter, sugar and brown sugar in bowl until fluffy.
Beat . . . . in egg.
Add . . . . 1/2 cup peanut butter and vanilla, mixing well.
Add . . . . sifted dry ingredients and oats gradually, mixing well.
Spread . . . . . in greased 9 x 13-inch baking pan.
Bake . . . . at 350 degrees for 20 to 25 minutes or until brown.
Top . . . . with chocolate chips.
Let . . . . stand for 5 minutes.
Spread . . . . . over top.
Blend . . . . . . 1/4 cup peanut butter, confectioners' sugar and enough milk to make thin icing in bowl.
Drizzle . . . . . over chocolate.
Cool . . . . in pan on wire rack.
Cut . . . . into 1 x 3-inch bars.
Yields . . . . . . 36 servings.

Approx Per Serv: Cal 123, Prot 2.2 g, T Fat 6.8 g, Chl 15.1 mg, Car 14.8 g, Sod 86.2 mg, Pot 68.1 mg.

Janeen Beck, Forest

WHOLE WHEAT TOLLHOUSE-PEANUT BUTTER COOKIES

1 c. margarine
1 c. crunchy peanut butter
1 c. packed brown sugar
1 1/2 c. sugar
2 eggs
4 tbsp. milk
2 tsp. vanilla extract
1 c. chocolate chips
1 1/2 c. flour
2 c. whole wheat flour
2 tsp. soda
1 tsp. salt

Cream . . . . . . margarine, peanut butter, brown sugar and 1 cup sugar in bowl.
Add . . . . eggs, milk and vanilla, beating well after each addition.
Stir . . . . in chocolate chips.
Add . . . . sifted dry ingredients, mixing well.
Shape . . . . . . into 1-inch balls.
Roll . . . . in remaining 1/2 cup sugar.
Place . . . . on cookie sheet.
Bake . . . . at 375 degrees for 8 to 10 minutes or until golden brown.
Yields . . . . . . 96 servings.

Approx Per Serv: Cal 79, Prot 1.4 g, T Fat 4.1 g, Chl 2.7 mg, Car 10.1 g, Sod 80.6 mg, Pot 43.7 mg.

Tori L. Hughes, Venango

WELSH COOKIES

4 c. flour
1 1/2 c. sugar
1 tbsp. baking powder
3/4 tsp. salt
1 tsp. nutmeg
1 c. shortening
Milk
3 eggs, beaten
1 c. currants

Mix . . . . flour, sugar, baking powder, salt and nutmeg in bowl.
Cut . . . . in shortening until crumbly.
Add . . . . enough milk to eggs to measure 1 cup.
Stir . . . . into flour mixture with currants.
Chill . . . . in refrigerator.
Roll . . . . on floured surface and cut into circles.
Bake . . . . on griddle over medium heat, turning once.
Yields . . . . . . 36 servings.

Approx Per Serv: Cal 158, Prot 2.2 g, T Fat 6.9 g, Chl 21.4 mg, Car 22.2 g, Sod 79.5 mg, Pot 53.2 mg.

Phyllis McNamara, Susquehanna

Recipe on page 100.

MOLASSES SUGAR COOKIES

3/4 c. shortening, melted
1 1/2 c. (or more) sugar
1/4 c. molasses
1 egg
2 c. sifted flour
1 tbsp. soda
1/2 tsp. salt
1/2 tsp. each cloves, ginger
1 tsp. cinnamon

Combine .... shortening, 1 cup sugar, molasses and egg in bowl.
Add .... sifted flour, soda, salt and spices to sugar mixture, mixing well.
Chill .... in refrigerator.
Shape ...... into 1-inch balls.
Roll .... in remaining sugar.
Place .... 2 inches apart on greased cookie sheet.
Bake .... at 375 degrees for 8 to 10 minutes or until brown.
Yields ...... 36 servings.

Approx Per Serv: Cal 105, Prot .9 g, T Fat 4.9 g, Chl 7 mg, Car 14.7 g, Sod 59.2 mg, Pot 29.4 mg.

Christine Dutko, Indiana

RAISIN-FILLED SUGAR COOKIES

6 c. raisins
3 c. sugar
4 or 5 eggs, beaten
2 tsp. vanilla extract
Flour
1 c. chopped walnuts
2 c. applesauce
1 c. lard
3/4 c. milk
2 tsp. baking powder
1/8 tsp. salt

Combine .... raisins, 3/4 cup sugar, 2 or 3 eggs, 1 teaspoon vanilla and 1 1/2 cups water in saucepan, mixing well.
Cook .... until slightly thickened, stirring occasionally.

Mix .... 2 heaping teaspoons flour with enough water to make thick paste in small bowl.
Add .... to raisin mixture with walnuts and applesauce.
Cook .... until thick, stirring constantly; cool.
Cream ...... 2 cups sugar and lard together in large bowl until light and fluffy.
Add .... milk, baking powder, salt, 2 eggs, 4 cups flour and remaining 1 teaspoon vanilla, mixing well.
Roll .... dough on floured surface to desired thickness.
Cut .... into circles.
Spread ..... raisin mixture over half the circles.
Place .... remaining circles on top, pressing to enclose filling.
Place .... on cookie sheet.
Sprinkle .... remaining sugar over top.
Bake .... at 350 degrees for 10 to 12 minutes or until brown.
Yields ...... 24 servings.

Approx Per Serv: Cal 442, Prot 5.6 g, T Fat 14.3 g, Chl 63.7 mg, Car 77.4 g, Sod 66 mg, Pot 374.1 mg.

Lucille A. Dashem, Centre

PINEAPPLE-PECAN COOKIES

1/2 c. shortening
1 c. sugar
1 1/2 c. flour
2 tsp. baking powder
1/4 tsp. salt
1 egg
1 c. drained crushed pineapple
1/2 c. pineapple juice
1 1/2 c. oats
1/2 c. chopped pecans

Cream ...... shortening and sugar in bowl.
Add .... next 6 ingredients, mixing well.
Stir .... in oats and pecans.
Drop .... by teaspoonfuls onto greased cookie sheet.
Bake .... at 350 degrees for 15 minutes.
Yields ...... 72 servings.

Approx Per Serv: Cal 51, Prot .7 g, T Fat 3.5 g, Chl 3.5 mg, Car 7 g, Sod 17.5 mg, Pot 20.4 mg.

Mildred Butchkovitz, Lackawanna

Recipes on pages 15, 82, 83 and 101.

PINEAPPLE SQUARES

1 20-oz. can crushed pineapple
1 1/2 c. sugar
4 tbsp. cornstarch
3 c. flour
2 tsp. baking powder
1 tsp. salt
1 c. margarine
1/2 c. milk
1 egg white, beaten
1/2 c. chopped pecans

Combine .... pineapple, sugar and cornstarch in saucepan.
Cook .... for 10 minutes, stirring constantly; cool.
Sift .... dry ingredients together into bowl.
Cut .... in margarine until crumbly.
Add .... milk to make soft dough.
Divide ...... into 2 portions.
Cover ...... cookie sheet with 1 portion.
Spread ..... with pineapple mixture.
Top .... with remaining pastry.
Brush ...... with egg white.
Sprinkle .... with pecans.
Bake .... at 375 degrees for 30 to 40 minutes or until golden.
Cut .... into squares when cool.
Yields ...... 16 servings.

Approx Per Serv: Cal 328, Prot 3.5 g, T Fat 14.7 g, Chl 1.1 mg, Car 47.1 g, Sod 322.3 mg, Pot 101 mg.

Linda Beatty, Indiana

PUMPKIN WHOOPEE PIES

1 1-lb. box brown sugar
1 c. oil
2 eggs
2 c. cooked pumpkin
1 tsp. each cinnamon, cloves, ginger
1 tsp. soda
1 tsp. baking powder
2 tsp. vanilla extract
Flour
1 egg white
2 tbsp. milk
2 c. confectioners' sugar
3/4 c. shortening

Combine .... first 4 ingredients and spices in large bowl, mixing well.

Add .... soda, baking powder and 1 teaspoon vanilla, mixing well.
Stir .... in 3 1/2 cups flour, 1 cup at a time, mixing well after each addition.
Drop .... by teaspoonfuls onto baking sheet.
Bake .... at 350 degrees for 8 to 10 minutes or until cookies test done; cool.
Mix .... egg white, 1 teaspoon vanilla, 2 tablespoons flour, milk, confectioners' sugar and shortening in medium bowl.
Spread ..... icing on half the cookies.
Top .... with remaining cookies.
Yields ...... 36 servings.

Approx Per Serv: Cal 219, Prot 1.8 g, T Fat 11.2 g, Chl 14.2 mg, Car 28.5 g, Sod 41.5 mg, Pot 65.6 mg.

Velma Sherman, Tioga

RASPBERRY DREAM BARS

2 1/2 c. flour
1/2 tsp. salt
2 tsp. baking powder
1 c. butter
4 eggs, well beaten
2 tsp. vanilla extract
1 12-oz. jar red raspberry preserves
1 1/2 c. sugar
1 7-oz. package coconut
3 tbsp. melted butter

Mix .... flour, salt and baking powder in bowl.
Cut .... in butter until crumbly.
Add .... 2 eggs and 1 teaspoon vanilla, mixing well.
Press .... over bottom and 1 inch up sides of buttered 10 x 16-inch baking pan.
Spread ..... preserves over dough.
Beat .... 2 eggs, 1 teaspoon vanilla and remaining 3 ingredients in bowl.
Spread ..... over preserves.
Bake .... at 350 degrees for 35 minutes.
Yields ...... 48 servings.

Approx Per Serv: Cal 122, Prot 1.4 g, T Fat 5.6 g, Chl 35.1 mg, Car 16.9 g, Sod 101.2 mg, Pot 25.1 mg.

Janice Blose, Delaware

SKILLET STRAWBERRY COOKIES

1   8-oz. package pitted dates,
      finely chopped
1/2 c. flaked coconut
1/2 c. sugar
4 tbsp. butter
1 egg, beaten
1/8 tsp. salt
1 1/2 c. crisp rice cereal
1/2 c. chopped walnuts
1 tsp. vanilla extract
2 jars fine red sugar crystals
1 can green decorator frosting

Combine .... first 6 ingredients in skillet.
Cook .... over medium-low heat for 5 to 10 minutes or until thick and bubbly, stirring constantly; remove from heat.
Stir .... in cereal, walnuts and vanilla.
Cool .... for 10 minutes.
Shape ...... by tablespoonfuls into strawberries with moistened fingers.
Roll .... in red sugar.
Trim .... with green frosting leaves.
Yields ...... 30 servings.

Approx Per Serv: Cal 77, Prot .8 g, T Fat 3.5 g, Chl 13.2 mg, Car 11.7 g, Sod 48.6 mg, Pot 69.6 mg.

Mrs. Homer Poulos, Blair

OATMEAL PIES

4 eggs
2 c. sugar
1 1/2 c. dark corn syrup
1 c. milk
1 1/2 c. quick oats
1/2 c. melted butter
1/2 tsp. salt
2 tsp. vanilla extract
1/2 c. chopped pecans
1/2 c. coconut
2 unbaked 9-in. pie shells

Mix .... first 10 ingredients in bowl.
Spoon ...... into pie shells.
Bake .... at 350 degrees for 45 to 50 minutes or until pies test done.
Yields ...... 12 servings.

Approx Per Serv: Cal 593, Prot 6.7 g, T Fat 25.6 g, Chl 110.8 mg, Car 87.1 g, Sod 432.2 mg, Pot 146.6 mg.

Esther Beaver, Franklin

EGG CUSTARD PIE

1 c. sugar
2 tbsp. butter
2 1/2 tbsp. cornstarch
1/8 tsp. salt
2 eggs, separated
1 c. milk
1 unbaked 9-in. pie shell

Cream ...... sugar and butter together in medium bowl.
Add .... cornstarch and salt, mixing well.
Stir .... in egg yolks and milk, mixing well after each addition.
Fold .... in stiffly beaten egg whites.
Spoon ...... into pie shell.
Bake .... at 375 degrees for 15 to 20 minutes.
Reduce ..... temperature to 350 degrees.
Bake .... for several minutes longer or until custard tests done.
Yields ...... 6 servings.

Strawberries may be added to bottom of pie shell before adding custard.

Approx Per Serv: Cal 226, Prot 3.6 g, T Fat 7 g, Chl 101.4 mg, Car 38.2 g, Sod 130.8 mg, Pot 81.5 mg.

Cynthia Newhard, Lehigh

LEMON SPONGE PIE

1 c. sugar
2 tbsp. butter, melted
2 tbsp. (scant) flour
3 eggs, separated
Juice of 1 lemon
Grated rind of 1 lemon
1 1/4 c. milk
1 unbaked 9-in. pie shell

Mix .... sugar, butter, flour and egg yolks in bowl.
Stir .... in lemon juice and rind.
Add .... milk gradually, stirring constantly.
Fold .... stiffly beaten egg whites into sugar mixture.
Spoon ...... into pie shell.
Bake .... at 375 degrees for 50 minutes.
Yields ...... 6 servings.

Approx Per Serv: Cal 396, Prot 7.2 g, T Fat 18.5 g, Chl 145.4 mg, Car 51.1 g, Sod 286.8 mg, Pot 125.5 mg.

Edith Hemminger, Cumberland

AUTUMN PUMPKIN PIES

1 1/2 c. cooked pumpkin
1 c. packed brown sugar
1/2 tsp. salt
1 tsp. cinnamon
1 tbsp. flour
2 tbsp. molasses
2 eggs, beaten
1 c. each evaporated milk, milk
2 unbaked 9-in. pie shells

Combine .... first 5 ingredients in mixer bowl, mixing well.
Mix .... in molasses and eggs.
Add .... evaporated milk and milk, mixing well.
Pour .... into pie shells.
Bake .... at 350 degrees for 1 hour.
Yields ...... 12 servings.

Approx Per Serv: Cal 295, Prot 5.5 g, T Fat 13.5 g, Chl 51.5 mg, Car 39.1 g, Sod 395.9 mg, Pot 287.1 mg.

Shirley A. Womer, Snyder

ICE CREAM PUMPKIN PIE

1 c. cooked pumpkin
1/2 c. packed brown sugar
1/2 tsp. each salt, cinnamon, ginger
1/4 tsp. nutmeg
1 qt. vanilla ice cream, softened
1 graham cracker crust

Mix .... pumpkin, brown sugar, salt and spices in bowl.
Add .... ice cream, mixing well.
Spoon ...... into pie crust.
Freeze ...... until firm.
Garnish ..... with whipped cream.
Yields ...... 8 servings.

Approx Per Serv: Cal 393, Prot 3.3 g, T Fat 18.7 g, Chl 57.7 mg, Car 56.5 g, Sod 288.2 mg, Pot 276.3 mg.

Debby Long, Union

IMPOSSIBLE PUMPKIN PIE

3/4 c. sugar
1/2 c. biscuit mix
2 tbsp. margarine
1 13-oz. can evaporated milk
2 eggs
1 16-oz. can pumpkin
2 1/2 tsp. pumpkin pie spice
2 tsp. vanilla extract

Place .... all ingredients in blender container.
Process ..... on high for 1 minute.
Pour .... into greased 8-inch pie plate.
Bake .... at 350 degrees for 50 to 55 minutes or until knife inserted in center comes out clean.
Yields ...... 6 servings.

Approx Per Serv: Cal 323, Prot 8.7 g, T Fat 12.8 g, Chl 106 mg, Car 45.2 g, Sod 281.8 mg, Pot 439.9 mg.

Peggy Lewis, Susquehanna

FRESH STRAWBERRY PIE

1 carton strawberries
1 9-in. baked pie shell
2 tbsp. cornstarch
3/4 c. sugar
1 3-oz. package strawberry gelatin

Arrange ..... strawberries in bottom of pie shell.
Mix .... cornstarch, sugar and 1 1/2 cups water in saucepan.
Boil .... for 2 minutes.
Add .... gelatin, stirring until dissolved.
Cool .... slightly.
Pour .... over strawberries.
Chill .... until set.
Yields ...... 6 servings.

Approx Per Serv: Cal 344, Prot 3.7 g, T Fat 10.3 g, Chl 0 mg, Car 57.5 g, Sod 229.1 mg, Pot 54.5 mg.

Kim Boyer, Dauphin

SOUR CREAM PASTRIES

1 c. butter
2 1/2 c. flour
1 egg, beaten
1/2 c. sour cream
1/2 c. apricot preserves
1/2 c. coconut
1/4 c. chopped walnuts
1/4 c. sugar

Cut .... butter into flour in bowl until crumbly.
Mix .... egg and sour cream in small bowl.
Add .... to flour mixture, blending well.
Chill .... dough for several hours.
Divide ...... into 4 equal portions.

Roll .... into 10-inch circles on floured surface.
Spread ..... preserves on circles.
Sprinkle .... with coconut and walnuts.
Cut .... each circle into 12 wedges.
Roll .... wedges into crescent shapes.
Sprinkle .... with sugar.
Place .... on baking sheet.
Bake .... at 350 degrees for 20 minutes.
Yields ...... 48 servings.

Approx Per Serv: Cal 84, Prot 1.1 g, T Fat 5.2 g, Chl 18.2 mg, Car 8.6 g, Sod 51.6 mg, Pot 20.3 mg.

Judy Muller, Wayne

PIE CRUSTS

4 c. flour
1 tbsp. sugar
2 3/4 c. shortening
1 tbsp. vinegar
1 egg, beaten

Combine .... flour and sugar in bowl.
Cut .... in shortening until crumbly.
Add .... vinegar, egg and 1/2 cup water, stirring until well mixed.
Knead ...... lightly.
Roll .... on floured surface.
Fit .... into 3 pie plates.
Yields ...... 3 crusts.

Approx Per Crust: Cal 2702, Prot 19.7 g, T Fat 205 g, Chl 84.3 mg, Car 131.3 g, Sod 23.8 mg, Pot 185 mg.

Verna Manjone, Schuylkill

NOODLE PUDDING

1 8-oz. package thin noodles, cooked
1 c. sugar
1/2 tsp. vanilla extract
5 eggs, beaten
2 c. milk
1/4 c. margarine
8 oz. cream-style cottage cheese
1 3-oz. package cream cheese, softened
1 c. sour cream
Graham cracker crumbs

Combine .... all ingredients except graham cracker crumbs in large bowl, mixing well.
Spoon ...... into greased 9 x 13-inch baking dish.

Bake .... at 350 degrees for 1/2 hour.
Top .... with crumbs.
Bake .... for 1/2 hour longer.
Yields ...... 8 servings.

Approx Per Serv: Cal 65.4, Prot 1.9 g, T Fat 3.7 g, Car 5.9 g, Sod 30.1 mg, Pot 49.6 mg.

Nutritional information does not include graham cracker crumbs.

Sue Arner, Armstrong

APPLE-BREAD PUDDING

3 tbsp. butter, softened
10 thin slices bread
3 or 4 apples, peeled, sliced
3 tbsp. sugar
2 eggs
2 c. milk

Spread ..... butter on bread.
Place .... in buttered 5 x 9-inch loaf pan.
Arrange ..... apples on bread.
Sprinkle .... with sugar.
Beat .... eggs and milk together in bowl.
Pour .... over apples.
Let .... stand for 15 minutes.
Bake .... at 450 degrees for 40 minutes or until set.
Yields ...... 6 servings.

Approx Per Serv: Cal 725, Prot 9.4 g, T Fat 12.9 g, Chl 14.8 mg, Car 148 g, Sod 373.1 mg, Pot 348.1 mg.

Gayle Clyde, Lawrence

QUICK BREAD PUDDING

8 slices dry bread, cut into 1-in. cubes
3 eggs, beaten
1/2 c. sugar
1 tsp. vanilla extract
1 1/2 c. milk
1/2 c. raisins

Pour .... hot water over bread in bowl to moisten; drain excess water.
Add .... next 4 ingredients, mixing well.
Stir .... in raisins.
Spoon ...... into greased baking pan.
Bake .... at 350 degrees for 1 hour.
Yields ...... 6 servings.

Approx Per Serv: Cal 282, Prot 9 g, T Fat 6.3 g, Chl 136.1 mg, Car 48.2 g, Sod 256.2 mg, Pot 252.6 mg.

Kathy Yemm, Schuylkill

CHERRY PUDDING

1 tbsp. butter, softened
Sugar
1 1/2 c. flour
2 tsp. baking powder
1/8 tsp. (about) salt
1 c. milk
1 c. sour cherries
1 c. cherry juice

Cream . . . . . . butter and 1 cup sugar in bowl.
Sift . . . . flour, baking powder and salt together.
Add . . . . to sugar mixture alternately with milk, ending with flour mixture and beating well after each addition.
Stir . . . . in cherries.
Pour . . . . into greased 2-quart casserole.
Mix . . . . cherry juice, 1/4 to 1 cup sugar and 1 cup boiling water in bowl until sugar is dissolved.
Pour . . . . into casserole.
Bake . . . . at 350 degrees for 45 minutes.
Yields . . . . . . 15 servings.

Approx Per Serv: Cal 180, Prot 1.9 g, T Fat 1.5 g, Chl 4.6 mg, Car 40.3 g, Sod 80.1 mg, Pot 74.2 mg.

Lee Eisler, Butler

OLD-FASHIONED RICE PUDDING

1/2 c. rice
8 c. milk
2 tsp. vanilla extract
2/3 c. sugar
1/8 tsp. salt
1/2 c. (or more) raisins (opt.)

Combine . . . . all ingredients except raisins in large bowl, mixing well.
Pour . . . . into well-greased 2 1/2-quart casserole.
Bake . . . . at 325 degrees for 2 1/2 hours, stirring twice during first hour.
Stir . . . . in raisins.
Bake . . . . for 30 minutes longer.
Yields . . . . . . 20 servings.

Approx Per Serv: Cal 117, Prot 3.8 g, T Fat 3.4 g, Chl 13.7 mg, Car 18 g, Sod 63.4 mg, Pot 172.7 mg.

Doris Koenig, Lehigh

BOILED RICE PUDDING

1 c. rice
1 c. sugar
1/2 tsp. salt
6 1/2 c. milk
2 eggs
2 tsp. vanilla extract
Cinnamon

Combine . . . . rice, sugar, salt, 6 cups milk and 2 cups water in saucepan.
Boil . . . . for 25 minutes, stirring frequently.
Mix . . . . remaining 1/2 cup milk, eggs and vanilla in bowl.
Stir . . . . a small amount of rice mixture into egg mixture; stir egg mixture into rice.
Pour . . . . into large serving bowl.
Sprinkle . . . . cinnamon over top.
Chill . . . . in refrigerator.
Yields . . . . . . 10 servings.

Approx Per Serv: Cal 264, Prot 8.1 g, T Fat 6.8 g, Chl 72.8 mg, Car 42.6 g, Sod 199.2 mg, Pot 259 mg.

Dawn L. Blocker, Carbon

FAVORITE RICE PUDDING

4 c. milk
1 lg. can evaporated milk
1 c. sugar
2 eggs
3 tbsp. cornstarch
1 c. rice, cooked
1 c. raisins (opt.)

Bring . . . . milk, evaporated milk and sugar to a boil in large saucepan.
Beat . . . . eggs and cornstarch together in bowl until smooth.
Stir . . . . a small amount of milk mixture into eggs; stir eggs into milk mixture.
Cook . . . . until thick, stirring constantly.
Stir . . . . in rice and raisins; cool.
Spoon . . . . . . into serving dish.
Garnish . . . . . with cinnamon.
Yields . . . . . . 15 servings.

Approx Per Serv: Cal 192, Prot 5.6 g, T Fat 5.3 g, Chl 51.5 mg, Car 31.4 g, Sod 127.7 mg, Pot 265.3 mg.

Christine McCahren, Juniata

Ethnic Favorites

ITALIAN RATATOUILLE, recipe on page 117.

BARBADIAN COCONUT BREAD

4 c. flour
2 tsp. baking powder
1/2 tsp. salt
3/4 c. sugar
1 egg, beaten
3/4 c. each milk, coconut water
1/4 lb. shortening, melted
1 tsp. vanilla extract
6 oz. raisins
2 c. grated coconut
Confectioners' sugar

Sift .... flour, baking powder and salt together in bowl.
Add .... sugar, egg, milk, coconut water, shortening and vanilla, mixing well.
Coat .... raisins with a small amount additional flour.
Stir .... raisins and coconut into dough.
Knead ...... lightly on floured surface.
Shape ...... into 2 loaves.
Place .... in greased loaf pans.
Dust .... lightly with confectioners' sugar.
Bake .... in moderate oven until bread tests done.
Yields ...... 24 servings.

Approx Per Serv: Cal 192, Prot 2.9 g, T Fat 7.4 g, Chl 11.1 mg, Car 28.6 g, Sod 93.6 mg, Pot 90.8 mg.

Janet M. Pifer, Jefferson

CANADIAN EGG BRUNCH

3 English muffins, split, toasted
6 slices Velveeta cheese
6 slices Canadian bacon, cooked
6 eggs, fried

Place .... muffins on rack in broiler pan.
Layer ...... each half with remaining 3 ingredients.
Broil .... until cheese melts.
Yields ...... 6 servings.

Approx Per Serv: Cal 231, Prot 17.8 g, T Fat 16.2 g, Chl 290.6 mg, Car 2.5 g, Sod 1050.2 mg, Pot 220.3 mg.

Nutritional information does not include English muffins.

Natalie Wagner, Lebanon

MICROWAVE CHINESE-STYLE STIR-FRY

1/2 lb. round steak, thinly sliced
1 onion, sliced
1 pkg. Chinese pea pods
5 or 6 fresh mushrooms
1/2 c. bean sprouts
1 tbsp. (about) soy sauce

Preheat ..... browning dish for 1 to 2 minutes.
Place .... steak and onion slices in dish.
Microwave .. for 3 minutes.
Add .... remaining ingredients.
Microwave .. for 4 minutes longer; stir.
Let .... stand for 3 minutes before serving.
Yields ...... 2 servings.

Approx Per Serv: Cal 298, Prot 43.6 g, T Fat 8.1 g, Chl 116 mg, Car 11.5 g, Sod 772.1 mg, Pot 816.8 mg.

Nutritional information does not include chinese pea pods.

Helen D. Tunison, Adams

CHINESE-STYLE CHICKEN

2 whole boned chicken breasts, cut into thin strips
2 tbsp. oil
3/4 c. each slivered celery, green pepper, carrot
1/2 c. chicken broth
1/4 c. soy sauce
1 sm. clove of garlic, chopped
1/4 tsp. ginger
2 tbsp. cornstarch
2 tbsp. parsley flakes
Juice of 1/2 lemon
1/2 tsp. (or more) salt
Pepper to taste

Stir-fry ..... chicken in oil in wok over high heat for 3 minutes.
Add .... vegetables.
Stir-fry ..... for 3 minutes longer.
Combine .... remaining ingredients in small bowl, mixing well.
Pour .... over chicken and vegetables.
Bring .... to a boil.
Cook .... for 2 minutes longer, stirring constantly.

Serve . . . . over rice.
Yields . . . . . . 6 servings.

Approx Per Serv: Cal 382, Prot 31.4 g, T Fat 9 g, Chl 74 mg, Car 41.5 g, Sod 1208.1 mg, Pot 457.3 mg.

Elisabeth Brown, Allegheny

ENGLISH MUFFIN LOAVES

2 pkg. dry yeast
1 tbsp. sugar
2 tsp. salt
1/4 tsp. soda
6 c. flour
2 c. milk
4 tbsp. butter, melted
2 tbsp. (about) cornmeal

Combine . . . . first 4 ingredients and 3 cups flour in large bowl.
Heat . . . . milk, 1/2 cup water and butter in saucepan until very warm.
Add . . . . to dry ingredients, beating well.
Stir . . . . in remaining 3 cups flour.
Shape . . . . . . into 2 loaves on floured surface.
Place . . . . in greased loaf pans sprinkled with cornmeal.
Let . . . . rise, covered, for 45 minutes.
Bake . . . . at 400 degrees for 25 minutes; cool.
Serve . . . . sliced and toasted.
Yields . . . . . . 12 servings.

Approx Per Serv: Cal 300, Prot 8.6 g, T Fat 5.9 g, Chl 17.5 mg, Car 52.1 g, Sod 441.3 mg. Pot 144.1 mg.

Jessie Puzo, Susquehanna

BUBBLE-AND-SQUEAK (ENGLAND)

4 tbsp. butter, melted
4 tbsp. flour
2 c. cold milk
1/4 tsp. (or more) each salt, pepper
1 lb. sausage, cooked, drained
2 c. chopped cooked cabbage
2 tbsp. wheat germ

Blend . . . . . . butter and flour in saucepan.
Stir . . . . in milk gradually.
Bring . . . . to a boil over low heat, stirring constantly.
Cook . . . . for 2 minutes, stirring constantly.
Season . . . . . with salt and pepper.
Layer . . . . . . sausage, cabbage and sauce in 2-quart casserole.

Sprinkle . . . . with wheat germ.
Bake . . . . at 350 degrees for 30 minutes.
Yields . . . . . . 4 servings.

Approx Per Serv: Cal 627, Prot 24 g, T Fat 51.6 g, Chl 122.9 mg, Car 16.6 g, Sod 1431 mg, Pot 638 mg.

Erin Peterhaensel, Erie

POULET CORDON BLEU

3 chicken breasts, split, skinned, boned
3 slices Swiss cheese, cut in half
3 slices boiled ham, cut in half
2 tbsp. butter
1 can cream of chicken soup
1/4 c. milk

Flatten . . . . . chicken breasts with meat mallet.
Top . . . . each with cheese and ham, rolling to enclose filling; secure with toothpick.
Brown . . . . . . in butter in skillet.
Add . . . . soup and milk.
Simmer . . . . . covered, for 20 minutes or until tender, stirring occasionally.
Garnish . . . . . with parsley.
Yields . . . . . . 3 servings.

Approx Per Serv: Cal 534, Prot 50.6 g, T Fat 32.2 g, Chl 221.4 mg, Car 8.2 g, Sod 1368.1 mg, Pot 513.5 mg.

Nancy Honeywell, Luzerne

ZUCCHINI QUICHE

4 eggs
1/3 c. oil
3/4 c. biscuit mix
1/4 tsp. salt
1/8 tsp. (about) garlic powder
2 c. shredded zucchini
1/2 c. chopped onion
1 c. shredded Cheddar cheese

Beat . . . . eggs with oil in bowl.
Add . . . . dry ingredients, mixing well.
Stir . . . . in zucchini, onion and cheese.
Pour . . . . into greased pie plate.
Bake . . . . at 350 degrees for 40 to 45 minutes or until knife inserted in center comes out clean.
Yields . . . . . . 6 servings.

Approx Per Serv: Cal 316, Prot 11.2 g, T Fat 24 g, Chl 187.2 mg, Car 14.6 g, Sod 458.5 mg, Pot 224.1 mg.

Renee Mullowney, Bucks

MICROWAVE QUICHE LORRAINE

9 or 10 slices crisp-cooked bacon,
  crumbled
1 c. shredded Swiss cheese
1/4 c. minced onion
4 eggs
1 c. evaporated milk
3/4 tsp. salt
1/4 tsp. sugar
1/8 tsp. pepper

Sprinkle .... first 3 ingredients in 9-inch glass pie plate.
Combine .... eggs and remaining ingredients in bowl, beating well.
Pour .... over bacon mixture.
Microwave .. on Medium-High for 9 1/2 to 11 minutes or until knife inserted near center comes out clean.
Let .... stand for 1 minute before serving.
Yields ...... 6 servings.

Approx Per Serv: Cal 418, Prot 15.1 g, T Fat 22.6 g, Chl 512.9 mg, Car 39.4 g, Sod 782.7 mg, Pot 248.6 mg.

Carol Garling, Franklin

CLASSIC QUICHE LORRAINE

6 slices crisp-fried bacon, crumbled
1 4 1/2-oz. can sliced mushrooms,
  drained
1 1/2 c. shredded Swiss cheese
1 med. onion, chopped
1 tbsp. flour
1/2 tsp. salt
1/4 tsp. garlic powder
2 eggs, beaten
1 c. evaporated milk
1 baked 9-in. pie shell

Combine .... first 7 ingredients in bowl, mixing well.
Stir .... in eggs and evaporated milk.
Pour .... into pie shell.
Bake .... at 325 degrees for 1 hour.
Cool .... for 10 to 15 minutes before serving.
Yields ...... 8 servings.

Approx Per Serv: Cal 314, Prot 12.8 g, T Fat 21.9 g, Chl 233.9 mg, Car 16.8 g, Sod 668 mg, Pot 235.8 mg.

Brenda Watkins, Huntingdon

BROWN POTATO SOUP (GERMANY)

5 c. chopped potatoes
1 1/2 c. flour
1/2 c. oil
1 tsp. (about) salt
Pepper to taste

Cook .... potatoes in water to cover in saucepan until just tender.
Brown ...... flour in hot oil in skillet, stirring constantly.
Stir .... flour into boiling potatoes.
Cook .... until thick, stirring constantly.
Season ..... with salt and pepper to taste.
Yields ...... 10 servings.

Approx Per Serv: Cal 221, Prot 3.5 g, T Fat 11.1 g, Chl 0 mg, Car 27.1 g, Sod 215.6 mg, Pot 323.1 mg.

Tracy Zoe Gourley, Adams

GERMAN-STYLE NOODLE CASSEROLE

1 lb. bacon, crisp-cooked, crumbled
1 lb. twist noodles, cooked, drained
2 cans golden mushroom soup
1 28-oz. can sauerkraut

Combine .... all ingredients in 1/2-inch bacon drippings in skillet, stirring gently.
Cook .... over medium heat until heated through.
Yields ...... 12 servings.

Approx Per Serv: Cal 218, Prot 7 g, T Fat 10.4 g, Chl 37.7 mg, Car 23.9 g, Sod 644.8 mg, Pot 126.9 mg.

Amy Knepper, Erie

HOT GERMAN GREEN BEANS

1 1/2 lb. fresh green beans, cut into
  1-in. pieces
2 tbsp. sugar
1/2 tsp. salt
1 tbsp. lemon juice
1 sm. onion, sliced
2 tbsp. bacon drippings
2 tsp. cornstarch
3 slices crisp-cooked bacon, crumbled

Cook .... beans in 1 cup water in covered saucepan until tender; drain, reserving 1/4 cup liquid.
Combine .... next 5 ingredients in skillet.

Cook . . . . until onion is tender.

Blend . . . . . . cornstarch with reserved bean liquid.

Stir . . . . into onion mixture.

Cook . . . . . . until thick and clear, stirring constantly.

Add . . . . beans.

Cook . . . . . . until heated through.

Sprinkle . . . . with bacon.

Yields . . . . . . 6 servings.

Approx Per Serv: Cal 152, Prot 3.5 g, T Fat 9.7 g, Chl 9.5 mg, Car 14.6 g, Sod 457.2 mg, Pot 319.2 mg.

Phyllis M. Paine, Lebanon

SAUERKRAUT AND KIELBASA (GERMANY)

    1   2-lb. package sauerkraut
    1 c. applesauce
    1/2 c. orange juice
    1/2 c. packed brown sugar
    2 tbsp. chopped onion
    1 tsp. caraway seed
    1 1/2 lb. kielbasa, cut into
        serving-sized pieces

Combine . . . . all ingredients, except kielbasa, in large skillet, mixing well.

Arrange . . . . . kielbasa over top.

Simmer . . . . . covered, for 1 hour or longer.

Yields . . . . . . 12 servings.

Approx Per Serv: Cal 225, Prot 10.3 g, T Fat 15.2 g, Chl 2.2 mg, Car 18.9 g, Sod 613.5 mg, Pot 182.6 mg.

Edna Minich, Clarion

ICED GERMAN APPLE CAKE

    2 c. sugar
    1 1/2 c. oil
    3 eggs
    2 tsp. vanilla extract
    3 c. flour
    2 tsp. soda
    1 tsp. salt
    3 c. chopped apples
    1 c. chopped pecans
    1/2 c. butter, melted
    1 c. packed light brown sugar
    1/4 c. evaporated milk

Combine . . . . first 7 ingredients in large bowl, mixing well.

Fold . . . . in apples and pecans.

Spoon . . . . . . into greased and floured baking pan.

Place . . . . in cold oven.

Bake . . . . at 325 degrees for 1 hour.

Blend . . . . . . butter, brown sugar and evaporated milk in saucepan.

Bring . . . . to a boil, stirring constantly; cool.

Spread . . . . . over cake.

Yields . . . . . . 12 servings.

May substitute sprinkle of confectioners' sugar for icing.

Approx Per Serv: Cal 729, Prot 6.3 g, T Fat 44.1 g, Chl 88.5 mg, Car 80.6 g, Sod 436.1 mg, Pot 217.6 mg.

Audrey Ridinger, Adams

GERMAN POOR MAN'S CAKE

    1 c. chopped dates
    1/2 c. butter, melted
    1 c. sugar
    2 eggs, beaten
    2 c. flour
    1 tsp. soda
    1/2 tsp. salt
    1/4 tsp. each nutmeg, ground cloves
    3/4 tsp. cinnamon
    1/2 c. chopped pecans
    1 c. confectioners' sugar
    2 tbsp. milk

Simmer . . . . . dates in 1 1/4 cups water in large saucepan for 20 minutes.

Mix . . . . in butter; cool.

Add . . . . sugar and eggs, mixing well.

Sift . . . . next 3 ingredients with spices into bowl.

Add . . . . pecans, mixing well.

Stir . . . . into date mixture.

Spread . . . . . in prepared 10 x 15-inch baking pan.

Bake . . . . at 325 degrees for 20 minutes.

Blend . . . . . . confectioners' sugar and milk in bowl.

Spread . . . . . over hot cake.

Cool . . . . before cutting.

Yields . . . . . . 20 servings.

Approx Per Serv: Cal 197, Prot 2.5 g, T Fat 7.4 g, Chl 39.5 mg, Car 31.4 g, Sod 157 mg, Pot 95.6 mg.

Elsie G. Brown, Delaware

HAWAIIAN CAKE

2 c. flour
2 c. sugar
2 eggs
2 tsp. soda
1 20-oz. can crushed pineapple
1 c. coconut
1 c. chopped walnuts
1 8-oz. package cream cheese, softened
4 tbsp. margarine, softened
1 tsp. vanilla extract
1 c. confectioners' sugar

Combine .... first 7 ingredients in bowl, mixing well.
Spoon ...... into greased and floured 9 x 13-inch baking pan.
Bake .... at 350 degrees for 40 minutes.
Combine .... cream cheese, margarine, vanilla and confectioners' sugar in bowl, beating until smooth.
Spread ..... over cake.
Yields ...... 12 servings.

Approx Per Serv: Cal 489, Prot 6.7 g, T Fat 20.7 g, Chl 63.1 mg, Car 72.3 g, Sod 257.3 mg, Pot 165.3 mg.

Natalie Wagner, Lebanon

KING KAMEHAMEHA PIE (HAWAII)

3/4 c. sugar
1 12-oz. can pineapple juice
1 med. cooking apple, sliced
3 tbsp. cornstarch
1 tbsp. butter
1/2 tsp. vanilla extract
1/4 tsp. salt
1 baked 9-in. pie shell

Bring .... sugar and 1 1/4 cups juice to a boil in large saucepan.
Add .... apple.
Simmer ..... covered, for 3 to 4 minutes or until just tender; drain apple, reserving syrup.
Blend ...... remaining 1/4 cup juice with cornstarch in small bowl.
Stir .... into syrup in saucepan.
Simmer ..... until thickened, stirring constantly.
Stir .... in butter, vanilla and salt.
Cool .... for 10 minutes.
Pour .... half the syrup into pie shell.

Arrange ..... apple over top.
Spoon ...... remaining syrup over apples.
Chill .... until serving time.
Garnish ..... with whipped cream.
Yields ...... 6 servings.

Approx Per Serv: Cal 332, Prot 2.2 g, T Fat 12.2 g, Chl 5.9 mg, Car 55.1 g, Sod 296.7 mg, Pot 148.2 mg.

Janice Freeman, Schuylkill

HAWAIIAN CHICKEN

1/2 c. each soy sauce, pineapple juice
1/4 c. oil
1 tsp. each dry mustard, garlic salt
1 tbsp. brown sugar
2 tsp. ginger
1/4 tsp. pepper
1 3-lb. chicken, boned, cut into 1 1/4-in. pieces

Combine .... all ingredients except chicken in saucepan, mixing well.
Simmer ..... for 5 minutes; cool.
Place .... chicken in mixture.
Marinate .... for 1 hour.
Place .... chicken on rack in broiler pan.
Broil .... for 5 minutes on each side.
Yields ...... 4 servings.

Approx Per Serv: Cal 274, Prot 22.1 g, T Fat 17.2 g, Chl 76.7 mg, Car 7 g, Sod 1910.8 mg, Pot 342.2 mg.

Lenora Aquilani, Montgomery

HUNGARIAN CREAM CHEESE KIFLIKS

3 c. sifted flour
1/2 lb. cream cheese, softened
1/2 lb. margarine
1 lb. ground walnuts
1 tsp. cinnamon
1/3 c. sugar
1 jar raspberry jam
Confectioners' sugar

Combine .... first 3 ingredients in bowl, mixing well.
Shape ...... into 1-inch balls.
Chill .... covered, overnight.
Mix .... walnuts, cinnamon and sugar in bowl.
Fold .... in jam.
Roll .... out each ball on confectioners' sugar-covered board.

Place . . . . a small amount of jam mixture in center, rolling to enclose filling.

Shape . . . . . . into crescent on baking sheet.

Bake . . . . at 350 degrees for 20 to 25 minutes or until golden.

Sprinkle . . . . with confectioners' sugar.

Yields . . . . . . 50 servings.

Approx Per Serv: Cal 160, Prot 2.6 g, T Fat 11.6 g, Chl 5 mg, Car 12.6 g, Sod 57.2 mg, Pot 59.8 mg.

Nutritional information does not include confectioners' sugar.

Beth Hemminger, Cumberland

CROCK•POT ITALIAN MEATBALLS

1 c. dry bread crumbs
1 lb. ground beef
2 eggs
1/2 c. grated Romano cheese
2 tbsp. parsley flakes
1 tsp. each oregano, salt
1/2 tsp. garlic salt
Pepper to taste
1 jar spaghetti sauce

Combine . . . . all ingredients except spaghetti sauce in bowl, mixing well.

Shape . . . . . . into sixteen 1-inch balls.

Brown . . . . . . in skillet.

Place . . . . in Crock•Pot.

Cover . . . . . . with spaghetti sauce.

Cook . . . . on High for 1 1/2 hours.

Serve . . . . over rice.

Yields . . . . . . 8 servings.

Approx Per Serv: Cal 171, Prot 16.7 g, T Fat 9.3 g, Chl 109 mg, Car 4.1 g, Sod 547.1 mg, Pot 235.2 mg.

Nutritional information does not include spaghetti sauce.

Marjorie F. Aurand, Snyder

CHICKEN CACCIATORE (ITALY)

1   3 to 3 1/2-lb. chicken, cut up
1 sm. clove of garlic
2 tbsp. oil
1 tsp. oregano
1   16-oz. can stewed tomatoes
1/8 tsp. (or more) salt
Pepper to taste
1 1/2 c. sliced mushrooms

Brown . . . . . . chicken with garlic in oil in skillet until lightly browned; remove garlic.

Add . . . . remaining 5 ingredients, mixing well.

Simmer . . . . . covered, for 30 minutes or until chicken is tender.

Serve . . . . with spaghetti.

Yields . . . . . . 5 servings.

Approx Per Serv: Cal 170, Prot 18.3 g, T Fat 8.3 g, Chl 61.4 mg, Car 5 g, Sod 221.2 mg, Pot 480.4 mg.

Annette Wright, Philadelphia

ITALIAN RATATOUILLE

1 med. eggplant, peeled
2 med. zucchini, cut into 1/2-in. slices
2 tsp. salt
1/2 c. olive oil
2 each med. yellow onions, green peppers, thinly sliced
2 cloves of garlic, minced
3 med. firm tomatoes, peeled, cut into strips
1 c. sliced pimento-stuffed olives
1/4 c. chopped parsley
1/4 tsp. pepper

Cut . . . . eggplant into 1/2 x 3-inch strips.

Combine . . . . with zucchini and 1 teaspoon salt in bowl.

Let . . . . stand for 30 minutes; drain and pat dry.

Saute . . . . . . in 1/4 cup oil in large skillet for 2 minutes or until lightly browned on both sides; remove vegetables.

Add . . . . remaining 1/4 cup oil, onions and peppers to skillet.

Cook . . . . until tender, stirring frequently.

Stir . . . . in garlic.

Place . . . . tomatoes on top.

Cook . . . . covered, for 5 minutes.

Stir . . . . in eggplant, zucchini, olives, parsley, pepper and remaining 1 teaspoon salt.

Simmer . . . . . covered, for 20 minutes.

Simmer . . . . . uncovered, for 5 minutes longer, basting frequently.

Serve . . . . hot or chilled.

Photograph for this recipe on page 111.

TERIYAKI STEAK (JAPAN)

1/2 c. soy sauce
3 tbsp. sesame seed
4 tbsp. finely chopped green onion
1 tbsp. crushed garlic
1 tbsp. sugar
1 tsp. pepper
1 1/2 lb. beef filet, cut into
　　1/4-in. slices
3 tbsp. oil

Combine .... first 6 ingredients in bowl.
Add .... beef, stirring to coat.
Marinate .... for 1 hour or longer.
Stir .... in oil.
Grill .... beef over hot coals to desired de-
gree of doneness.
Serve .... with fried rice.
Yields ...... 6 servings.

Approx Per Serv: Cal 522, Prot 19.3 g, T Fat 46.6 g,
Chl 77.1 mg, Car 5.9 g, Sod 1820.5 mg, Pot 402.2 mg.

Nancy Heverly, Blair

KOLACHE

1 c. shortening
3 eggs, separated
1 3/4 c. light cream
1 cake yeast, crumbled
3 1/2 to 4 c. flour
1/8 tsp. salt
1 1/2 c. confectioners' sugar
1 lb. walnuts, ground
3/4 c. sugar
1 tbsp. melted butter

Cream ...... shortening.
Add .... egg yolks and 1 cup cream, mix-
ing well.
Dissolve .... yeast in 1/4 cup cream.
Stir .... into creamed mixture.
Sift .... in flour and salt.
Knead ...... on floured surface until smooth
and elastic.
Shape ...... into 3 balls.
Chill .... overnight.
Roll .... to 1/4 inch thickness on surface
covered with confectioners'
sugar.
Cut .... into 2 1/2-inch squares.

Combine .... walnuts, sugar and butter with
remaining 1/2 cup cream in
bowl, mixing well.
Spread ..... over dough.
Roll .... squares diagonally.
Place .... on cookie sheet.
Beat .... egg whites with 1 tablespoon
water in bowl.
Brush ...... over cookies.
Bake .... at 375 degrees for 15 minutes.
Yields ...... 48 servings.

Approx Per Serv: Cal 196, Prot 3.3 g, T Fat 13.8 g,
Chl 21.5 mg, Car 16.1 g, Sod 16.1 mg, Pot 72.4 mg.

Nancy Honeywell, Luzerne

KRAUPHEN

3 c. flour
1 tbsp. salt
1 1/2 c. shortening
1 tbsp. vinegar
1 egg, beaten
2 lb. dates, chopped
1 20-oz. can pears, drained, chopped
1 c. ground walnuts
1/2 c. (about) sugar

Combine .... flour and salt in large bowl, mix-
ing well.
Cut .... in shortening until crumbly.
Blend ...... vinegar, egg and 6 tablespoons
water in bowl.
Pour .... into flour mixture, blending
well.
Divide ...... dough in half.
Roll .... out on floured surface.
Cook .... dates in a small amount of water
in saucepan until thick, stirring
constantly.
Mix .... in pears and walnuts.
Spread ..... over 1 portion pastry.
Top .... with remaining pastry.
Cut .... into diamond shapes.
Sprinkle .... with sugar.
Place .... on cookie sheet.
Bake .... at 350 degrees for 12 to 15 min-
utes or until lightly browned.
Yields ...... 24 servings.

Approx Per Serv: Cal 349, Prot 3.5 g, T Fat 17.8 g,
Chl 10.5 mg, Car 47.4 g, Sod 270 mg, Pot 299.2 mg.

Linda Werneth, Elk

MEXICAN DISH

2 cans hot chili peppers, seeded
12 oz. Cheddar cheese, grated
1/2 c. evaporated milk
6 eggs, beaten
2 tbsp. flour
1/8 tsp. (about) salt
1 sm. can tomato sauce

Arrange . . . . . chili peppers in greased 7 x 11-inch baking pan.
Sprinkle . . . . cheese over peppers.
Combine . . . . next 4 ingredients in bowl, beating well.
Pour . . . . over cheese.
Bake . . . . at 350 degrees for 30 minutes.
Top . . . . with tomato sauce.
Bake . . . . for 10 minutes longer.
Yields . . . . . . 10 servings.

Approx Per Serv: Cal 214, Prot 13.8 g, T Fat 15.5 g, Chl 189.3 mg, Car 4.9 g, Sod 383.2 mg, Pot 172.8 mg.

Lenora Aquilani, Montgomery

RELLENOS DE PAPA (MEXICO)

2 lb. potatoes, cooked, mashed
1 1/2 tsp. salt
4 tbsp. butter
1 egg, slightly beaten
Cornstarch
1 lb. lean ground beef
1 green pepper, chopped
1 onion, chopped
2 cloves of garlic, minced
1 tbsp. oil
1 tsp. oregano
1/4 tsp. vinegar
1/4 c. tomato sauce
Oil for deep frying

Combine . . . . hot mashed potatoes, 1/2 teaspoon salt, butter, egg and 1 tablespoon cornstarch in bowl, mixing well.
Cool . . . . to room temperature.
Brown . . . . . . ground beef in skillet, stirring until crumbly; drain.
Saute . . . . . . green pepper, onion and garlic in 1 tablespoon oil in skillet.
Mix . . . . in remaining 1 teaspoon salt, oregano, vinegar, tomato sauce and ground beef.

Shape . . . . . . potato mixture into 12 balls.
Flatten . . . . . each in cornstarch-coated hand.
Spoon . . . . . . ground beef mixture into center, shaping to enclose filling.
Coat . . . . lightly with cornstarch.
Fry . . . . in deep 375-degree oil until golden brown; drain on paper towel.
Serve . . . . immediately.
Yields . . . . . . 12 servings.

Approx Per Serv: Cal 103, Prot 2.1 g, T Fat 5.5 g, Chl 32.9 mg, Car 11.8 g, Sod 348.8 mg, Pot 290.7 mg.

Nutritional information does not include cornstarch for coating or oil for deep frying.

Efrain and Nohemi Munoz, Erie

CHICKEN WITH CASHEWS (ORIENTAL)

1/4 c. peanut oil
2 whole boned chicken breasts, cut into 1-in. pieces
1/2 c. chopped green pepper
1/2 c. cashews
2 tbsp. chopped green onion
2 cloves of garlic, finely chopped
1/4 tsp. ginger
1/4 c. soy sauce
2 tbsp. dark corn syrup
1 tbsp. vinegar
4 tsp. cornstarch

Preheat . . . . . wok for 2 minutes.
Pour . . . . oil around sides of wok.
Heat . . . . over high heat for 2 minutes longer.
Stir-fry . . . . . chicken in wok for 2 to 3 minutes or until partially cooked; push to side.
Add . . . . green pepper and cashews.
Stir-fry . . . . . for 30 seconds; push to side.
Add . . . . green onion, garlic and ginger.
Stir-fry . . . . . for 1 minute; push to side.
Blend . . . . . . remaining 4 ingredients with 1/2 cup water in bowl.
Stir . . . . into chicken mixture.
Boil . . . . for 1 minute, stirring to mix stir-fried ingredients into sauce.
Yields . . . . . . 6 servings.

Approx Per Serv: Cal 288, Prot 15.4 g, T Fat 19.5 g, Chl 27.6 mg, Car 14.5 g, Sod 904.9 mg, Pot 270.1 mg.

Marcia Fehl, York

SWEET AND SOUR PORK (ORIENTAL)

1 1/2 lb. pork, cut into chunks
1/4 c. soy sauce
1 c. tomatoes
1 green pepper, chopped
1/2 c. chopped onion
2/3 c. pineapple chunks
1/2 c. vinegar
1/4 c. packed brown sugar
1/4 c. sugar
1/4 c. cornstarch
1/2 c. pineapple juice

Cook . . . . pork in 2 cups water in saucepan until tender.
Add . . . . next 5 ingredients, mixing well.
Combine . . . . remaining ingredients with 1/2 cup water in bowl, mixing well.
Stir . . . . into pork mixture.
Bring . . . . to a boil, stirring constantly.
Serve . . . . over rice.
Yields . . . . . . 6 servings.

Approx Per Serv: Cal 483, Prot 21 g, T Fat 28.6 g, Chl 70.3 mg, Car 35.8 g, Sod 1002 mg, Pot 586.7 mg.

Mollie Geise, Northumberland

PENNSYLVANIA DUTCH POTPIE

2 lb. roast beef, cut into chunks
Chopped parsley
1/4 tsp. (or more) salt
Pepper to taste
2 c. flour
1 egg, beaten
1/4 c. (about) milk
2 onions, chopped
6 potatoes, cubed

Cook . . . . beef in water to cover in stock pot with parsley, 1/8 teaspoon salt and pepper for 2 hours; remove beef, reserving broth.
Combine . . . . flour, egg and 1/8 teaspoon salt in bowl.
Stir . . . . in enough milk to make stiff dough.
Roll . . . . into thin rectangle on floured surface.
Cut . . . . into 2-inch square noodles.
Layer . . . . . . beef, noodles, onions and potatoes alternately in broth until all ingredients are used.

Cook . . . . covered, for 20 minutes.
Yields . . . . . . 10 servings.

Approx Per Serv: Cal 380, Prot 24.8 g, T Fat 12.3 g, Chl 87.5 mg, Car 41.7 g, Sod 134.9 mg, Pot 850.5 mg.

Joy Hornberger, Fayette

PENNSYLVANIA DUTCH PEPPER CABBAGE

1 med. head cabbage, shredded
2 lg. green peppers, chopped
1 tsp. salt
2 c. sugar
1 c. vinegar
1 tsp. celery seed

Combine . . . . cabbage, green peppers and salt in bowl, mixing well.
Let . . . . stand for 10 minutes.
Mix . . . . sugar, vinegar, 1/2 cup water and celery seed in saucepan.
Boil . . . . for 1 minute.
Pour . . . . over cabbage mixture, mixing well.
Freeze . . . . . . until firm.
Thaw . . . . . . before serving.
Yields . . . . . . 60 servings.

Approx Per Serv: Cal 28, Prot 1 g, T Fat 0 g, Chl 0 mg, Car 7.3 g, Sod 37.1 mg, Pot 25.2 mg.

Evelyn Conklin, Snyder

IMPOSSIBLE REUBEN PIE

1/2 lb. cooked corned beef, chopped
4 oz. Swiss cheese, shredded
1 8-oz. can sauerkraut, drained
1 c. milk
3/4 c. biscuit mix
1/3 c. mayonnaise
2 tbsp. chili sauce
3 eggs

Layer . . . . . . corned beef, cheese and sauerkraut in buttered 9-inch pie plate.
Place . . . . remaining 5 ingredients in blender container.
Process . . . . . until smooth.
Pour . . . . into pie plate.
Bake . . . . at 400 degrees for 30 minutes or until golden.

Let ....stand for 5 minutes before serving.

Yields ......6 servings.

Approx Per Serv: Cal 443, Prot 20.3 g, T Fat 33 g, Chl 195.2 mg, Car 15.9 g, Sod 1170.3 mg, Pot 222.8 mg.

Nancy Myers, Columbia

RODNEY'S SOFT PRETZELS

1 pkg. dry yeast
1/3 c. packed brown sugar
5 c. flour
Soda
Coarse Kosher salt

Dissolve ....yeast in 2 tablespoons hot water in large bowl.

Stir ....in 1 1/3 cups warm water and brown sugar.

Mix ....in flour gradually until smooth and dough leaves side of bowl.

Knead ......on lightly floured surface.

Divide ......into 1/4 cup portions and roll each into a rope on floured surface.

Shape ......into pretzels.

Fill ....skillet with water.

Add ....1 tablespoon soda per cup of water.

Bring ....to a boil.

Lower ......pretzels 1 at a time with spatula into water.

Cook ....for 30 seconds.

Place ....on greased baking sheet sprinkled with Kosher salt.

Sprinkle ....with additional Kosher salt.

Bake ....at 475 degrees for 8 minutes or until golden brown.

Serve ....warm from oven.

Yields ......24 servings.

Approx Per Serv: Cal 107, Prot 2.8 g, T Fat .3 g, Chl 0 mg, Car 22.8 g, Sod 412.1 mg, Pot 41 mg.

Nutritional information does not include Kosher salt.

Rodney Garling, Franklin

SOFT PRETZELS WITH SESAME SEED

1 pkg. dry yeast
1 tbsp. sugar
1/2 tsp. salt

3 1/2 to 4 c. flour
1 egg
2 tbsp. sesame seed

Dissolve ....yeast in 1 1/3 cups warm water.

Add ....sugar and salt, stirring to dissolve.

Mix ....in flour gradually until stiff dough forms.

Knead ......on floured surface for 5 to 7 minutes or until smooth, adding 1/2 cup or more flour if necessary.

Divide ......dough into 12 portions.

Let ....rest for 5 to 10 minutes.

Roll ....into 15-inch ropes on floured surface.

Shape ......into pretzels.

Place ....on greased baking sheets.

Beat ....egg with a small amount of water in bowl.

Brush ......over pretzels.

Sprinkle   with sesame seed.

Bake ....at 425 degrees for 15 to 25 minutes or until golden brown.

Yields ......12 servings.

Approx Per Serv: Cal 172, Prot 5.4 g, T Fat 1.6 g, Chl 21.1 mg, Car 33.2 g, Sod 95.9 mg, Pot 66.3 mg.

Loree Karlinsey, Indiana

POLISH PIZZA LASKOWSKI

1 lb. ground beef
1   15-oz. can tomato sauce
1/8 tsp. garlic salt
Pinch of pepper
2 loaves frozen bread, thawed
12 slices American cheese

Brown ......ground beef in skillet, stirring until crumbly.

Stir ....in next 3 ingredients.

Simmer .....for 5 minutes.

Press ....bread dough over bottom of greased baking sheet.

Arrange .....cheese slices on dough.

Spoon ......ground beef mixture onto cheese slices.

Bake ....at 350 degrees for 40 minutes.

Yields ......12 servings.

Approx Per Serv: Cal 375, Prot 20.7 g, T Fat 18.6 g, Chl 53.2 mg, Car 34 g, Sod 828.6 mg, Pot 390.1 mg.

Kara Laskowski, Dauphin

PIROGI CASSEROLE (POLAND)

6 c. mashed potatoes
1 8-oz. package cream cheese, softened
1 tsp. salt
1 sm. jar Cheez Whiz
1 lg. onion, sliced
3 sticks butter
1 lb. lasagna noodles, cooked

Mix . . . . mashed potatoes, cream cheese, salt and Cheez Whiz in bowl.
Saute . . . . . . onion in butter in skillet until brown.
Layer . . . . . . noodles, potatoes and onion mixture alternately in buttered 9 x 13-inch baking dish until all ingredients are used, ending with onion mixture.
Bake . . . . covered, at 300 degrees for 20 minutes; uncover.
Broil . . . . until brown.
Yields . . . . . . 12 servings.

Approx Per Serv: Cal 586, Prot 12.5 g, T Fat 40.2 g, Chl 83.8 mg, Car 43.1 g, Sod 1157.4 mg, Pot 393.4 mg.

Nancy Honeywell, Luzerne

LAZY GOLOBKI CASSEROLE (POLAND)

1 lg. head cabbage, shredded
1 can tomato soup
1 c. tomatoes
1/2 c. each chopped celery, green pepper
Chopped onion
1 1/2 lb. ground beef
1/2 c. rice, cooked
1 egg
1/2 tsp. (or more) salt
Pepper to taste

Boil . . . . cabbage in salted water in saucepan for 1/2 hour; drain.
Combine . . . . soup, tomatoes, celery, green pepper and 1/2 cup onion with 1 soup can water in bowl, mixing well.
Mix . . . . ground beef, rice, egg, 1 tablespoon onion, salt and pepper in bowl.

Layer . . . . . . half the cabbage and tomato mixture and all the ground beef mixture in large casserole.
Top . . . . with remaining cabbage and tomato mixture.
Bake . . . . at 350 degrees for 2 hours.
Yields . . . . . . 8 servings.

Approx Per Serv: Cal 306, Prot 18.2 g, T Fat 19.8 g, Chl 89.4 mg, Car 13.9 g, Sod 605.5 mg, Pot 578.9 mg.

Ann Stanislawczyk, Cambria

GAZPACHO (SPAIN)

2 c. peeled tomatoes
1 cucumber, chopped
1 green pepper, chopped
1 onion, chopped
2 tbsp. oil
3 tbsp. vinegar
1/2 tsp. salt
1/4 tsp. pepper
1/8 tsp. garlic salt

Combine . . . . all ingredients in blender container.
Process . . . . . for 10 seconds or until smooth.
Chill . . . . for 1 hour.
Yields . . . . . . 10 servings.

Approx Per Serv: Cal 39.9, Prot .7 g, T Fat 2.8 g, Chl 0 mg, Car 3.6 g, Sod 137.2 mg, Pot 125.2 mg.

Mary T. Hosterman, Centre

SPANISH RICE

2 c. stewing tomatoes
1 tbsp. rice
3 tbsp. butter, melted
1/2 c. grated cheese
3 tbsp. chopped onion
1/8 tsp. salt
Pepper and paprika to taste

Combine . . . . all ingredients and 1 cup hot water in baking dish, mixing well.
Bake . . . . at 350 degrees for 1 hour or until rice is tender.
Yields . . . . . . 6 servings.

Approx Per Serv: Cal 114, Prot 3.4 g, T Fat 9 g, Chl 27.1 mg, Car 5.6 g, Sod 285.5 mg, Pot 193.7 mg.

Ann Powell, Lackawanna

Calorie Chart

Almonds, shelled, 1/4 cup	213
Apples: 1 med	70
chopped, 1/2 cup	30
Apple juice, 1 cup	117
Applesauce: sweetened, 1/2 cup	115
unsweetened, 1/2 cup	50
Apricots: fresh, 3	55
canned, 1/2 cup	110
dried, 10 halves	100
Apricot nectar, 1 cup	140
Asparagus: fresh, 6 spears	19
canned, 1/2 cup	18
Avocado, 1 med.	265
Bacon, 2 sl. crisp-cooked, drained	90
Banana, 1 med.	100
Beans: baked, 1/2 cup	160
dry, 1/2 cup	350
green, 1/2 cup	20
lima, 1/2 cup	95
soy, 1/2 cup	95
Bean sprouts, 1/2 cup	18
Beef, cooked, 3 oz. serving:	
roast, rib	375
roast, heel of round	165
steak, sirloin	330
Beer, 12 oz.	150
Beets, cooked, 1/2 cup	40
Biscuit, from mix, 1	90
Bologna, all meat, 3 oz.	235
Bread: roll, 1	85
white, 1 slice	65
whole wheat, 1 slice	65
Bread crumbs, dry, 1 cup	390
Broccoli, cooked, 1/2 cup	20
Butter: 1/2 cup	800
1 tbsp.	100
Buttermilk, 1 cup	90
Cabbage: cooked, 1/2 cup	15
fresh, shredded, 1/2 cup	10
Cake: angel food, 1/12 pkg. prepared	140
devil's food, 1/12 pkg. prepared	195
yellow, 1/12 pkg. prepared	200
Candy: caramel, 1 oz.	115
chocolate, sweet, 1 oz.	145
hard candy, 1 oz.	110
marshmallows, 1 oz.	90
Cantaloupe, 1/2 med.	60
Carrots, cooked, 1/2 cup	23
fresh, 1 med.	20
Catsup, 1 tbsp.	18
Cauliflower: cooked, 1/2 cup	13
fresh, 1/2 lb.	60
Celery, chopped, 1/2 cup	8
Cereals: bran flakes, 1/2 cup	53
corn flakes, 1/2 cup	50

oatmeal, cooked, 1/2 cup	65
Cheese: American, 1 oz.	105
Cheddar: 1 oz.	113
shredded, 1 cup	452
cottage: creamed, 1/2 cup	130
uncreamed 1/2 cup	85
cream: 1 oz.	107
mozzarella, 1 oz.	80
shredded, 1 cup	320
Parmesan, 1 oz.	110
Velveeta, 1 oz.	84
Cherries: canned, sour in water, 1/2 cup	53
fresh, sweet, 1/2 cup	40
Chicken, meat only, 4 oz. serving:	
boned, chopped, 1/2 cup	170
broiled	155
canned, boned	230
roast, dark meat	210
roast, light meat	207
Chili peppers: green, fresh, 1/2 lb.	62
red, fresh, 1/2 lb.	108
Chili powder with seasoning, 1 tbsp.	51
Chocolate, baking, 1 oz.	143
Cocoa mix, 1-oz. package	115
Cocoa powder, baking, 1/3 cup	120
Coconut, dried, shredded, 1/4 cup	166
Coffee	0
Corn: canned, cream-style, 1/2 cup	100
canned, whole kernel, 1/2 cup	85
Corn bread, mix, prepared, 1 x 4-in. piece	125
Corn chips, 1 oz.	130
Cornmeal, 1/2 cup	264
Cornstarch, 1 tbsp.	29
Crab, fresh, meat only, 3 oz.	80
canned, 3 oz.	85
Crackers: graham, 2 1/2-in. square	28
Ritz, each	17
saltine, 2-in. square	13
Cracker crumbs, 1/2 cup	281
Cranberries: fresh, 1/2 lb.	100
juice, cocktail, 1 cup	163
sauce, 1/2 cup	190
Cream: half-and-half, 1 tbsp.	20
heavy, 1 tbsp	55
light, 1 tbsp.	30
Creamer, imitation powdered, 1 tsp.	10
Cucumber, 1 med.	30
Dates, dried, chopped, 1/2 cup	244
Eggs: 1 whole, large	80
1 white	17
1 yolk	59
Eggplant, cooked, 1/2 cup	19
Fish sticks, 5	200
Flour: rye, 1 cup	286
white: 1 cup	420

Puddings, instant, prepared:
  banana, 1/2 cup 175
  butterscotch, 1/2 cup 175
  chocolate, 1/2 cup 200
  lemon, 1/2 cup 180
Pumpkin, canned, 1/2 cup 38
Raisins, dried, 1/2 cup 231
Rice: cooked, white, 1/2 cup 90
  cooked, brown, 1/2 cup 100
  precooked, 1/2 cup 105
Salad dressings, commercial:
  blue cheese, 1 tbsp....................... 75
  French, 1 tbsp.......................... 70
  Italian, 1 tbsp. 83
  mayonnaise, 1 tbsp. 100
  mayonnaise-type, 1 tbsp. 65
  Russian, 1 tbsp......................... 75
  Thousand Island, 1 tbsp................. 80
Salami, cooked, 2 oz......................180
Salmon: canned, 4 oz. 180
  steak, 4 oz. 220
Sardines, canned, 3 oz.....................175
Sauces: barbecue, 1 tbsp.................. 17
  hot pepper, 1 tbsp. 3
  soy, 1 tbsp............................ 9
  white, med., 1/2 cup 215
  Worcestershire, 1 tbsp. 15
Sauerkraut, 1/2 cup 21
Sausage, cooked, 2 oz.....................260
Sherbet, 1/2 cup 130
Shrimp: cooked, 3 oz. 50
  canned, 4 oz. 130
Soft drinks, 1 cup 100
Soup, 1 can, condensed:
  chicken with rice 116
  cream of celery 215
  cream of chicken 235
  cream of mushroom 331
  tomato 220
  vegetable-beef 198
Sour cream, 1/2 cup 240
Spaghetti, cooked, 1/2 cup 80
Spinach: fresh, 1/2 lb. 60
  cooked, 1/2 cup 20

Squash: summer, cooked, 1/2 cup 15
  winter, cooked, 1/2 cup 65
Strawberries, fresh, 1/2 cup 23
Sugar: brown, packed, 1/2 cup 410
  confectioners', sifted, 1/2 cup 240
  granulated: 1/2 cup 385
    1 tbsp......................... 48
Syrups: chocolate, 1 tbsp................. 50
  corn, 1 tbsp........................... 58
  maple, 1 tbsp.......................... 50
Taco shell, 1 shell 50
Tea, 1 cup 0
Tomatoes: fresh, 1 med. 40
  canned, 1/2 cup 25
  juice, 1 cup 45
  paste, 6 oz. can 150
  sauce, 8-oz. can 34
Toppings: caramel, 1 tbsp................ 70
  chocolate fudge, 1 tbsp. 65
  Cool Whip, 1 tbsp. 14
  Dream Whip, prepared, 1 tbsp. 8
  strawberry, 1 tbsp. 60
Tortilla, corn, 1 65
Tuna: canned in oil, drained, 4 oz. 230
  canned in water, 4 oz. 144
Turkey: dark meat, roasted, 4 oz. 230
  light meat, roasted, 4 oz. 200
Veal: cutlet, broiled, 3 oz. 185
  roast, 3 oz. 230
Vegetable juice cocktail, 1 cup 43
Vinegar, 1 tbsp.......................... 2
Waffles, 1 130
Walnuts, chopped, 1/2 cup 410
Water chestnuts, sliced, 1/2 cup 25
Watermelon, fresh, cubed, 1/2 cup 26
Wheat germ, 1 tbsp....................... 29
Wine: dessert, 1/2 cup 140
  table, 1/2 cup 85
Yeast: compressed, 1 oz. 24
  dry, 1 oz. 80
Yogurt: plain, w/whole milk, 1 cup 153
  plain, w/skim milk, 1 cup 123
  with fruit, 1 cup 260

Nutrition Labeling Chart

Modern Americans have become very diet and nutrition conscious, and in response, commercial food producers have begun to include nutrition information on the labels of their products. Nutrition Labeling is an invaluable service in many ways. There are many persons on special diets (diabetic, low-sodium, low-cholesterol) who must know the specifics of the foods they eat. However, whether the homemaker cooks for a special diet or not, Nutrition Labeling on the foods she buys helps her to know the part they play in her overall nutrition and menu planning.

The United States Food and Drug Administration has determined how much of every important nutrient is needed by the average healthy person in the United States, well known as the Recommended Daily Dietary Allowance (RDA). The United States RDA reflects the highest amounts of nutritives for all ages and sexes. Pregnant and nursing women, as well as persons with special dietary needs, should consult their doctors for any recommended increases or decreases in their daily diet.

UNITED STATES RECOMMENDED DAILY ALLOWANCE CHART

Protein	45-65 Grams
Carbohydrates	125 Grams
Vitamin A	5,000 International Units
Thiamine (Vitamin B_1)	1.5 Milligrams
Riboflavin (Vitamin B_2)	1.7 Milligrams
Vitamin B_6	2 Milligrams
Vitamin B_{12}	6 Micrograms
Folic Acid (B Vitamin)	0.4 Milligrams
Pantothenic Acid (B Vitamin)	10 Milligrams
Vitamin C (Ascorbic Acid)	55-60 Milligrams
Vitamin D	400 International Units
Vitamin E	30 International Units
Iron	18 Milligrams
Calcium	1 Gram
Niacin (Nicotinic Acid)	13-20 Milligrams
Magnesium	400 Milligrams
Zinc	15 Milligrams
Copper	2 Milligrams
Phosphorus	1 Gram
Iodine	150 Micrograms
Biotin (Vitamin H)	0.3 Milligrams

IMPORTANT NUTRIENTS YOUR DIET REQUIRES

PROTEIN

Why? Absolutely essential in building, repairing and renewing of all body tissue. Helps body resist infection. Builds enzymes and hormones, helps form and maintain body fluids.

Where? Milk, eggs, lean meats, poultry, fish, soybeans, peanuts, dried peas and beans, grains and cereals.

CARBOHYDRATES

Why?   Provide needed energy for bodily functions, provide warmth, as well as fuel for brain and nerve tissues, Lack of carbohydrates will cause body to use protein for energy rather than for repair and building.

Where?   Sugars: sugar, table syrups, jellies and jams, etc., as well as dried and fresh fruits. Starches: cereals, pasta, rice, corn, dried beans and peas, potatoes, stem and leafy vegetables, and milk.

FATS

Why?   Essential in the use of fat soluble vitamins (A, D, E, K), and fatty acids. Have more than twice the concentrated energy than equal amount of carbohydrate for body energy and warmth.

Where?   Margarine, butter, cooking oil, mayonnaise, vegetable shortening, milk, cream, ice cream, cheese, meat, fish, eggs, poultry, chocolate, coconut, nuts.

VITAMIN A

Why?   Needed for healthy skin and hair, as well as for healthy, infection-resistant mucous membranes.

Where?   Dark green, leafy and yellow vegetables, liver. Deep yellow fruits, such as apricots and cantaloupe. Milk, cheese, eggs, as well as fortified margarine and butter.

THIAMINE (VITAMIN B_1)

Why?   Aids in the release of energy of foods, as well as in normal appetite and digestion. Promotes healthy nervous system.

Where?   Pork, liver, kidney. Dried peas and beans. Whole grain and enriched breads and cereals.

RIBOFLAVIN (VITAMIN B_2)

Why?   Helps to oxidize foods. Promotes healthy eyes and skin, especially around mouth and eyes. Prevents pellagra.

Where?   Meat, especially liver and kidney, as well as milk, cheese, eggs. Dark green leafy vegetables. Enriched bread and cereal products. Almonds, dried peas and beans.

VITAMIN B_6

Why?   Helps protein in building body tissues. Needed for healthy nerves, skin and digestion. Also helps body to use fats and carbohydrates for energy.

Where?   Milk, wheat germ, whole grain and fortified cereals. Liver and kidney, pork and beef.

VITAMIN B_{12}

Why?   Aids body in formation of red blood cells, as well as in regular work of all body cells.

Where?   Lean meats, milk, eggs, fish, cheese, as well as liver and kidney.

FOLIC ACID

Why?   Aids in healthy blood system, as well as intestinal tract. Helps to prevent anemia.

Where?   Green leaves of vegetables and herbs, as well as liver and milk. Wheat germ and soybeans.

PANTOTHENIC ACID

Why?   Aids in proper function of digestive system.

Where?   Liver, kidney and eggs. Peanuts and molasses. Broccoli and other vegetables.

VITAMIN C (ASCORBIC ACID)

Why?   Promotes proper bone and tooth formation. Helps body utilize iron and resist infection. Strengthens blood vessels. Lack of it causes bones to heal slowly, failure of wounds to heal and fragile vessels to bleed easily.

Where? Citrus fruits, cantaloupe and strawberries. Broccoli, kale, green peppers, raw cabbage, sweet potatoes, cauliflower, tomatoes.

VITAMIN D

Why? Builds strong bones and teeth by aiding utilization of calcium and phosphorus.

Where? Fortified milk, fish liver oils, as well as salmon, tuna and sardines. Also eggs.

VITAMIN E

Why? Needed in maintaining red blood cells.

Where? Whole grain cereals, wheat germ, and beans and peas, lettuce and eggs.

IRON

Why? Used with protein for hemoglobin production. Forms nucleus of each cell, and helps them to use oxygen.

Where? Kidney and liver, as well as shellfish, lean meats, and eggs. Deep yellow and dark green leafy vegetables. Dried peas, beans, fruits. Potatoes, whole grain cereals and bread. Enriched flour and bread. Dark molasses.

CALCIUM

Why? Builds and renews bones, teeth, other tissues, as well as aiding in the proper function of muscles, nerves and heart. Controls normal blood clotting. With protein, aids in oxidation of foods.

Where? Milk and milk products, excluding butter. Dark green vegetables, oysters, clams and sardines.

NIACIN

Why? Helps body to oxidize food. Aids in digestion, and helps to keep nervous system and skin healthy.

Where? Peanuts, liver, tuna, as well as fish, poultry and lean meats. Enriched breads, cereals and peas.

MAGNESIUM

Why? Aids nervous system and sleep.

Where? Almonds, peanuts, raisins and prunes. Vegetables, fruits, milk, fish and meats.

ZINC

Why? Needed for cell formation.

Where? Nuts and leafy green vegetables. Shellfish.

PHOSPHORUS

Why? Maintains normal blood clotting function, as well as builds bones, teeth and nerve tissue. Aids in utilization of sugar and fats.

Where? Oatmeal and whole wheat products. Eggs and cheese, dried beans and peas. Nuts, lean meats, and fish and poultry.

IODINE

Why? Enables thyroid gland to maintain proper body metabolism.

Where? Iodized salt. Saltwater fish and seafood. Milk and vegetables.

BIOTIN (VITAMIN H)

Why? Helps to maintain body cells.

Where? Eggs and liver. Any foods rich in Vitamin B.

Equivalent Chart

	WHEN RECIPE CALLS FOR:	YOU NEED:
BREAD & CEREAL	1 c. soft bread crumbs	2 slices
	1 c. fine dry bread crumbs	4-5 slices
	1 c. small bread cubes	2 slices
	1 c. fine cracker crumbs	24 saltines
	1 c. fine graham cracker crumbs	14 crackers
	1 c. vanilla wafer crumbs	22 wafers
	1 c. crushed corn flakes	3 c. uncrushed
	4 c. cooked macaroni	1 8-oz. package
	3 1/2 c. cooked rice	1 c. uncooked
DAIRY	1 c. freshly grated cheese	1/4 lb.
	1 c. cottage cheese or sour cream	1 8-oz. carton
	2/3 c. evaporated milk	1 sm. can
	1 2/3 c. evaporated milk	1 tall can
	1 c. whipped cream	1/2 c. heavy cream
SWEET	1 c. semisweet chocolate pieces	1 6-oz. package
	2 c. granulated sugar	1 lb.
	4 c. sifted confectioners' sugar	1 lb.
	2 1/4 c. packed brown sugar	1 lb.
MEAT	3 c. diced cooked meat	1 lb., cooked
	2 c. ground cooked meat	1 lb., cooked
	4 c. diced cooked chicken	1 5-lb. chicken
NUTS	1 c. chopped nuts	4 oz. shelled / 1 lb. unshelled
VEGETABLES	4 c. sliced or diced raw potatoes	4 medium
	2 c. cooked green beans	1/2 lb. fresh or 1 16-oz. can
	1 c. chopped onion	1 large
	4 c. shredded cabbage	1 lb.
	2 c. canned tomatoes	1 16-oz. can
	1 c. grated carrot	1 large
	2 1/2 c. lima beans or red beans	1 c. dried, cooked
	1 4-oz. can mushrooms	1/2 lb. fresh
FRUIT	4 c. sliced or chopped apples	4 medium
	2 c. pitted cherries	4 c. unpitted
	3 to 4 tbsp. lemon juice plus 1 tsp. grated peel	1 lemon
	1/3 c. orange juice plus 2 tsp. grated peel	1 orange
	1 c. mashed banana	3 medium
	4 c. cranberries	1 lb.
	3 c. shredded coconut	1/2 lb.
	4 c. sliced peaches	8 medium
	1 c. pitted dates or candied fruit	1 8-oz. package
	2 c. pitted prunes	1 12-oz. package
	3 c. raisins	1 15-oz. package

Common Equivalents

1 tbsp. = 3 tsp.	4 qt. = 1 gal.
2 tbsp. = 1 oz.	6 1/2 to 8-oz. can = 1 c.
4 tbsp. = 1/4 c.	10 1/2 to 12-oz. can = 1 1/4 c.
5 tbsp. + 1 tsp. = 1/3 c.	14 to 16-oz. can (No. 300) = 1 3/4 c.
8 tbsp. = 1/2 c.	16 to 17-oz. can (No. 303) = 2 c.
12 tbsp. = 3/4 c.	1-lb. 4-oz. can or 1-pt. 2-oz. can (No. 2) = 2 1/2 c.
16 tbsp. = 1 c.	1-lb. 13-oz. can (No. 2 1/2) = 3 1/2 c.
1 c. = 8 oz. or 1/2 pt.	3-lb. 3-oz. can or 46-oz. can or 1-qt. 14-oz. can = 5 3/4 c.
4 c. = 1 qt.	6 1/2-lb. or 7-lb. 5-oz. can (No. 10) = 12 to 13 c.

Metric Conversion Chart

VOLUME

1 tsp.	=	4.9 cc
1 tbsp.	=	14.7 cc
1/3 c.	=	28.9 cc
1/8 c.	=	29.5 cc
1/4 c.	=	59.1 cc
1/2 c.	=	118.3 cc
3/4 c.	=	177.5 cc
1 c.	=	236.7 cc
2 c.	=	473.4 cc
1 fl. oz.	=	29.5 cc
4 oz.	=	118.3 cc
8 oz.	=	236.7 cc

1 pt.	=	473.4 cc
1 qt.	=	.946 liters
1 gal.	=	3.7 liters

CONVERSION FACTORS

Liters	X	1.056	=	Liquid quarts
Quarts	X	0.946	=	Liters
Liters	X	0.264	=	Gallons
Gallons	X	3.785	=	Liters
Fluid ounces	X	29.563	=	Cubic centimeters
Cubic centimeters	X	0.034	=	Fluid ounces
Cups	X	236.575	=	Cubic centimeters
Tablespoons	X	14.797	=	Cubic centimeters
Teaspoons	X	4.932	=	Cubic centimeters
Bushels	X	0.352	=	Hectoliters
Hectoliters	X	2.837	=	Bushels

WEIGHT

1 dry oz.	=	28.3 Grams
1 lb.	=	.454 Kilograms

CONVERSION FACTORS:

Ounces (Avoir.)	X	28.349	=	Grams
Grams	X	0.035	=	Ounces
Pounds	X	0.454	=	Kilograms
Kilograms	X	2.205	=	Pounds

Substitution Chart

	INSTEAD OF:	USE:
BAKING	1 tsp. baking powder	1/4 tsp. soda plus 1/2 tsp. cream of tartar
	1 c. sifted all-purpose flour	1 c. plus 2 tbsp. sifted cake flour
	1 c. sifted cake flour	1 c. minus 2 tbsp. sifted all-purpose flour
	1 tsp. cornstarch (for thickening)	2 tbsp. flour or 1 tbsp. tapioca
SWEET	1 1-oz. square chocolate	3 to 4 tbsp. cocoa plus 1 tsp. shortening
	1 2/3 oz. semisweet chocolate	1 oz. unsweetened chocolate plus 4 tsp. sugar
	1 c. granulated sugar	1 c. packed brown sugar or 1 c. corn syrup, molasses, honey minus 1/4 c. liquid
	1 c. honey	1 to 1 1/4 c. sugar plus 1/4 c. liquid or 1 c. molasses or corn syrup
DAIRY	1 c. sweet milk	1 c. sour milk or buttermilk plus 1/2 tsp. soda
	1 c. sour milk	1 c. sweet milk plus 1 tbsp. vinegar or lemon juice of 1 c. buttermilk
	1 c. buttermilk	1 c. sour milk or 1 c. yogurt
	1 c. light cream	7/8 c. skim milk plus 3 tbsp. butter
	1 c. heavy cream	3/4 c. skim milk plus 1/3 c. butter
	1 c. sour cream	7/8 c. sour milk plus 3 tbsp. butter
	1 c. bread crumbs	3/4 c. cracker crumbs
SEASONINGS	1 c. catsup	1 c. tomato sauce plus 1/2 c. sugar plus 2 tbsp. vinegar
	1 tbsp. prepared mustard	1 tsp. dry mustard
	1 tsp. Italian spice	1/4 tsp. each oregano, basil, thyme, rosemary plus dash of cayenne
	1 tsp. allspice	1/2 tsp. cinnamon plus 1/8 tsp. cloves
	1 medium onion	1 tbsp. dried minced onion or 1 tsp. onion powder
	1 clove of garlic	1/8 tsp. garlic powder or 1/8 tsp. instant minced garlic or 3/4 tsp. garlic salt or 5 drops of liquid garlic
	1 tsp. lemon juice	1/2 tsp. vinegar

Index

FOR ORDER INFORMATION
WRITE TO:

State 4-H Office
405 Ag Administration
University Park, Pennsylvania 16802

OR CALL:

Your Local County Extension Office

Library of Congress Cataloging in Publication Data
Main entry under title:

Appetite pleasers.
    Includes index.
    1. Cookery, American — Pennsylvania. I. Favorite
Recipes Press.
TX715.A625 1983   641.5   83-11513
ISBN 0-87197-153-4